I CAME AS A SHADOW

I CAME AS A SHADOW

AN AUTOBIOGRAPHY

JOHN THOMPSON

with Jesse Washington

HENRY HOLT AND COMPANY

NEW YORK

Henry Holt and Company
Publishers since 1866
120 Broadway
New York, New York 10271
www.henryholt.com

Henry Holt® and ® are registered trademarks of Macmillan Publishing Group, LLC.

Distributed in Canada by Raincoast Book Distribution Limited

Library of Congress Cataloging-in-Publication Data

Names: Thompson, John, 1941 September 2– author. | Washington, Jesse John, 1969– author.
Title: I came as a shadow : an autobiography / John Thompson with Jesse Washington.
Description: First edition. | New York : Henry Holt and Company, 2020. | Includes index.
Identifiers: LCCN 2020034400 (print) | LCCN 2020034401 (ebook) | ISBN 9781250619358 (hardcover) | ISBN 9781250619341 (ebook)
Subjects: LCSH: Thompson, John, 1941 September 2– | Basketball coaches—United States—Biography. | African American basketball coaches—Biography. | Georgetown Hoyas (Basketball team—History. | United States—Race relations.
Classification: LCC GV884.T48 A3 2020 (print) | LCC GV884.T48 (ebook) | DDC 796.323092 [B]—dc23
LC record available at https://lccn.loc.gov/2020034400
LC ebook record available at https://lccn.loc.gov/2020034401

Our books may be purchased in bulk for promotional, educational, or business use. Please contact your local bookseller or the Macmillan Corporate and Premium Sales Department at (800) 221-7945, extension 5442, or by e-mail at MacmillanSpecialMarkets@macmillan.com.

First Edition 2020

Designed by Kelly S. Too

Printed in the United States of America

1 3 5 7 9 10 8 6 4 2

To Mary Fenlon,
my right-hand man who was a woman

CONTENTS

A Note from the Co-Author xi

Introduction 1

1. Anna and Rob 7
2. The Rabbit 20
3. Red 35
4. Providence 48
5. The Celtics 61
6. The Game Behind the Game 76
7. Seventy Percent 94
8. "My Mortgage" 108
9. Bay Bay, Big Sky, and the Big East 126
10. Patrick 143
11. The Mountaintop 161
12. Bet the Jockey, Not the Horse 182
13. Sometimes the Lion Kills You 196

14. Rayful 208
15. Proposition 42 221
16. Alonzo and Dikembe 238
17. Iverson 250
18. Nike 273
19. Time to Go 290
20. To Be a Coach 305
21. Do Not Forget 317
Acknowledgments 325
Index 327

A NOTE FROM THE CO-AUTHOR

The door was unmarked. It opened into a tiny office, barely big enough for the man's substantial frame, and our feet almost touched as we sat alone together for the first time. The room had no windows, no trophies, only photos of people he admired and loved, from Rosa Parks and Nelson Mandela to Patrick Ewing and Allen Iverson. A small statuette of the Virgin Mary rested on his desk.

We were on the first floor of Georgetown's John R. Thompson Jr. Intercollegiate Athletic Center, down the hall from his larger-than-life statue. Coach Thompson made no small talk when I arrived; there was no conversational layup line to warm up for the writing of his autobiography. He started in a full-court press, flooding my recorder with a wide range of stories. His gaze was penetrating, challenging, and occasionally amused by all the things I did not yet understand. He focused on the time before he became basketball coach at Georgetown, when the only Black people on campus were servants and mascots, and the university had yet to acknowledge the fact that its very existence had been secured by the sale of 272 enslaved Black people.

Two years later, several months before the publication of this book, John Thompson died at age seventy-eight. The outpouring of testimonials to his legacy demonstrates how his impact on higher education, athletics, and Black empowerment remains deeply relevant today. Yet even many of his greatest admirers were unaware of the full meaning of his singular life—the extent of the obstacles he faced, the mentors who taught him how to succeed, why he refused to play the role expected of Black people, what he believed we all must overcome in order to turn our tortured American history into triumph. These are the things he wanted people to learn through his life story, and why he periodically told me, "I don't want this to be a book about basketball."

Soon after we met, Coach moved our sessions to another room at the athletic center, where we sat amid scrapbooks containing newspaper and magazine articles that chronicled his entire coaching career. But Coach had little interest in rehashing what happened in all those famous games. He cared most about the intellectual aspects of "the game behind the game"—the layers of variables and barriers, mostly psychological instead of physical, that he encountered during his career. And he cared intensely about his players, whose well-being dictated his thoughts and actions. Almost every negative headline in those scrapbooks came from his mission to protect and educate his "kids" at all costs—while obtaining equality for Black people.

During countless hours of conversations over those two years, Coach told me on more than one occasion, "We have to get this right," and he deliberated over every word on these pages to make sure they were exactly what he wanted to say. He knew this would be his final testimony, and how much it is still needed.

Thank you, Coach, for opening the door.

Jesse Washington
September 8, 2020

I CAME AS A SHADOW

INTRODUCTION

I always planned to be a teacher, not a basketball coach. I used basketball as an instrument to teach.

My classroom was the court.

When I say teach, I'm not talking about how to run 2-2-1 zone press or the fast break, although we did those things quite well. I felt a responsibility to broaden my players' perspectives, of the world and of themselves. I had to expose my kids to their own intellects and give them a sense of self-worth beyond their physical attributes. I tried to praise them for their minds as much as for making the quick trap off the inbounds pass. But I always knew the reason I had their attention was basketball. Basketball was my instrument to make them listen to everything else.

Basketball also became a vehicle for me to challenge injustices. I didn't think about it that way when I started coaching Georgetown's team in 1972. I just did what came naturally based on how I was raised by my mother and father, the environments that I lived in, and the amount of time I was exposed to certain things. I reacted based on heredity, environment, and time. It wasn't like I strategized or planned to be an outspoken person. If I thought my team, myself, or people in general were being treated unfairly, I tried to say something about it. Sometimes I did not speak up when I should have. Other times, I should have kept my mouth shut. But as I got further in my career, basketball became a way of kicking down a door that had been closed to Black people. It was a way for me to express that we don't have to act apologetic for obtaining what God intended us to have, and that we should be recognized more for our minds than our bodies. All this came out of the strong responsibility I felt to teach kids more than how to throw a ball through a hoop.

Too many Black kids are conditioned to seek recognition based on physical instead of intellectual attributes. We have to stop thinking about power as being able to dunk on somebody or lay somebody out on the football field. Real power is defined by the capacity to think and excel in various situations. Compared with physical abilities, intelligence places you in a better position for a longer period of time. Far more money is made sitting down than standing up.

These are some of the things I felt it was important to teach. But I have to be honest about my motivations. I also wanted to win basketball games. I wanted to win an awful lot. Let's not act like I was Saint John out there, only concerned with education and uplifting the race. Winning was incredibly important to me, and you best believe I was good at it.

People only listen to you if you win. I intended to be heard.

I knew that my success or failure would influence opportunities not only for other Black coaches, but for Black people in general. I couldn't be just a coach because my cause was not the same as most other coaches. My cause was more serious. I had to win because Black people didn't have the right *not* to be successful.

Years ago, I read a quote by Mahatma Gandhi that affected me deeply: "Freedom is not worth having if it does not include the freedom to make mistakes." In other words, to be truly free, we must have the freedom not to be successful, too. When I arrived at Georgetown, I knew of only four other Black head basketball coaches at white colleges. If I didn't win, and win fast, I would have been run out of there and you never would have heard from me again. The next Black coach in line probably wouldn't have gotten hired, either. Most Black people, myself included, did not have the freedom not to be successful.

America is finally realizing that even today, after all that Black people have fought for and achieved, far too many of us are still not free.

As I finish this book, the nation is being torn apart by protests and riots over the death of George Floyd. This man did not have the freedom to make a tiny mistake—allegedly passing a fake twenty-dollar bill. I empathized with Floyd when I heard him cry out "Mama!" as he died beneath that policeman's knee. I was a mama's boy growing up. The safest place I ever felt was in my mother's arms. The protests have forced everyone to confront a lot of deeper injustices, which is something I have always tried to get people to consider. Yes, Black people are being needlessly killed by police, but there are many ways of killing a person. You can kill people by depriving them of opportunity and hope. You can kill people by saying that society is equal, then starting a hundred-yard race with most white people at the fifty-yard line. Discrimination is a lot more complicated today than when I was growing up and they made Black people sit in the back. Trying to fight discrimination today can feel like shooting at ghosts.

But I am proud of the way today's generation is protesting and refusing to be apologetic for insisting on their God-given rights. We have entered a new era of vocalizing our humanity. To reach this point is one reason I did the things I did, to help demonstrate that we should not accept the unacceptable. I never would have imagined years ago that a Black female mayor of D.C. would paint BLACK LIVES MATTER on the street leading to the White House. I respect that young man Colin Kaepernick because he sacrificed his career to protest police brutality. He was a hell of a quarterback who could have played many more years and made a lot more money, but after he kneeled during the national anthem, football was taken away from him. Let's not forget that he was protesting exactly what happened to Floyd.

That said, I disagree with the method Kaepernick chose to protest. I love America. We as Black people are not guests here. We paid a heavy price for our citizenship, which makes me cherish it. I know people who have fought in wars, and I would never personally kneel during the anthem because it would hurt some of them. But I will defend what Kaepernick did with all my heart. I think he showed the utmost love and respect for what the flag represents, which is the right to demonstrate against injustice. I think Kaepernick was honoring every American who died in uniform.

I don't agree with people who riot, either. The looting and burning over Floyd's killing made me disappointed, sad, and angry. But I always said that fear of the riot is more powerful than the riot itself. Now, the fear of the riot has returned.

Some people try to translate Kaepernick's protest as hating America, or they tell LeBron James to "shut up and dribble." Tell me, when do these people think it is appropriate to speak up? When have certain white people ever said it was the right time to protest injustice? Never, that's when. "There goes John again," is what I always heard. I refused to be quiet, but a good deal of the time, I felt like I was by myself. Now, I'd like to see them try to shut up the millions of people who marched in the streets for George Floyd.

Reflecting back on my life, I said and did things that I regret. I hope God forgives me for all the mistakes I made. I do not intend to cast the first stone in this book. But I hope that some of the things I said and did helped us get closer to obtaining real freedom. Ralph Waldo Emerson said we should call our employment by its lowest name, and so take from evil tongues their sharpest weapon. People tried to define me as many things during my career, both good and bad. In my own mind, I just considered myself a secondhand teacher. But this book is not about teaching Allen Iverson to handle the basketball, or Patrick Ewing to control the paint, or Dikembe Mutombo and Alonzo Mourning to block shots. I always told my players not to define themselves by the eight to nine pounds of air inside a round piece of leather, and I apply that same principle to myself. I'm extremely proud of the fact that Patrick, Dikembe, Alonzo, and Allen are in the Naismith Memorial Basketball Hall of Fame. I'm in there, too, although it took them three tries to vote me in because of the stances I took and the statements I made. But when people ask what I'd like to be remembered for, I say, "All the things that kept me *out* of the Hall of Fame."

Here's what happened with all those things. I might be wrong sometimes. But this is how I feel.

1

ANNA AND ROB

My mother always told me to speak my mind.

My father always said, "Son, study the white man."

Growing up, I didn't fully understand what they meant. Now I know my father was teaching me to figure out how things operated beyond our segregated corner of Washington, D.C. And my mother was saying I should not let myself be interpreted or defined as something I was not. They were preparing me for what I would deal with in the future.

The two people who had the greatest influence on my life are my mother and father, Anna Alexander Thompson and John Robert Thompson Senior. I know what they had to go through for me to accomplish anything.

My mother was born and raised in Washington and graduated from Dunbar High School, where a lot of legendary Black people were educated, like Carter G. Woodson, General Benjamin Davis, Charles Hamilton Houston, and Dr. Charles Drew. After high school, my mother earned a degree from Miner Teachers College in Washington. Then she went to teach in a one-room schoolhouse in the tiny town of Compton, in rural St. Mary's County, Maryland. That's where she met my father. They got married and moved back to Washington, but my mother couldn't get work as a teacher. I'm not exactly sure why, but I do know that in the 1930s and '40s, the District of Columbia didn't properly fund the segregated Black schools. Despite the fact that my mother was a trained educator, she took what we called "day's work" to make ends meet.

"Day's work" sounds better than "cleaning white folks' houses," doesn't it?

My mother did day's work mostly on the west side of Rock Creek Park, which was the dividing line for Black people in the city. We called everything over there Across the Park. Most everything Across the Park was white. Georgetown University was Across the Park, too. Georgetown might as well have been the moon, as far as we were concerned. The moon felt more familiar to us than a place like Georgetown.

My father woke up at five every morning, without an alarm clock, to go to work at the Standard Art, Marble and Tile Company at 117 D Street Northwest. My father could not read or write. He was born and raised down in St. Mary's County, working the fields and farms, oystering on the water, and doing other types of manual labor. Some of the children in his family had to work, and some of them went to school. He got the bad roll of the dice. His lack of education feels tragic now, but back then it didn't make much of an impression on us, because we were conditioned to think that a man never being taught to read or write was normal.

I was born in 1941, in my parents' house at 523 2nd Street Southwest. I was the youngest of four children, behind my sisters, Inez, Barbara, and Roberta. When I was maybe a year old, we moved to the Frederick Douglass housing projects in Southeast Washington, also known as Anacostia. Until I was ten, these projects were the center of my world. They consisted of several dozen two-story wooden buildings, not crammed together but spread out with some grass and packed dirt in between. Our apartment had five rooms, maybe six. Behind our apartment was a tiny plot of land, just a few steps wide, where my father grew some vegetables. Everybody in the projects kept their yards clean and looked out for one another. And everybody in the projects was Black, I mean that literally. I never saw a white person there, ever. I had no idea we were living under segregation and poverty, because my parents kept food on the table and clothes on our backs. Everything seemed good to me.

We didn't have any playgrounds in the projects, but we found amusement all over the place. Kids today buy their fun; we learned how to make our fun. We nailed two pieces of wood together in the shape of a cross, attached some wheels from a broken-down bicycle to the short piece, then put some old roller skates on the long piece. We called that a skatemobile. You'd lie on the long piece of wood and race down the hill. We played stickball in the street. I fell in love with baseball on a field that had more bumps than smooth parts. When a ground ball came your way, you'd better watch out that it didn't hit a rock and fly up in your face.

Across the street from the projects the woods began. People in Washington used to call Anacostia "the country" because you had to cross a bridge to get there, and we had grass and some trees. My friends and I had a great time in those woods. You could go in there, get a limb from a tree, put it between your legs, and that was your horse. Go get your cap guns and run around playing cowboy. We picked flowers, apples, and pears. We caught rabbits in shoeboxes: set the box up on a stick, put some food behind the stick, the rabbit hits the stick, and the box comes down over the rabbit. We gazed at horses in a nearby field, collected tadpoles and frogs. I learned that blackberries grow on a vine and mulberries grow on a tree.

There was a popular song when I was growing up that said even though folks might be uneducated or underprivileged, "still they get from A to Z, doin' what comes naturally." That's how we lived, just doing what came naturally.

I always had some sort of little hustle job. Money has never been something I was reluctant to get. I took my Radio Flyer wagon up to the Safeway grocery store and asked people if I could carry their bags home. I sold crepe flowers door to door for Mother's Day. All the houses in the projects were heated with stoves that burned wood or coal, so my friends and I collected scrap wood in bushel baskets and sold it for people to burn in their stoves. Or when coal got dropped off in the street, I could shovel it into an old lady's house and get a few coins.

My sisters liked taking me to the movies at the Carver Theater on Nichols Street, which is now Martin Luther King Avenue. They showed these pictures where the white hero with big guns ran all through the jungle. He always had a bunch of Black natives with him, and the natives went up ahead carrying sticks and spears. If anything went wrong, if they got attacked by a tiger or some enemy, the natives always got killed first.

I used to think, *Why is the Black guy with the stick in the front, and the white guy with all the heavy artillery in the back?*

My father liked to come home from work, sit on the porch, light his pipe or a cigar, and listen to baseball games on the radio with me. I was crazy about baseball as a kid. The Cleveland Indians were our favorite team, because they signed Larry Doby, the first Black player in the American League. Doby went through everything Jackie Robinson did, but without the same recognition. The Indians also had the Black players Luke Easter and Harry "Suitcase" Simpson. Some of the biggest inspirations of my earliest years were Larry Doby and the boxer Joe Louis, because those were the only successful Blacks that society permitted to be visible to us. All we saw were athletes, which had a powerful effect on us.

Boxing was the most popular sport in the projects, by far. When a Joe Louis fight was on the radio, everything stopped, I mean the babies wouldn't even cry. We all gathered to watch the radio. Not listen to the radio—we watched it like it was a television. If Joe knocked one of them suckers out, so many people would come outside yelling and hollering, you thought it was a parade. That's how much respect Black people had for Joe Louis. Educated Black people and Black thinkers were not visible to us.

I may have lived in the Frederick Douglass projects, but I never knew who Frederick Douglass was when I grew up. He wasn't someone we talked about. Black people were too busy surviving.

Money was a constant problem in our household, although my parents kept that hidden from us. The government limited the amount you could earn and remain in public housing, and they sent people to the projects to snoop around. My mother worried that we would lose our home if they found out she made extra money doing day's work. My father took me to the Christmas party at the tile factory every year, and there was a lot of extra food left over. We gathered it up and took it home. I don't know exactly what my father's job was at the factory, but when he came home from work his hands never got clean. He washed them in the kitchen sink, even rubbed lard from a can on his hands, but the dirt was ground in so deep his hands stayed dirty all the time. Despite all this, I never once heard my father complain about having to wake up so early every morning. My mother never complained about scrubbing floors and cleaning toilets, or having to bring home secondhand clothing from houses she cleaned. They kept us fed and clothed and did not raise us to feel we were deprived of anything. Most important, they showed us a tremendous amount of love. As a result, I had an extremely happy childhood.

Let me say right now, this is no sob story about "Oh, look at us poor Blacks suffering in the projects." I never felt oppressed or inferior. I felt very secure. I actually thought we were middle class, because my parents provided for us. We had very little exposure to the outside world. I was a mama's boy, and my sisters called me "little Jesus baby" because they said I could do no wrong in our mother's eyes. I never felt safer than in my mother's arms.

Some of my earliest memories are of my father hugging me and smiling at me. Here's something I think about a lot in my later years: my father always stood behind us and ate what we left behind. At the time, I just thought, *He doesn't want us to waste food.* Now I realize the man must have been hungry but sacrificed so we could have more than him. Was I so selfish that I didn't realize the reason he chewed on that pork chop bone I left behind, why he sopped up the gravy on my plate? My father was providing. He didn't eat so we could eat.

A common stereotype about low-income Black people is they're not loved, the fathers are missing, they're always fighting with each other. My childhood was the opposite of that. My parents made sure I had everything I wanted.

But I also knew what not to want. My parents made sure of that, too.

I knew not to want a new pair of tennis shoes until you could see my sock through the hole. I knew not to want two pairs of dungarees. I knew not to want more than one slice of baloney on a sandwich. When I lived in public housing, I didn't have my own bedroom to sleep in, I had a spot. Bedrooms were for the wealthy. I had a place to sleep, and I was happy.

My mother and father always stressed that education is the most important thing a person can have. My mother is the one who took me to school and dealt with all my teachers, since she was a trained teacher herself. My father spent more time teaching me about life. It started with telling me to study the white man, which did not mean to ingratiate myself, but to learn how his world functioned. He also taught me about things to be ready for at school, how to deal with kids in the neighborhood and people in the wider world. He instructed me to watch and listen to my surroundings, especially when I was someplace new. He always told me, "Watch the person who doesn't say anything, because they're the one who's really listening."

Once he took me to the tile factory, and I saw the way his bosses trusted him for guidance and information. He knew far more than they did about what kind of tile or cement to use in certain situations. I once saw him rip open a bag of mortar, put a little in his mouth, spit it out, and say exactly what kind it was. He did that because he couldn't read the bag. My father told me he trained every new boss they gave him. That taught me how to value people who worked for me, because they might know more than me about certain things.

Forget that line about people without formal education being dumb.

My father taught me more about life than someone with a doctorate. Our family didn't make a big deal out of the fact that he was illiterate, and when I got older I realized that people covered it up for him. We avoided situations where he had to read or write anything. If someone brought a newspaper over to our house with something they wanted him to know, we read the article out loud. If we ate at a restaurant, my mother made a meal suggestion instead of him reading the menu. Think about that for a second. My father grew up only fifty-six miles from the nation's capital, and he could not obtain a basic education. He was one of the most intelligent people I've ever been around, and he couldn't spell "John Thompson."

We all acted like it was no big deal. Being conditioned to think it was normal—that almost feels worse than the fact that it happened.

THE FIRST SCHOOL I went to was Turner Elementary, right on the edge of the projects. I didn't want to go. Forget about kindergarten, I wanted to stay home with my mother. But that wasn't what my mother wanted. Our family was Catholic, like many other Black families in Washington, and after the second or third grade I left Turner and went to the local Catholic school, Our Lady of Perpetual Help. The school was about a mile from the projects. We walked down a hill through some woods along Stanton Road, which was dirt at the time. When we got to the Suitland Parkway, we'd peek up and down to make sure it was safe, cross the parkway, and walk up another hill to get to school. Our Lady of Perpetual Help sat up high on a plateau, you could see the whole city laid out beneath you. People still go up there to watch fireworks on the Fourth of July.

All the students at Our Lady of Perpetual Help were Black, but the nuns and priests were white. This was my first direct, daily exposure to white people.

This was also when I experienced my first problem in life. I couldn't read.

To this day, I don't know why. My mother read to me and tried to help me. My sisters could read, but not me. The nuns thought I was "retarded," that's the word they used at the time. The classrooms had a gold star row, a blue star row, and a baby row. Literally a baby row: the nuns put a picture of a baby at the end of that row. The gold star row was the smartest. The blue was average. They stuck me in the baby row.

Did I know they thought I was stupid? You bet I knew. I never thought of myself as stupid. I was more embarrassed by the fact they put me in the baby row. But that wasn't the only thing. The nun teaching the class had candy, and she'd give you some as a reward if you did the best on the test or you answered a question right.

I always wanted that candy. I never got it.

It didn't take long for my friends and me to give Our Lady of Perpetual Help a different name. We called it Our Little Prison Home. We were too young to say that for any specific reason other than making a joke, but we must have sensed it was not a loving or welcoming place.

My temper started to bubble up then. Once, a classmate started a conflict with me. He was very light-skinned, to the point of looking almost white, and he sat in the gold star row. He did something to me and I plucked him or retaliated in some way. He ran and told the nun. She assumed I was the instigator and grabbed me. I reacted very strongly, told her to take her hands off me, and called her a "white witch."

For me to explode like that was not typical. I wasn't a troublemaker or knocking people down or robbing them. But I was beginning to sense that the light-skinned kids were treated better than those of us with dark skin. They were more pampered and got more praise. I had some vague idea that this was not right, so I resisted strongly. That may have been the birth of me resisting, because that was not in my personality up to that time.

The nun sent me home, and my mother brought me back to school to find out what happened. The nun told my mother I called her a white bitch.

In those days, I didn't curse at all. My mother would have killed me for that. Fortunately there was a girl in my class, Patsy Stewart, who had been sitting beside me and heard what happened. Patsy said, "Mrs. Thompson, he didn't say a bad word, he said 'witch.' "

My behavior was probably a way for me to camouflage what I didn't know. I think I was insecure about not being able to read, or about being dark-skinned. At that age, all the abusive things that were said to me about color came not from whites, but from Black people. We were never around any white people except the nuns and priests. For another Black person to call you dark or black was one of the worst insults you could get. That was to be expected, because Black people wanted acceptance. We transferred what the oppressor was doing to us and inflicted it on someone else. Before I ever encountered white society, I was taught that it was a disadvantage in life to be a darker Black person.

After the situation with the nun, the pastor at the school made a big deal out of taking me for a drive down Suitland Parkway to talk to me about controlling my temper. He said, "You have to be careful, you might grow up and kill somebody and go to jail." In those days, if you were a Black boy and didn't end up in jail, or if you were a Black girl and didn't end up pregnant before you got married, that was considered a successful life. Black folks thought that way, too. Think about how low those expectations were: don't go to jail, and don't get pregnant. The pastor thought he was doing his job.

But I remember one white nun at the school, Sister Eunice, whispering to me later, "A man without any temper is not much of a man at all."

WE DIDN'T HAVE a car, and neither of my parents knew how to drive, so we took the Greyhound bus once or twice a year to visit my father's family down in St. Mary's County. Sometimes all six of us would go together. Other times, my father rode down with me and one of my sisters and dropped us off to stay with our aunts, uncles, and cousins. The only time I saw my father wear a suit was when he visited his hometown. He wanted to show his family he was doing well up in the big city.

We called the Greyhound bus the Hound. It made a rest stop in Waldorf, Maryland, not far outside Washington. Maryland used to be a slave state, and then it had Jim Crow. When we stopped at the little Waldorf rest area, which had snacks and restrooms, Black people had to enter through the back of the building. We couldn't go in the front. When we returned to the bus, we always sat in the back. None of this made an impression on me at the time.

One trip I was sitting next to my father in the back of the Hound when we pulled into the rest stop. My father needed to use the bathroom and walked around to the back entrance. I waited on the bus by myself, looking out the window toward the front of the rest stop, where the white people entered.

All the white folks came back out and got back on the bus. We waited another minute or two. The bus driver closed the door and started rolling.

I sat there by myself, silent and terrified, looking out the window. The bus kept rolling.

My father ran around the corner of the building. The bus stopped. He got on, came to the back, and sat down beside me.

"Why didn't you say something?" my father asked. I couldn't articulate an answer. I was scared to death, a little Black boy on a strange bus full of white people.

My father's hometown of Compton was this tiny place surrounded by farmland as far as you could see. All my relatives lived in little houses on long country lanes, with no electricity or running water. I was fascinated by their way of life, which exposed me to things I had never seen in the projects. To get water, we had to walk down the lane to the pump. To bathe, they heated water on a woodstove, then filled up a metal washtub. You stood up in the middle of the tub and washed yourself. Light came from kerosene lamps. There was no toilet; you went out back to the outhouse. We never thought about it as being a disadvantage. I loved going down there.

I admired how my cousins could walk a mile barefoot on the side of the hot asphalt road to get groceries. They had some tough feet. We walked to a white man's farm and got fresh milk from his cows. I didn't like the taste, but my cousins drank it like water. I thought it was really funny when a fly or a bug flew around the house and my cousins gave it the name of somebody they didn't like. They'd swat the bug and say "Get outta here, Sam!" or "Betty, you better keep away from my porch!"

My cousins taught me to walk along the left side of the road, where the cars came toward you, not from behind you. They showed me to always mount a horse from the left side. I respected my cousins for how hard they worked on the farms. When they took me through the tobacco fields, I saw huge green worms on the tobacco leaves that scared me to death, but my cousins flicked them out of the way like they were nothing. Sometimes I went out to work with them just for fun and didn't last more than fifteen minutes. They stayed out there all day, making money.

When I coached, we called sprinting back on defense or hustling on the fast break "working hard." I wonder if I would feel differently about that phrase if I'd grown up like some of my cousins, working in those fields cutting down tobacco and corn in the sun.

My first time in a boat was with my father in St. Mary's County. We caught a big fish and it frightened me flopping around in the boat. That was nothing compared with my terror when he caught an eel. It was wriggling all over the place until he beat it on the side of the boat to kill it. The first time we went fishing, I caught three fish and he got four. But when we got back to the house, my father said he caught three and I caught four. I was proud of that.

My father was the first person I ever saw play a slot machine, in a little corner store down there called Abel's. I'll never forget it. My father would drop a nickel in the machine, turn, and walk away—but then he'd pause by the door to listen for the sound that would tell whether he hit or not. What I remember is the smile on his face as he turned and listened. If any coins fell in the big metal cup, he would break out laughing. That's how I got into playing the slots.

In the evenings, people sat on the porch and played instruments. I had a cousin who played the guitar like nobody I had ever heard. On Saturdays, my relatives took me into Leonardtown, which had a back street with speakeasy-type joints where Black folks danced and had a good time. I'd be on the sidelines, peeping at what was going on. My sister Barbara was the best dancer I'd ever seen. On Sundays, baseball was a big deal. Teams representing the different parts of St. Mary's County played each other, and people treated it almost like a major league game.

The other thing we did on Sundays was go to St. Francis Xavier Church.

The Jesuits had come to southeastern Maryland about the year 1640. They bought 850 acres of land and started farming it with slave labor. In 1662, they built St. Francis Xavier. It's still there today, a small wood and brick building with ten or eleven pews, one of the oldest churches in America.

Up in Washington, our Catholic church was all Black. Down in St. Mary's County, there were white people in the church, too, and all of us Blacks had to sit in the back. When they passed the collection plate, they took our collection second. When Holy Communion was given, the whites went up to the altar first, and the Blacks followed only after they were finished. When the Catholic festivals came, they had one for Blacks and one for whites. Everything about the church was segregated.

To say I accepted all this would be incorrect. I hardly even identified it. Everyone acted like Blacks sitting in the back was the way things were supposed to be. We were mentally conditioned. I didn't get angry in the back of the church and want to throw a brick through the stained-glass window. Later, I got mad that I *didn't* get mad about it. I got mad that I wasn't aware of it, because that's the bigger danger.

I was just a little boy at the time. Sometimes I asked questions: "Why can't we go to Communion with them? Why can't we do our collection now?" Whatever the adults told me, it was enough to make me settle down at that moment. But before long, I started thinking more about what happened, like, *This priest was saying Jesus loves everybody the same, but I had to go to Communion second, after the white folks. You're telling me one thing about God and Jesus, and you're practicing another thing.* That was the first time I recognized racism. In the Catholic Church.

This isn't some story I heard from the elders. The segregation in our church, I saw that. I lived that. All that stuff people said later about me being hung up on race, where do they think I learned to be racially conscious? I didn't teach myself. I was taught by the things I experienced, and then I responded based on heredity, environment, and time.

I do forgive people. A lot of white people today weren't alive then, although they are still benefiting from the injustices of the past. But I can forgive. I can live with white people and have fun with them and trust and love them. Jesus said we have to forgive.

But Jesus never told us to forget. That's why I'm haunted by my past.

My mother and father deserve more credit than anybody else for the things I accomplished. I had a fantastic childhood because they loved and protected me. But just because my parents gave me happiness, that doesn't mean the happiness they gave me was right. Happiness isn't an indication of fairness. We were trained what to be happy about. We were trained what not to want. We were trained not to wonder why my mother had to clean toilets instead of teach school, and not to question why someone as smart as my father couldn't spell his own name.

This was the training America gave us.

Did America do this consciously, subconsciously, intentionally, unintentionally?

Whatever. It happened.

2

THE RABBIT

At the end of the fifth grade, the nuns told my mother that because I was "retarded," I had to leave Our Lady of Perpetual Help. I guess the help wasn't so perpetual after all. My mother knew there was nothing wrong with me intellectually. Now I realize that when my mother always told me to speak my mind, she was teaching me more than that I had the right to say what I thought. She also was saying I should not let myself be interpreted or defined as something I was not. She had a lot of wisdom about how the world operated. She wanted me to stand up for myself and not be apologetic for the things God intended everyone to have.

My mother enrolled me in the sixth grade in the Washington public school system, at Harrison Elementary School at 13th and V Streets Northwest. My teacher there was a tall, no-nonsense Black woman named Sametta Wallace Jackson.

I would not be where I am today if not for Sametta Wallace Jackson.

One of the first things she told us in her classroom was, "Good odor or no odor. Good hair or no hair. Comb it or cut it off." Then she put her feet up where we all could see them. She had some big feet. She said, "Go ahead and laugh now. Laugh as loud as you want, because this is the last day laughing at these big feet will be allowed." She focused as much on how to behave with manners and respect as she did on reading, writing, and arithmetic. We knew not to yawn in her class. We would never even imply Mrs. Jackson was boring. We knew someone was in charge, and it wasn't us.

After a few days in her classroom, Mrs. Jackson told me, "You're not stupid. You just can't read." At that moment, she changed my life. She was able to see potential and ability in me that those nuns could not. She cared enough about me as a person not to make assumptions based on what things looked like from the outside.

Mrs. Jackson called my mother in to school and told her I needed a reading specialist. We went all over the city looking for one. I saw some troubled children at these places, kids with behavioral problems, maybe some mental health issues. I saw kids reading books upside down. I didn't know what all that meant at my young age, but I knew something wasn't right, and I knew I was being lumped in with them. Once I was taken into a room where a white man sat behind a desk. He said, "Name everything you can think of." I'm thinking it had to be a trick, because there was no end to what I could think of. It would take all day just to go through what I played with in the woods behind the projects. I named some things I saw in the room, then named some other things, but after a while it felt silly and awkward. No matter what you say, you're leaving a whole lot out. I think it was the same sort of test they employed to keep Black people from voting—asking how many jelly beans in a jar, or how many bubbles in a bar of soap. No matter what, you can't really answer the question. The man behind the desk gave my mother an official diagnosis that I had a learning disability.

After a few experiences like that, I started to wonder, in my unformed mind, if there really was something wrong with me. But my mother remained supportive and reassuring, and the fact she and Mrs. Jackson had confidence in me is what got me through. I knew they didn't think I was stupid.

Finally my mother found Dr. Harry Lewis, one of the first Black reading specialists in Washington. He made me bite a pencil while I read to myself so I wouldn't move my lips and sound out the words. He sat patiently with me and showed me other techniques that I don't remember now, but obviously they worked. The fact that he was a Black man made an impression on me. Mrs. Jackson coordinated what Dr. Lewis taught me with her instruction at Harrison Elementary, and that was when I started to be able to handle things academically in school. I still have no idea why I couldn't read before that.

There's a theme here, which is that Black educators were able to help me and white ones did not. I'm not saying there were no good white educators, or that no white people would have helped me. Maybe at another school with white teachers, I would have had a different experience. But it's a fact that for whatever reason, most of the white people I had encountered in the educational system up to that point in my life thought I was "retarded." You can read that however you want to.

About this time, when I was ten years old, I observed a lot of discussion and huddling between my mother and father at home, and then they told us children that our family had to move. I later learned the people who ran the projects found out about some of the day's work my mother did Across the Park, and they said that this disqualified us from living there. In 1951, we moved from the Frederick Douglass projects to 1425 W Street Northwest, where my mother's sister lived, not far from Harrison Elementary.

The apartment on W Street was in bad shape, far worse than the projects. We were on the first floor, and a public hallway ran through the set of rooms we lived in. You had to cross the public hall to go into the living room, where my sisters Barbara and Roberta slept. The public hall went up to the second floor, where my aunt and her daughter lived. I slept in the kitchen on a foldout sofa. At night you would see mice running around. My entertainment was blowing a bean through a tube at the mice scampering through the house. I thought it was fun to play with rat traps like they were toys. Sometimes we had problems keeping the electricity on, and I remember needing to open the back door and stand in the doorway to get enough light to comb my hair.

That's when I learned that bricks hide poverty. Back in Southeast we could tell which were the poor people's houses because they were made of wood and would be falling apart. The house on W Street had a nice brick front and looked fine from the outside, but was so terrible inside it was condemned by the city after we moved out.

My parents protected me from a lot of things I could have been insecure about, and, most important, they provided psychological security through the power of their love. So life on W Street was fine despite the living conditions. It was better than fine, because the neighborhood made life exciting.

We had a store on every corner and three movie theaters nearby. We could walk everywhere and didn't have to catch the bus. We had options. No more grass and trees, everything was concrete. Now I understood why they called Anacostia the country. Each alleyway and rooftop held the promise of something new and exciting. My friends and I played stoopball on our block, throwing a tennis ball up against the front steps. We played touch football in the alleys. I played my first organized sport, on a baseball team whose uniforms were purchased by a local numbers runner named Simpson. He had a restaurant on North Capitol Street, where one of my sisters worked. We tried to play basketball in the schoolyards, but the people who ran the schools didn't like us in there. Sometimes when we played there, we had to catch the basketball before it hit the ground so nobody would hear it bounce and kick us out. One day I found some books that a student had left on the playground of one of those Catholic schools. I figured I would get some brownie points, so I picked up the books and ran them over to the convent. The nun thanked me and God-blessed me. I strutted back out to the court and started bouncing my basketball with no fear. Man, that nun came out and chased us out so fast. Those books didn't mean a thing to her.

Over the next few years, I had all kinds of jobs on W Street. We collected bushel baskets of clear glass bottles in the alleys and sold them. Soon I knew all the alleys like the back of my hand, and the winos would tell you where they left a bottle for you. The store on our corner, at 14th and W, was Carl's Meat Market. People got paid on Fridays, so every Thursday, Mr. Carl would print up handbills with the sale prices for his meats. He paid us to slide handbills under doors in our neighborhood. I delivered the *Washington Daily News*, they called it "serving the paper." I served the paper to people's homes and collected the subscription money. I was good at it so they made me the route captain, which I didn't like because that meant I had to get out of my neighborhood all the way to Adams Morgan to collect from the people who wouldn't pay the other delivery boys. Some of the places I served the paper were pretty rough, but it was home to us. Sometimes when people opened the door, I knew they were doing something illegal. They usually gave the biggest tips.

One of those alleys around W Street is where I first saw the famous picture of Emmett Till, the fourteen-year-old boy lynched in Mississippi for talking to a white woman. *Jet* magazine printed the photograph of Emmett in his casket. His face was grotesque, from having been beaten and shot in the head and thrown in the river. Kids in the neighborhood were passing the picture around, talking about how a boy our age got lynched. I also remember being in class at Harrison Elementary when they announced the Supreme Court decision in *Brown v. Board of Education*. When the news came over the loudspeakers, everybody started cheering and yelling. But I was so young, and so protected by my parents, I didn't make a direct connection between these events and my own life, even though much of Washington was still segregated.

Mr. Carl, who owned the meat market, was white. Sometimes his son Jimmy used to go around with us to pass out the handbills. Jimmy was my age. Once we went into a lunch counter on 14th Street, and the owner said no Black people could sit down at the counter. Jimmy couldn't understand and made a fuss about it. It didn't bother me, because we as Black people were conditioned to accept it. We were conditioned not to think beyond the way things were.

There's an old story about a dog who was tied up on a long chain in his yard. Every day, people walked by the yard and the dog would get all ferocious, he growled and barked and chased the passersby. Then the dog would yank up against the end of his chain, and he couldn't chase the people any farther. One day they took the chain off the dog. The next person who walked by, the dog took off running and chased him like hell—then stopped where the chain used to end. The dog had been conditioned to place that limit on himself.

When I was growing up, a lot of us Black people were like that dog. Some of us still are.

In addition to helping me learn to read, Sametta Wallace Jackson did something else extremely important. At the end of the school year, in the spring of 1953, she informed my mother I would not be promoted to the seventh grade. She didn't ask. She told my mother I would repeat sixth grade.

Sixth grade was the last year of elementary school. I was over six feet tall at the time. I was the biggest kid in the building, by a lot. I was supposed to be leaving for junior high school. Now I'm staying another year? It wasn't like nobody would notice this giant kid coming back to the same school again. Repeating the sixth grade had the potential to be humiliating for me. But what Mrs. Jackson did, which I will never forget, is protect my feelings. When my classmates had graduation preparations or other activities, she came up with reasons for me to be someplace else. She would invent some activity in another part of the school, or send me on an errand to the store. She was conscious of my dignity as a young person.

Remember how I thought that my family was middle class, because we never missed a meal and had all the things we needed? Reality started to dawn on me when Mrs. Jackson sent me to the store to get some food for the principal's dog. They instructed me to buy this special hamburger. I knew my meats from passing out flyers for Mr. Carl. I remember thinking, *This dog is eating better food than my family ate for dinner last night.*

But the point is that Mrs. Jackson not only recognized that I could think, she also protected my feelings. This stuck with me when I coached at Georgetown. If a player had to sit out some games because of bad grades, I didn't announce it to the media. I might even tell the trainer, "Put a knee brace on him," to protect the kid. When I recruited players, I never assumed they were stupid if they had bad grades or test scores. A lot of them had been stuck under low expectations like those at Our Little Prison Home, where all we were expected to achieve was staying out of jail. Mrs. Jackson planted the idea in me to look deeper at a ballplayer's life and figure out if he was capable of academic success with the proper support.

I wasn't trying to look deeper at a kid who couldn't shoot, though. I didn't offer the proper support to any slow, short guys. Let's be honest about my motivations. I was trying to support kids who could help me win basketball games.

Once these players got to Georgetown, they had to take their education seriously. They had to study and go to class. That part was on them. I always told my players, "If you want to be a slave, I refuse to be the master." In other words, if you want to allow Georgetown to make all this money and prestige off you and not get an education in return, I won't be part of it. I will put you out.

All of this connects back to Sametta Wallace Jackson. She saved my life, and she had as much influence on my coaching as some of the greatest minds in basketball.

When Mrs. Jackson died, the people who handled her estate said she had a newspaper article about me in her dresser drawer. That brought a tear to my eye.

After I repeated the sixth grade, I entered the seventh grade at Brown Junior High School in the fall of 1954. We also left our house on W Street and moved to 766 19th Street Northeast, just off Benning Road. This was the first house my parents owned, and the first time I had my own bedroom. I was still obsessed with baseball. I played first base and sometimes the outfield. I'll never forget hitting a home run with runners on first and second to end a game. In addition to the few

Black major league stars, I worshipped Stan Musial, Herb Score, and a bunch of other white ballplayers. I hardly knew anything about the Negro Leagues. I wanted to break Babe Ruth's home run record, not Josh Gibson's.

My father would take me to Griffith Stadium to see the Washington Senators play Larry Doby's Cleveland Indians, and the field itself amazed me. I had never seen grass that pretty and dirt that smooth. Nobody could miss a ground ball on that. My father always took me home during the seventh inning stretch, which made me mad, but I wasn't thinking about the fact that he had to get up for work at five in the morning.

I played baseball all over the neighborhood, but people saw this tall kid walking around with a baseball glove and started making remarks. Like, "Hey, you need to get over to the basketball court, because all that height is wasted with that glove." So I started dipping into basketball a bit more. I wasn't very good when I started.

Two young neighborhood guys around Benning Road, Ellsworth "Sandy" Freeman and Bob Grier, liked to help local kids with sports. They were in their early twenties and became like my older brothers as they introduced me to a different element of Washington basketball. They were the first people to recognize that I could get a college scholarship and to push me in that direction. Sandy got his nickname because he was light-skinned with reddish hair. He was a quiet person. Whenever Sandy got angry, he smiled. Bob had thick glasses, and everybody called him Batman. Both of them were good non-scholarship type of playground basketball players. They had regular jobs, and Sandy had a car. Sandy and Bob would pull up in the alley next to my house and beep the horn. "Batman's here," my mom would say. I'd hop in the car and we'd go looking for a game. I was still a mama's boy and not tough at all, but nobody ever messed with me with Sandy and Bob around.

The gym teacher at Brown Junior High, Mr. Kermit Trigg, also played an important role in my development. Between Sandy, Bob, and Mr. Trigg, I started to improve. I got my name in the paper for the first time, a little article in the school publication that mentioned me scoring a few points in some game. One of my sisters read it to my father, and my family was proud of me. But I clearly recall my sisters telling me, "Don't take this too seriously, because the same people will come back and criticize you." Years later, both the *Washington Post* and *Sports Illustrated* published articles about me with the title "The Gospel According to John." My sister Roberta saw them and told me something very simple and humbling: "We know you." My sisters always kept me grounded.

While I mostly played pickup with Sandy and Bob, Mr. Trigg made me do different drills like jump rope, or leap up and make a chalk mark as high as I could on the wall. I hated all this because I just wanted to play ball with the other kids. But Mr. Trigg was preparing me for something I had not yet seen.

This is when I started hearing about the Rabbit.

Everywhere you went in the neighborhood, people were talking about what this Rabbit person did on the basketball court. He sounded to me like Superman. People said he could leap way over the rim, shoot from deep, make all kinds of difficult runners and floaters and bank shots. They said he could change direction in midair. Guys on the playground were trying to demonstrate a trick shot where Rabbit looked like he jumped into the air but kept one foot on the ground. I had to ask my sisters, who is this Rabbit? They said, "That's that boy over at Spingarn High School. His name is Elgin Baylor."

Elgin was seven years older than me. He quickly became my hero. No, he was something above a hero. This didn't happen through television or the Internet. It happened organically, through word of mouth, sitting under a tree at the playground court with Sandy and Bob telling me what sounded like tall tales but I knew were true. I have a statue in my house right now of an African man sitting down and talking to three little Black children. That's how it was with me learning about Rabbit, like receiving a message in the village through a drumbeat. It didn't take long for me to idolize Rabbit and want to excel in basketball because of him.

But think about this for a second. At this point, I had never seen Elgin Baylor play. He was just a name. But he was a name that got so much respect and attention, from so many people, and there were no other examples of Black achievement that felt close enough to touch. Nobody in the neighborhood was talking about Dr. Charles Drew. But Spingarn was right next door to my school, Brown Junior High, so I wanted to be like Rabbit. That made me practice and play a lot more.

In the summer of 1957, when I had just finished the ninth grade, Elgin came home from college in Seattle and word shot though the city: "Rabbit's home." I finally got to see him play, at Randall playground down by the baseball stadium. The bus drivers were on strike, so Sandy and I walked an hour from Benning Road all the way down to Randall. About a thousand spectators showed up, no lie. I was completely starstruck. I swear Elgin had on regular shoes, like loafers or something, and still won every game. The whole walk home, literally all I talked about was Rabbit. Later that summer word came down that Rabbit was going to play Wilt Chamberlain at Kelly Miller playground. Wilt was still in college, at Kansas, but we all knew he was seven feet tall and strong as a bull. When we arrived, there had to be two thousand people there, just from word of mouth. That's not at all exaggerated. They were playing five-on-five, and even though Wilt was dominant, Elgin did more than Wilt and won every game.

Soon I knew everything there was to know about Rabbit. How he tied his shoes, how he ran, his mannerisms. He had some sort of nervous twitch with his head, it would quiver when he caught the ball, and he wasn't trying to fake you out. I knew how he liked to shoot with one hand. I had a friend who would go to the newsstand and buy us all the national newspapers just to read how Rabbit was doing. Now, there was no way in hell I was going to be as good a player as Rabbit. When I tried to lift up one leg and shoot, I was lucky if I hit the rim. But striving for what he represented was important to me.

One day some months later, I was playing ball with Sandy and Bob across the street from Brown Junior High. The park was jumping that day, lots of guys waiting for next, people laughing and joking, guys smoking and shooting dice. A car pulled up and Rabbit got out.

I swear, a hush fell over the entire park. His mere presence stopped everybody in their tracks. I think the squirrels stopped gathering nuts. Rabbit came down the hill to the court, and I ended up on his team. That was the first time I played in a game with him. I wasn't very good then, so all I remember is trying to stay out of the way.

Let me tell you right now, none of Elgin's reputation was exaggerated. He was six foot five, with unbelievable quickness and strength in the air. When people talk about the best ever to come out of Washington, you need to put Elgin at number one, skip over two, three, four, and five, then count the rest of the guys from there, including Kevin Durant. When I was on the Celtics, my teammates used to tease me about how I idolized Elgin. They respected him, but they liked to mess around and say that Elgin could only go to his right. Okay. In the 1962 NBA Finals at the Boston Garden, Elgin was guarded by Satch Sanders, the best defensive forward in the league. If he got by Satch, he had to deal with Bill Russell, probably the best shot blocker in the history of the game.

Elgin scored 61. But he could only go to his right, huh?

Later in life, Elgin and I got to be good friends, but to this day he doesn't know how responsible he is for the course of my life in basketball and in general. You could never convince me, rightly or wrongly, that Kevin Durant or LeBron James is a better player than Rabbit. I couldn't even compare Michael Jordan objectively and fairly with Elgin Baylor. That's how much of an influence Rabbit had on my life. I wouldn't say anybody is better than Rabbit. That would be heresy.

This is one of the dangerous things with athletes. Athletes don't choose to be role models. The public chooses them. Setting an example is part of an athlete's responsibility, particularly with African Americans, because there still are not enough examples for Black kids of pathways to success other than sports.

The bigger picture of the influence Elgin had on my life is how

Black people were not praised or acknowledged for intellectual accomplishments. I was deprived of being exposed to Black thinkers. My mother was a teacher with a college degree but cleaned houses. Practically the only Black people we saw on TV were Amos and Andy. When you read the classified ads in the newspaper, the jobs collecting garbage and laying bricks stipulated "blacks only." The jobs in an office said "whites only." They actually printed those things, right there in the newspaper.

What else did we have to strive for, other than being an athlete?

WHEN I WAS still in junior high school, Sandy and Bob took me down to the Police Boys Club No. 2 on 3rd and K Streets Northwest. That's where I met three men who had an enormous influence on my life, starting with James "Jabbo" Kenner.

Mr. Jabbo was a retired boxer who started Boys Club No. 2 in 1936. The boys clubs in Washington were white-only until Mr. Jabbo started No. 2 for Black kids. He was a big, tall, dark-skinned man, jolly and kind. He was well known for getting free stuff all around Washington and giving it to kids in need. Clothes, food, shoes, furniture, you name it. Even though he was clean-shaven, Mr. Jabbo's appearance and demeanor made him look like a Black Santa Claus.

Two counselors who worked with Mr. Jabbo were Bill Butler and Julius Wyatt. Mr. Butler was a cool guy, always immaculately dressed in slacks and nice shirts. He had won a Lincoln in a contest, and he liked to hang out in front of the club polishing his car while talking to all the kids. Mr. Wyatt was a smaller guy with a limp. These men cared about us, and we knew it. They were always advising kids about school and helped a lot of them get athletic scholarships. They stayed on your case about being respectful, but in a loving way. To this day, when I go into Boys Club No. 2, I can hear Mr. Butler saying, "Hey baby, take your hat off." We learned there were rules and protocols we had to follow. They coached us in a lot of sports, but they taught us much more than how to play ball. They were the first people to show me that good coaching is more about life guidance than about sports. I admired Mr. Jabbo, Mr. Butler, and Mr. Wyatt, and I wanted to be like them. They weren't working with you just to win a championship or get recognition from a shoe company. They wanted to help you as a person.

The basketball court at Boys Club No. 2 was a converted classroom. The ceiling was so low, you had to shoot jumpers flat. A water pipe on the wall went around the court and under the basket. If the ball hit the water pipe, that was out of bounds. But we didn't mind because there were very few places to play basketball indoors.

As time went on, more boys clubs were opened for Black kids, and guys identified themselves by the clubs they played for. We were from the Deuce. I've spent the rest of my life hanging around Boys Club No. 2. My sons, John and Ronny, grew up playing there. When I was coaching at Georgetown I would bring my sons down on Saturday morning and stay the entire day, just hanging out, talking, and watching the games. We'd go across the street to get a fish sandwich for lunch and be set. People started complaining I was there to recruit, especially after the NCAA made rules about where coaches could interact with recruitable athletes. Yeah, there were recruitable athletes there, and they might have gotten to know me while I was there, but I didn't go to No. 2 to recruit. I made it very clear to the enforcement people that I don't care what the NCAA says. I've been coming down here my whole life.

A lot of police officers were involved with Boys Club No. 2, and I experienced police doing wonderful things for Black kids. But at the same time, I had a natural suspicion of police based on how they were perceived in my neighborhood. A Black police officer named Dixon patrolled the area around my house on Benning Road. When my friends and I were playing in the streets and someone hollered "Dixon's coming!" we all took off running, even though we hadn't committed any crime. Even if we just heard a siren, we ran. We knew on a subconscious level that if the police got their hands on us, we could be harmed even if we were innocent. Dixon treated us fine, as far as I knew, and didn't have a bad reputation. But the police were a symbol, and not of friendship. Police meant run. We were trained from birth to think the police were our enemy. In some cases, for good reason.

JUNIOR HIGH SCHOOL went through the ninth grade in those days. I was improving as a player and dead set on going to Spingarn, because Rabbit had gone there. I wanted to play for his coach, Lieutenant Brown, who was good friends with Mr. Trigg. The Lieutenant was well known for being a tough, disciplinarian type of guy. People said before one game Rabbit did something wrong and the Lieutenant locked him in the dressing room at the start of the game. Spingarn was losing at halftime, so the Lieutenant let loose the Rabbit. Elgin went off in the second half and Spingarn won. Those type of legends made me determined to play there. You couldn't have bribed me to go anywhere else. Then I heard that the Lieutenant wasn't coaching basketball anymore, he was switching to football the next year. That opened the possibility for me to go to a different high school.

Bob Grier used to take me to the 12th Street YMCA, where we met a guy named Leo Miles who had associations with the white schools. Remember the jungle pictures I used to watch at the Carver Theater? Leo was like the Black guy who went ahead with the spear. He mentioned me to Bob Dwyer, the coach of Archbishop Carroll High School, who got my phone number and came over to our house on Benning Road.

Carroll was a white school that was just starting to integrate, mostly through its basketball team. There were no white people living in my neighborhood at all. I had never interacted with white people in a significant way, except for the nuns back at Our Little Prison Home. There was no real give-and-take with the white people down in St. Mary's County. Everything I knew about white people I'd heard secondhand. But my mother liked the idea of my going back to Catholic school, and Mr. Trigg said it was a good idea, too. Dwyer offered me a scholarship so I wouldn't have to pay for books or anything else.

I had an interview with the pastor at the school that we both knew was a formality. He asked why I wanted to come to Carroll. I told him, "To play basketball." Apparently that wasn't the right thing to say, and he gave me some sort of speech about bettering myself. On some level, I knew some white people were thinking that basketball was the only reason they would bring niggers up there anyway. They didn't do a good job of camouflaging their reasons for wanting me, so I didn't camouflage mine.

Mr. Trigg saw me walking down the hall one day holding the Carroll entrance application. He demanded to have a look and saw that I had checked the box for "general studies," which was a vocational track. On the spot, Mr. Trigg made me change my choice to the academic track. He told me, "John, you are going to college."

I laugh when people ask how many people in my family graduated from college. Forget college, only two of us graduated from high school—my other two sisters had to go to work and earn money. All of them were smart, probably smarter than me.

Five years earlier, I had arrived in Sametta Wallace Jackson's classroom almost illiterate. Once I could read, I did all right in school, just well enough to pass. Moving to the next grade was all I wanted to do. But now, when I looked at my classmates who were known for being smart, I noticed I was just as intelligent as they were, regardless of what the tests or the grades said. Still, as I prepared to enter the tenth grade at Archbishop Carroll High School in the fall of 1957, I was not an academically oriented person.

All I cared about was chasing the Rabbit.

3

RED

My father always told me to study the white man. I started to understand what he meant when I got to Archbishop Carroll High School in 1957. He was talking about more than how individual white people acted. He meant I should learn their system.

Carroll was the first place I interacted with white people on a regular and not superficial basis. I kept quiet. I observed. I was cautious. I immediately noticed that not all white people were bad. Not all of them hated us. But by the same token, a lot of the white people who were opposed to how we were treated didn't stand up and say anything about it. The price for doing that would have been too high. They might have been sympathetic to us, but they kept quiet, because they could have lost their jobs or their status. That doesn't make them bad people. I'm not sure I wouldn't have acted the same way. Lots of Black people didn't defy the system either. Martin Luther King didn't have all of Black America lining up behind him. A lot of Black folks wanted King to shut the hell up.

Our Carroll basketball team ended up as one of the best high school teams ever in Washington, and we won our last fifty-five games in a row. Not coincidentally, we were one of the city's first integrated teams, meaning a white school with Black players. Integration only happened in one direction. We had Tom Hoover at power forward, he was one of the best big men to ever come out of Washington. He taught me how to add a physical dimension to my game, although I never became an overpowering player. Our point guard was George Leftwich. He showed me what competition was all about. We'd be up by twenty points on somebody, and if they scored twice in a row Leftwich jumped down our throats. John Austin and Kenny Price were very good. The two white guys who contributed most were Walt Skinner and Monk Malloy, who later became president of the University of Notre Dame.

Bob Dwyer was a smart coach. I respected and admired him. He preached brotherhood and sacrificing for the good of the team. He did things to bring the team together like invite us all to his house for dinner. He also made racial appeals to motivate the team and cultivate an us-against-the-world mentality, and they worked. He said things like "Those people downtown think you're running wild on the court" or "The people downtown say you don't have any discipline." His phrase "downtown" was code for white people. We understood exactly what he was saying. We heard other coaches in the Catholic league say those same things about Black public school teams who pressed and ran the fast break. As a result, consciously or not, we went out on the court not only trying to win the game, but trying just as hard to prove that the people you thought were dumb niggers could play intelligently.

Dwyer also introduced us to the politics of high school basketball in Washington, explaining why certain schools got left out of tournaments or why suburban coaches wouldn't come into the city to play us. I started to understand that winning required way more than the storybook fairy tale about working hard. This game behind the game is what my father was talking about when he told me to study the white man. He wasn't telling me all whites are racist and I was supposed to dislike them. He meant that they live in a different world, so understand how it works. Understand how things get done when you're not in the room.

We won the Catholic league championship in 1958, when I was a sophomore, but in the city championship game we got killed by Cardozo, an all-Black public school. A kid named Rip Scott shot us out the gym. What made it worse is we had beaten Cardozo during the regular season. That loss devastated me. I refused to take the bus back to school and walked all the way home from the game with my best friend Fred Thomas, crying every step of the way. The next day I cut out a newspaper article about the loss, put it in my pocket, and carried it everywhere I went. I looked at it all the time and said to myself, *This ain't happening again.*

The 1959 city championship game was a rematch against Cardozo. I had 17 points at halftime. Game over.

Through all these basketball games, my parents almost never came to see me play. They were busy providing. They didn't associate basketball with something that would make them money or change their place in life, as many parents do today. They considered basketball recreation, until I started getting recruited by colleges. I once remarked to my mother, maybe in a selfish way, that Dad never came to my games. That's one of the few times she got truly angry at me. She said, "Your father works himself to the bone for this family! He loves you more than anything, which is why he makes sure that he puts food on your plate every night." When I thought about it, I realized she was right.

My father only saw me play one game in high school. Afterward, he walked across the floor to meet me, and he had tears in his eyes. That's the only time I ever saw him cry. I never felt so proud in my life.

AFTER MY FIRST year at Carroll, I played all through the summer. Sandy and Bob would pick me and a couple other guys up and we'd cruise around looking for a game. We would pass a playground, see some guys, slow the car down, and call out the window, "You got five?" The competition on the playgrounds was a lot tougher than at school, no question. So many terrific Black players didn't get an opportunity to play organized ball. Think about the fact that someone as incredible as Elgin Baylor didn't get recruited out of high school, and wound up at some obscure college in Idaho basically by accident before he went to Seattle University. Lots of other guys could have been outstanding in college or the pros. One cat named Chicken Breast could really get it done. I have no idea what his given name was, but everybody knew Chicken Breast. Another very tough player was Gary Mays, who had one arm and was known as the Bandit. You heard that right: Gary had one arm, but if there were fifty guys at the park and they chose up sides, Gary was always on the court. The tiny scoring guard Wil Jones could have been great in the NBA. Little Wil was a shooter's shooter, talked a whole lot of trash, and always backed it up. I could go on and on about all the great players you never heard of. That's one reason I laugh at people who argue about this or that player being the "greatest of all time." Some of the best basketball players in history never got the opportunity to put on a uniform. And yes, I saw both Michael Jordan and Bill Russell play, up close and personal. But we'll never know what some of these other guys could have been.

There was a white park out in Chevy Chase that had an indoor court plus a playground outside. Some of the white guys on the Carroll team took me there to play, but the people who ran the gym wouldn't let me inside. Then some of my Black friends wanted to go there and play outside, in the informal pickup games, where we were sometimes allowed to play. I couldn't understand why they wanted to do that and told them to go without me. The competition was much better in our neighborhood. Why go where we weren't wanted, to play in worse games? I didn't understand at the time that oppressed people often have an unconscious desire to prove themselves acceptable—in other words, human—to the people with power. Then someone spray-painted NIGGERS GO HOME right on the outdoor playground. I guess the niggers never did go home, because later Chevy Chase tore down the court and built a library in its place.

I also played in the summer with the Carroll team. Dwyer got us together to play in various local tournaments. That's how I met one of the greatest mentors and friends of my life.

Red Auerbach, the coach of the Boston Celtics, lived in Washington in the off-season. Red had gone to college in Washington, then coached high school and pro ball here before going to Boston. When I met him, the Celtics had just won their first championship. Red was friends with Dwyer, and I started to see him at some of our practices or summer games. Then I started seeing him at playgrounds in the city, all by himself. He never had an entourage. He'd be sitting there in shorts with a tennis racket and the newspaper, watching games on the playgrounds. Red was like a dope addict when it came to basketball.

He wasn't coming to watch me play. Hoover and Leftwich and some other guys were better than me then. He just loved the game. Before long, he was showing the other Carroll guys and me little things. He'd jump on the court and show us how to pivot or ball fake. Red always loved a good ball fake. I was quite inquisitive about basketball. Not about academics—I just wanted to get my C and get out of there. But when Red came around, I noticed he was always willing to give advice, so I began to ask a lot of questions. I wanted to know how to become a good player. I thought he could make me into another Rabbit.

None of us were awed by Red's presence. The NBA wasn't big in the late 1950s. The games were just starting to get on TV, and college coaches had way more publicity than Red. Nobody in the neighborhood was talking about us going to the NBA. They told us to get a college scholarship.

As my high school career progressed and I started to get taller and better, Red took more of a personal interest in me, and he invited me up to Kutsher's in the Catskill Mountains near Monticello, New York. Kutsher's was a Jewish resort that hosted lots of college players, and some pros, in the summer for exhibition games. We worked there as bellhops or waiters and played games at night in front of the guests.

Dwyer introduced Red to my parents, and he told them about Kutsher's. I don't think my mother and father could name any of the teams in the NBA. They paid very little attention to the game of basketball itself. About all they knew was if the ball went in the hoop, it was a good thing. But they paid a lot of attention to me. My mother said, "I don't know anything about this Kutsher's place, but I'll say a prayer, and you can go."

Over several summers, Red drove me up to Kutsher's and back, just the two of us in his big sporty car. Red talked the whole way. He told me little basketball things, like if you really want to understand a player, watch him "off the ball," when he doesn't have the ball in his hands. Red talked more about life than basketball, explaining his experiences and observations about the way things worked in the world. I mostly listened, and sometimes I asked questions. I didn't realize I was listening to the Aristotle of basketball. Can you imagine how many people would have paid money to sit and listen to Red talk?

His lessons ranged far and wide. Some of them were basic, like, "If you're around an older person, even if there's nothing you want to know, go ask them a question as a way of paying them respect." Other things he taught me were more complex. One situation he described was how one of his players he coached before the Celtics, with the Washington Capitols pro team, went behind his back to the owner and stole Red's job. He told me not everyone on your team or in your organization will have your best interests in mind. He talked a lot about the political side of basketball—who controls where the games are played, who assigns the referees, things like that. "This is a cutthroat business," Red would say. One of his favorite sayings was "Don't break the rules, figure out how to get around them. Find the loopholes." I'd watch his facial expression change when he told me things, his body language, and I could tell how intensely he felt about basketball.

On one drive we stopped by a plastics company that Red had an interest in, and I took note that he had business acumen. Another time, I was terrified as we drove through a thick fog. I wanted him to pull over, but Red kept driving. Pretty soon we heard several crashes behind us. "See, those are the people who stopped," Red said. "You have to keep moving when there's fog."

I distinctly remember Red being perplexed by his friends who took vacations. His work ethic was so strong, he couldn't understand the concept. "When they get there, what do they do?" he said.

What I mostly recall is Red explaining a world I could not yet see. For example, Red made me understand that some white people discriminated against other white people. Red didn't harp on anti-Semitism, but the way he mentioned it, I realized later what he was teaching me. When I told people I was going to Kutsher's, some of them would make negative remarks about Jews. I started to understand that although I looked at a Jewish or Polish or Irish person as white, other white people might look down on them. Red planted so much information in my mind at that young age, and then I would recall it years later. You know how your parents used to say, "One day you'll understand"? With Red, that day always came.

Red was not a racist in any way, but he abided by society's rules at the time. He could push back against the system only so far. As human beings, Red treated everyone equally. Except if you could put the ball in the basket—then he paid you extra attention. That was part of the basis of our relationship. The NBA had a territorial draft then, and franchises had first dibs on players from colleges close to their cities. Red wanted to steer me to a college team near Boston. But he was also interested in me as a person—that was very clear to me. I had no idea our relationship would get even stronger over the next fifty years.

WHILE I WAS in high school, my mother's older brother lived with us on Benning Road for a while. His name was Lewis Grandison Alexander. I had never met a Black person like him before. I had never met a Black person who was praised for using his mind.

Uncle Lewis was a poet who also worked in the theater and was active in the Harlem Renaissance. My mother and aunts used to talk about him admiringly. They would read his poems and talk about how Langston Hughes or Countee Cullen came by the house to see him. My mother said he had been recruited to be the principal of a Black school down south, and she almost went down there with him. That type of praise was new to me. The only people we heard about in the neighborhood were athletes. We elevated people for their physical abilities.

I admired my father because he could taste a bag of concrete and say what kind it was. I liked how Joe Louis knocked people unconscious. I wanted to jump over people like Rabbit.

My father wasn't one of the people praising Uncle Lewis. My father was a working man from the country. To him, the word "work" had a very specific meaning. Work meant labor, sweat, doing something physical that produced a physical result. My father always made fun of city folks in Washington who didn't like to sweat on the job. The idea of Lewis sitting on a sofa writing poetry, eating my father's food, while my father was out working? That just didn't compute. My father didn't dislike Lewis, but he'd say things like, "I'm the one doing the work around here." There was something else going on, too. Lewis was effeminate. He was probably gay, and that was another reason my father was skeptical of him.

But Lewis made an extremely positive impression on me, and I loved him dearly. He was the first person I knew who made a mark on the world with his intellectual abilities. He was another type of Rabbit to me. It makes me proud to know he was part of the Harlem Renaissance and was known for something other than running fast or jumping high. My favorite poem that Lewis wrote is titled "Nocturne Varial." I like to recite it sometimes:

I came as a shadow,
I stand now a light;
The depth of my darkness
Transfigures your night.
My soul is a nocturne
Each note is a star;
The light will not blind you
So look where you are.
The radiance is soothing.
There's warmth in the light.
I came as a shadow,
To dazzle your night!

I always identified with that shadow.

Years later, I named my second son Lewis Grandison Alexander Thompson. I gave him the entire name, to reflect the love I had for my uncle. But there was a problem with little Lewis's heart that went undetected when he was born. We were holding him and playing with him, smiling and laughing. Ten days later he was gone. He never came home from the hospital.

I always tell my sons John and Ronny, who are both about six foot four or five, "Lewis was bigger than both of y'all. He would have been my center."

I remember coming down the hospital elevator after Lewis died, with tears in my eyes. Two women were in the elevator, and they kept going on and on about my size. My child had just died and they want me to talk about how big I was. I could easily have snapped.

Within ten days, you are thinking of a newborn child as a family member. That made his death so much harder. When it came time to bury Lewis, his casket wasn't much bigger than a shoebox. That's always been one of the most upsetting things to me. To remember him buried in something that small reminds me of all the life we never got to see.

TOWARD THE END of that first summer with the Carroll team, I had an experience that changed something inside me. There were lots of prestigious all-star tournaments for the best players in the city, but when it was time to play at the Jelleff Boys Club and some of the other all-white tournaments, none of us Black players were invited to go.

Until that point, I had always accepted the discrimination I encountered. Even when I questioned it, like in our church down in St. Mary's County, the adults gave their standard, mentally conditioned explanation and I went about my business. But this time was different. Maybe because it was basketball, which I loved. Maybe because I had been studying the white man. But for whatever reason, being excluded from those summer tournaments hurt in the actual moment it happened.

I thought to myself, *Coach Dwyer has been talking about brotherhood and family and sacrificing for the team, but the white guys are playing at the best Boys Club and we can't?* And I distinctly recall wondering why Dwyer and the white players would agree to participate in these games when we could not play. After I finished wondering, which didn't take long, I determined that it was wrong. As I got older, I developed more forgiveness for white people who didn't resist segregation, because they had a lot to lose. But at age seventeen, all I felt was the raw injustice. This was the first time racism hurt me deeply. But I didn't raise hell or anything. I kept quiet.

Years later, when I was on the board of directors at Nike, another board member came up to me at a meeting and said, "You're a lot different than I expected you to be. One of your high school teammates told me you used to be so quiet, and he doesn't understand how you are now this loud racial person." I don't want to say which teammate it was, but he was white. His comment angered me, because it implied that I had not seen anything wrong back in high school, that I had changed, or that my public comments were inconsistent with how I used to think. It has never been in my nature to be quiet, but I had no other choice at Carroll. I was smart enough to listen and learn. We were some of the first Black people to go to Carroll. We knew we were constantly being evaluated as representatives of all the Black people in America, and probably Africa too. If we did something as simple as comb our nappy hair at school, we were self-conscious about it. I was sociable in high school. I wasn't aggressive. But that changed.

A few years after Jackie Robinson broke the color line, Branch Rickey told him, "Now you can talk." Well, I had a "Now you can talk" period of my life, too.

There was another challenge to being at Carroll. Some Black people criticized us for going there. One thing about the Black community is that too often, when we get the opportunities our elders sacrificed to obtain, the things that my parents and so many other Black folks sweated and bled for us to have, we might experience a certain amount of resentment from our own people.

I hitchhiked to Carroll every day from the corner of 17th Street and Benning Road. A tough kid from the neighborhood named Archie used to ride to school with me. Usually a man named Mr. Ford came by and gave us a ride, and if not him, somebody else always did.

One day we were waiting on the corner and Archie said, "John, do they think we're punks because we go to private school?"

The answer was yes. It still is, to a certain extent. That's something we have to overcome.

In 1960, my senior year, Tom Hoover introduced me to a girl from his neighborhood named Gwen Twitty, who attended a nearby high school. She asked me to go to her prom, I asked her to mine, and we began dating. I had reached my full height of six foot ten and had developed into a good player. Our Carroll team won another championship, and I played the last game of my high school career in Georgetown's McDonough Gymnasium. I liked Georgetown's basketball coach, Tom Nolan, and he was friendly with me. But Georgetown was basically segregated in 1960, and the basketball team remained entirely white until 1967. So Nolan never talked to me about playing at Georgetown, and I never expected him to. I was like the dog with that chain.

I was fine without Georgetown because lots of other top colleges recruited me, especially after I scored 26 points in the Dapper Dan national all-star game. The future legend Connie Hawkins showed up at halftime and scored 17, he got MVP and deserved it, but let's not forget I gave 'em 26. Some of the colleges that came to my house made illegal offers to my parents and me, including several schools I would rather not name that still have big-time basketball teams. My mother did day's work for one man who was an alumnus of a Big Ten university, and he offered to increase her salary if I went to his school. Another big school sent a guy over who talked all about the fraternities and girls and social life. My mother smiled and nodded through the conversation. The guy hadn't taken two steps out of our house when she said, "You're not going there." That taught me a great lesson for when

I was recruiting with Georgetown. Just because people react positively doesn't mean they accept what you are saying.

I went on recruiting trips to Syracuse, Cincinnati (because Oscar Robertson was there), Notre Dame, and Boston College. The first time I ever flew on an airplane was going to Boston College. The flight attendant asked me if I wanted a soda, and even though I was thirsty as hell I said no. I thought you had to pay for it, and I didn't have any money in my pocket.

When I got to Boston College they took me to see Cardinal Richard Cushing, because I was slightly curious about becoming a priest, and I think they overreacted to my questioning. What happened still makes me laugh, because the cardinal was not on the same page with the recruiting program. He kept repeating that colleges would use kids, ranting on and on about how they will dump you on the street when they're finished with you, so make sure you get your education. The Boston College coach looked like he wanted to sink right through the floor. That taught me not to ask people to speak on your behalf unless you know what they're going to say.

Red Auerbach told me point-blank to go to Providence College. Red was not a subtle person. The coach there was Joe Mullaney, who had played briefly for the Celtics, and Red would have first dibs on my rights in the territorial draft. Providence was the only trip my mother came on. She loved the Dominican branch of the Catholic Church. As we walked around campus, she knew more about the buildings and the Dominican history than they did. With two of the most influential people in my life telling me to go to Providence, the choice was clear.

By this time, I realized I wasn't going to be another Rabbit. But I thought I could be a Celtic.

When it was time to take the SAT I was nervous, because I was a poor test taker. I took the SAT at the Dominican House of Study in Washington. I never saw or heard the test results, but I knew I had enough intelligence to succeed in college. I was out of the baby row for good.

The summer before I left for Providence, I came outside our house one morning and there was an old Ford Galaxie sitting there. My mother and father had somehow saved up enough money to get me a car, which they still had to make payments on. They didn't even have their own automobile at that time. I knew they couldn't afford that Galaxie, and some people in the neighborhood thought it was an illegal recruiting gift. It makes me extremely emotional to think my parents were proud enough of me to make that kind of sacrifice. I also feel a little guilty. I think about my father not having the opportunity to learn how to read or write. And I wonder how many nights he had to eat my leftovers for me to drive up to college in that car.

4

PROVIDENCE

Providence, Rhode Island, in 1960 might as well have been a foreign country compared with 19th Street and Benning Road in Washington. It wasn't just going to school with white people during the daytime, like at Carroll. It wasn't playing ball in their neighborhood, like in Chevy Chase. This was total immersion, twenty-four hours a day. But I looked at it as an opportunity to learn something new, and I requested to live with a regular student in a normal dorm. Most of the time, colleges liked to room athletes with other athletes, or they searched the campus for one of the few other Black students and dumped you in with him. I didn't want any of that. I couldn't study the white man while living with Black people.

I had two white roommates my freshman year. One was from somewhere in Massachusetts; he flunked out quick. The other was Denny DeJesu from Oyster Bay, Long Island. We became good friends and stayed roommates for most of college. Living with white guys wasn't a problem. I would call it more of an adjustment, for all of us. I got more of an understanding that not all white people hated us. I also learned how some white people are incarcerated by their perception of us. Overall, I got a lot of informal education.

I heard guys talking about a pizza pie and thought it was some sort of dessert. Guys talked about going to swimming pools and country clubs; I grew up playing in the fire hydrant in the street, or maybe somebody sprayed you with a hose. I listened to my white friends' music and could eventually sing more of their songs than Motown—I enjoy country music to this day. One time I walked into our dorm and my roommates were looking through my *Ebony* magazine. They thought it would have naked pictures of Black women, or maybe they were just hoping. I was surprised by how openly the white guys talked about sex. We didn't have women on campus, Providence was all male then. White students had different terminology for sexual things than I had heard back home. I was shocked by how much alcohol was consumed, and how white students would stagger around openly drunk. I thought to myself, *And they like to say we Black people are out of control.*

I knew there were stereotypes about us, and I was careful not to live down to them. I told my roommates, half playfully, "I don't want anybody to come up missing anything. You're not going to blame any stealing on me." My sensitivity to these stereotypes probably contributed to an incident with the equipment manager of the basketball team freshman year. We practiced in cheap white T-shirts with PROVIDENCE stenciled on the front. After practice you would put all your sweaty gear on a big safety pin and they would wash it for you. My shirt must have fallen off the pin and gotten lost, because the equipment manager came at me and said, "Why can't I find your shirt?" As if I wanted that crummy white T-shirt. I went up to my room and got a white undershirt, gave it to the equipment manager, and said, "Don't you ever accuse me of something like that. I don't steal."

Maybe he didn't exactly accuse me of stealing, but in my mind, he was calling me a thief because I'm Black. I don't have any proof that's how he felt. But don't blame me for having the thought, because I knew that was how some white people saw us. Probably more than some.

I paid attention to my studies and did what was required to pass my classes. My real focus was basketball, and Providence had a very good team. A few years earlier, the university had decided to use basketball to raise its reputation, so they built a three-thousand-seat arena on campus and hired Joe Mullaney as head coach. Mullaney had played with Bob Cousy at Holy Cross and then played three dozen games with Red's Celtics. The season before I arrived, the future NBA Hall of Famer Lenny Wilkens took Providence to the finals of the National Invitation Tournament. The Friars lost that year, then won the NIT my freshman year, which back then was as important as winning the NCAA tournament. Freshmen weren't allowed to play on the varsity, but I averaged 32 points per game for the frosh squad. In one game I scored 52 points, and the point guard who kept throwing me the ball, Bill Stein, became one of my closest friends.

Billy was a six-foot white guy who also played on the baseball team. We may have looked like an odd couple, but I discovered we had a lot in common. We both loved baseball. We didn't drink alcohol or chase girls; I was still dating Gwen. When all the other students went out partying, Billy and I went to the gym to shoot around or play pickup, or we hung out in the dorm listening to music and talking about current events.

For some reason, my sophomore year I asked for a single room, which made me extremely lonely. Then I started to have problems on the basketball court. We had a senior center on the team, Jim Hadnot. When Mullaney tried to play both of us at once, it was a disaster, like having two thumbs on the same hand. I was moved to the power forward position, which I wasn't really suited for. I was a bit more mobile than Hadnot, could dribble the ball and shoot from outside. Today you might describe me as a European-style player. But I was put in a new position without any specific instructions. What made it worse was the distant relationship I had with Mullaney. I came to college knowing I needed to learn a lot about how to play, but I can't recall one time Mullaney took me under the basket to teach me any techniques, or sat me down to talk about life. He wasn't mean or hostile about it. He was a good Christian man and a nice guy. He did trivial things that he felt were a way to have fun with his players, but I needed more. Mullaney was unaware of my needs as a young person, let alone as a Black person living for the first time in an all-white environment. I was used to coaches like Red, or Mr. Jabbo, Mr. Wyatt, and Mr. Butler from the Boys Club, who talked to me about all kinds of things. That was not Mullaney's style. Years later, I remembered how unhappy I was, and it taught me to think more deeply about my players and their specific needs.

More than anything, though, I wanted to be a Celtic, and neither I nor the team was playing well. Between my frustrations on the court and my isolation off the court, my sophomore year was the most miserable time of my life. We were upset in the first round of the NIT in a two-point loss to Temple. I felt so bad, and my relationship with Mullaney was so distant, I intended to leave school. That's not uncommon with players. A lot of my former players don't say nice things about me, and they're not always wrong.

Everything changed when Dave Gavitt arrived as an assistant coach before my junior year. Dave was only a few years older than us players, and I could immediately tell that he genuinely cared about me as a person. We quickly became close friends. He would sit and talk with me about what was happening in the dorm, or advise me on how to adjust to a problematic teacher or class. Dave didn't let me wallow in self-pity. He had a natural comfort level with Black people, and not in a phony way like some guys who said they felt our pain because they grew up poor. Plus, he could get out on the court and play with us. Dave had some game. If it hadn't been for him, I would have left Providence for sure. I also ran into Denny DeJesu on campus and we decided to share a room again for our junior year, which made me a lot more comfortable.

My circle of white friends grew. I also enjoyed hanging out with some of the priests who lived on campus. Father Murray was a photographer who showed me how to take pictures and develop them in his darkroom. I got myself a little camera and took pictures of guys with their girlfriends to make some spare change. Father St. George played pickup with us in the gym. One game he fouled a student and the kid cursed at him. Father St. George cursed him out right back.

We often ate at Grady's Delicatessen, where Mr. and Mrs. Grady were big fans of the team. If you paid for something with a dollar bill, they gave you four quarters back for your change. Sometimes I went to Boston on the weekends, where Red introduced me to his friend Harold Furash and Harold's wife, Marty. The Furashes were tight with a lot of Celtics, and I hung out at their house or went to games with them. I would sit in their box seats if one was empty, and if not, I'd sit on the steps next to their box and watch the game.

White guys like Dave, Denny, and Billy Stein were my first white peers who became colorless to me. Some white people like to run around saying "I don't see color." That's ridiculous. I'm a large Black person, which is impossible not to see when you meet me. When I meet a white person, I bring all my history and experiences to that encounter. I have to sift through some of the assumptions I may have, because I'm haunted by my past. Maybe my assumptions are wrong, but you better not blame me for having them, because they're based on real history. At Providence, though, when I developed meaningful relationships with my white friends, their color became insignificant. If Dave or Denny or Billy said something I didn't like, I didn't interpret them as saying it because they were white. I didn't have to wonder about their motivations.

At Providence, I learned to accept the kindness of white people who were honest and true. I could confide in Billy or Dave. I could speak honestly about race with the Furashes. That helped me recognize there are a whole lot of terrific white people in this world.

On the court, things turned around for me in my junior year. Jim Hadnot had graduated, so I had the middle to myself and averaged 19 points and 14 rebounds per game. Ray Flynn, the future mayor of Boston, also averaged 19 points per game. Vinnie Ernst was only five foot eight but a helluva point guard. Jimmy Stone, one of only three Blacks on the team, was a great shooter. Stoney quit the team a thousand times. He'd always pack his bags to go home to Cleveland, then stop by my room so I could talk him out of it.

I declared an economics major, with a concentration in education.

I had the vague idea that I wanted to be some kind of youth counselor, like Mr. Jabbo, Mr. Butler, and Mr. Wyatt, or a gym teacher like Mr. Trigg. I did just enough to pass my classes. My grades were by no means outstanding, I didn't care what grade I got. Did I pass? Great, I'm gone, see y'all later.

I walked into the first day of one statistics course, and the professor said right off the bat, "If there are any athletes in here, you need to get out." He said the athletes would have to miss too many classes, and since we needed to master the early concepts to do the later work, we wouldn't be able to catch up. He didn't say it in a nice way, either. He was just being honest. I thought to myself, "I don't have control over when they make me go to practice and play the games." That realization left a big impression on me. I ended up staying in the class, and liking the teacher. I didn't fail, either. My grade might have been ugly, but I passed.

It's interesting that I didn't truly value education at Providence. I just wanted to play pro ball. When I got to Georgetown, I advocated for education much more than I had practiced it myself. I demanded more of my players than had been demanded of me. The Providence coaches said I should get good grades, but there were no repercussions when I didn't. Most of the coaches preached education, but their actions were all basketball. I don't fault them for it, but I believe some of them had certain notions about me. Maybe I'm wrong, but I'm the kid who the nuns put in the baby row.

On campus, the other students and faculty generally treated me well, although I was a special case because of being well known as a basketball player. I'm not sure the few other Black students at Providence would say they were treated well. I do remember this white kid from Alabama who lived next door in the dorm and refused even to look at me. I mean that literally. When we passed each other in the hallway, he would turn his head and conspicuously stare at the wall. Then, my junior year, I was walking through the dorm and saw some guys bullying him, acting like they were going to beat him up. I think they believed he was gay. I intervened and shooed the bullies away. Later, someone told me the Alabama kid said, "I could like Thompson if he wasn't Black."

The basketball team went 21–4 in the regular season that year, including losses to the University of Miami and Canisius. Then we beat both of those teams in the 1963 NIT and won the whole tournament, which was the equivalent of a national championship. On the bus ride home, cheering fans stood on the side of the road starting at the Rhode Island state line, and thousands of people gathered downtown to welcome us back to campus. Now I had a college championship to go along with the titles we had won at Carroll.

Winning the NIT raised my profile a few more notches. Mullaney started taking me to his speaking engagements at Catholic youth organizations and similar venues. He kept jelly beans in his car and would always give me some. I noticed that he got paid for speaking, while all I got was jelly beans. Mullaney didn't do it out of spite, that was how the system worked. I liked speaking at those places, and people were receptive to what I said. I also started getting invitations to talk to student groups on campus. When I spoke to the Spectrum Club, the auditorium was packed, and I felt comfortable onstage. Someone asked me what it was like to be Black at Providence. I said sometimes it felt like "Stop the world, I want to get off." I also told them that they cheered for me at games, and we had a good time socializing together on campus, but none of them would want me to date their sisters. People got real nervous when they heard that.

I was being exposed to a whole new way of life, things my mother and father never experienced. One of my sisters told me, "I don't know how you can stand being around all those white people." That's how far removed my new existence was from Benning Road. It was a tremendous opportunity for me to learn about the wider world, something many if not most other Black people were not then permitted to do. Basketball opened those doors for me, no question. No matter how much potential I had, if I couldn't put the ball in the basket I would have been stuck on Benning Road, wondering what life was like Across the Park.

All this exposure to white people came as the Civil Rights Movement gained speed. Watching Martin Luther King protest and hearing him speak so eloquently made me extremely proud. It reminded me of how my mother always told me to listen to Jackie Robinson, but she turned off the radio when Joe Louis was interviewed, because Louis was not articulate. Deep down, I was never sold on King's nonviolence philosophy. If somebody hits you, kneel down and pray? That's not for me. But I had tremendous respect for the people who were able to practice nonviolence. At the same time, I had to learn to accept Malcolm X. I was programmed to think he was going too far. The first time I heard Malcolm, I thought he was crazy. He came on the radio while I was driving across the George Washington Bridge into New York, on my way up to Providence. Malcolm was saying don't initiate, but retaliate. If somebody hits you, hit 'em back. I thought the white man would wipe us out if we did that. But over time, as I listened to more of his philosophy, I recognized his brilliance. The way he identified America's racial problems was powerful. You might question his solutions, and Malcolm himself even changed his solutions later, when he left the Nation of Islam and went in another Muslim direction. But Malcolm was never wrong when he described the reality of that time. I admired him for refusing to take abuse from anybody. His attitude was not apologetic or even accommodating. He demanded his rights in a strong way, which appealed to me. I also came to realize that Malcolm expedited white people listening to Dr. King. Most white people didn't agree with either one of them, but if they had to make a choice, they'd choose King eight days of the week. Malcolm scared the devil out of them.

DURING SUMMER BREAK, I went back to Washington and hit the playgrounds. That improved my game tremendously, and I realized I was now one of the best players in the city. One guy I played against a lot was a fella named Big Roy. Today people would say we worked out together, but back then it was just playing one-on-one. We went down to the naval annex all the time and played late into the night. Roy was a drug dealer, which was well known on the streets, but Roy never visited any of that upon me. We just played ball. He was six foot eight, and our games were a good matchup. Whenever we got something to eat, Roy had the money, and he paid for both of us. He also had a beautiful car that I admired. A few times he asked if I wanted to borrow it: "Go ahead and take my car, John, and I'll drive yours." I wasn't that stupid. Some time later I was watching the six o'clock news, and they took Roy out of a hotel, shot dead. I felt bad to see that. That was my man, and he never brought any criminal activity around me. He was just a guy from the neighborhood with a nice game.

I played even better my senior year at Providence, averaging 26 points and 15 rebounds per game. I finished as the all-time leading scorer in school history and set the single-game mark with 43 points against Fairfield. We had a freshman that year who would break all my scoring records, Jimmy Walker from Boston, Jalen Rose's father. Walk was incredible, he was the first player I ever saw dribble the ball between his legs on the run. Our team went to the 1964 NCAA tournament, but we lost to Villanova in the first round, 77–66.

Before I graduated, I was selected to travel through Eastern Europe on a team sponsored by the State Department. One of the assistants was the legendary Black coach John McLendon. Growing up, sitting under the tree at the playground, I heard everybody talking about Coach Mac's team at Tennessee State beating all the white schools to win three straight NAIA national championships in the 1950s. Nobody talked about Kentucky or North Carolina, because we couldn't go there. McLendon won eight Black college championships with North Carolina Central and beat Duke Medical School in the famous "secret game" in 1944, which was the first time a Black school and a white school played each other. McLendon had gone to college at the University of Kansas when the basketball team was segregated, and while he was there he learned from the inventor of basketball himself, James Naismith.

I'm not saying Naismith taught McLendon how to coach. Naismith had the idea to hang up the peach baskets, but he also said there should be a jump ball after every score. The Wright Brothers didn't teach people how to fly.

Coach Mac was one of the first coaches in basketball history, maybe the very first, to fully utilize the fast break and full court press. People say Red Auerbach pioneered running and pressing. I love Red, but McLendon ran and pressed way before him, like in the 1944 "secret game." Duke had literally never seen anything like it, and North Carolina Central ran them out the gym, 88–44. Coach Mac used a stall offense before Dean Smith, too. Here's the problem, though. When McLendon's Black teams played fast in the 1940s and '50s, people said it was undisciplined and disorganized. When Red did the same thing, people said it was smart and strategic. Racism doesn't get any more blatant than that.

Or maybe it does. McLendon was nominated for the Basketball Hall of Fame five times in the 1970s but never received enough votes to get in. When they finally inducted him in 1979, it was as a "contributor," not as a coach. How the hell do they think he made his contributions? The level of disrespect is infuriating. It makes me think about when I saw white children in St. Mary's County call older Black people by their first names. It took almost forty years for the Hall of Fame to put McLendon in as a coach, in 2016. As far as I'm concerned, that didn't make it right, because he died in 1999.

I spent much of our European trip sitting in Coach Mac's hotel room and walking around with him to see the sights. We played in Moscow, Leningrad, and Tbilisi, in Poland and Czechoslovakia. He bought a lot of books. He was a tiny person, about five foot eight, with a pleasant, calm demeanor. I was captivated by his stories about his Black teams. I also learned about how he had maneuvered to get Black colleges accepted into the national postseason tournaments, which was another early lesson for me in the political strategies needed to succeed. After one game I saw Coach Mac in the locker room, writing in a large notebook. I asked what he was doing. He said, "The reason they have to take me on these trips is because I document everything. Nobody knows more about international players than me."

During our games, McLendon sat in the middle of the bench. That was the first time I had seen a coach sit anywhere but at the front of the bench, closest to the scorer's table. When I asked Coach Mac why he sat there, he told me, "There's no end of the bench if you sit in the middle."

I had a much worse experience trying out for the Olympic team in 1964. Only college players were eligible then. The selection committee formed teams consisting of the players being considered, and those teams played against each other over a week's time. It quickly became apparent that I didn't have a shot to make the team, because I hardly got to play. Guys I had beaten in college got plenty of minutes. One day I was walking from the hotel to the gym and John Wooden, the UCLA coaching legend, was heading in the same direction. I had never met him, but we fell in step together and started talking. Wooden told me he was upset with the politics of the selection process. He said the team had a quota for guys from AAU teams, which were big at that time, and there was another quota for guys from the military teams. "They better take Walt," Wooden said, referring to his UCLA guard Walt Hazzard. He told me not to focus on the politics and just play, but that didn't make me feel better. A few days after that, one of the coaches was talking to the group and said we should be grateful that they put us up in nice hotels and fed us good food. I told them I could have stayed in Providence and ate just as well. I wasn't looking for a vacation. Give me an equal chance, and then if you want to cut me, fine.

Slats Gill from Oregon coached my team. In the final game of the tryouts, with about a minute left, he told me to check in. He's lucky I wasn't deeper into Malcolm X at that point, because that was a real slap in the face. I refused to enter the game. Afterward, Earl Lloyd, the first Black guy to play in an NBA game, came down from the stands to admonish me. Earl said, "I understand why you did that, but it was a mistake. It'll come back to haunt you later on." I respected Earl, but his comment made me sad, because he was conditioned by our oppressors to accept the unacceptable. Besides, it was too late for any regrets. Something burned inside me, and I let it out.

The Olympic disappointment didn't outweigh all my great experiences in college. I got a degree in economics and a teaching certificate in social studies, and my parents came up to Providence to see me graduate. That was extremely special, because my father hardly traveled anywhere. The man had to work. My parents didn't drive, and I don't even know how they got up to Rhode Island. I received a bunch of awards as a senior, including Man of the Year. Gwen and I were thinking about marriage. But my strongest memory is of something that happened a few months before I left.

Walking across campus one night, I happened to be headed in the same direction as a philosophy professor named Father Heath. He was well known on campus for being odd and different, a free spirit. Father Heath had served in the navy on submarines during World War II. He had four degrees, in physics, radio engineering, metallurgy, and philosophy, but he wasn't a snob. He noticed me and called me over. We had never met before, and we started talking while he puffed on his pipe.

Father Heath said, "I am an American white man. I have more privileges and status than you. And I don't ever want to make anybody equal to me. All of us white men, we don't really want to give up the privileges and advantages that we have."

Father Heath made it clear to me that he wasn't bragging or being mean. He was trying to teach me about an essential aspect of human nature: that people don't voluntarily relinquish their power. He was saying that white people will give Blacks a little bit of what we deserve, but never so much that white people lose their advantages. Not necessarily because they hate Black people, but because human beings instinctively care more about themselves. Everyone wants to keep what they have.

That was a great lesson for me, the final lecture in my collegiate study of the white man. From then on, I didn't want to be equal. I wanted to be better. This isn't a hateful thing toward white people. I wanted to be better than everybody. I strove for excellence, not mediocrity. I wanted to graduate more of my players and make more money than you. I wanted to win every single game. I was a basketball coach, man. I wasn't playing for no tie. I like to say that Black people and Indians are the only ones who run around talking about "We want to be equal to the white man." That's because we've been put in a position of inferiority for so long. Being equal looks like winning when you're taking a beating every day.

Who wants to be equal to the next guy? I want to kick his ass.

5

THE CELTICS

Red picked me in the third round of the 1964 NBA draft, No. 27 overall. I was home in Washington that summer, getting ready for my rookie training camp, when I got a phone call from Boston. Walter Brown, the team owner, wanted to discuss my salary.

I said I would rather have the discussion in person. There were no agents in those days, players dealt directly with their teams. I drove up to Boston in the Ford Galaxie my parents gave me and sat down with Mr. Brown. Before he could get started, I said, "I don't want to ask for anything right now. I haven't made the team. Hopefully after training camp I'll be on the team, and then we can decide on a salary."

After he got over his surprise, Mr. Brown asked, "Why didn't you just tell me that on the phone, and avoid that long drive all the way up here from Washington?"

I said, "I thought I owed it to you to tell you to your face."

That made an impression on him, but that's not why I did it. I knew people with money were respected, and I felt the only way to obtain money was to succeed. It had to happen in that order. Once I was successful, I would have the ability and the leverage to be properly compensated.

I'll never forget the day during training camp when Red sent the trainer, Buddy LeRoux, up to my hotel room to say that Red wanted to talk to me. That's what Red did when it was time to cut or keep people. I was scared to death. You work your whole life for something and it comes down to that moment. Going downstairs to Red's room was one of the longest walks of my life.

I knocked on the door and entered. Red was sitting there eating Chinese food.

"Welcome to the Celtics," he said.

As great as it felt to make the team, I didn't get to play for the Celtics. Yes, I was a member of the team for two seasons, from 1964 to 1966. I own two NBA championship rings. But I didn't get to *play* for the Celtics, because Bill Russell never came out of the damn game.

I had been a college All-American and had gone toe to toe with the best big men in the country, so I was extremely frustrated in Boston. Still, I couldn't argue with riding the bench. I was playing behind Russell, the greatest winner in the history of basketball. The man has eleven rings and only ten fingers. I'm exaggerating when I say Russ never got subbed out, but not by much. If games were close, he stayed in the whole time. I know exactly how Michael Jordan's backup feels. When you play behind a guy that great, you're not getting in the game in any meaningful way.

Statistics on the Internet say I played almost eleven minutes per game my rookie year, averaging 3.9 points and 3.9 rebounds. I don't care what the Internet says, me playing eleven minutes per game is a lie. That's how incredible Russ was.

Still, I wouldn't have wanted to play for any other team, based on my relationship with Red and the fact that the Celtics were in the middle of winning eight straight championships. Watching Red run the Celtics organization, on and off the court, was an incredible education for me.

But that doesn't mean everything that happened with the Celtics was right.

During my first training camp, I heard a lot of the newer Black players asking each other, "You think you'll be here tomorrow? How many of us do you think they'll take?" I quickly understood that we weren't competing for one of the twelve roster spots. We were competing for however many spots were in the Black quota. Everybody knew there was a maximum number of us on each team. The number itself was not announced. Most NBA teams kept no more than three. The Celtics had more Black players than most, but Red still had to follow the guidelines of that era, so the quota hung over our heads.

My roommate in training camp was a high-scoring guard named Levern Tart. This dude could really get it done, he led Bradley University to the NIT title in 1964 and was MVP of the championship game. He was clearly one of the best guards in camp. The Celtics already had the future Hall of Famers John Havlicek, K. C. Jones, and Sam Jones at the guard spots, but Levern tore up a half dozen other guys on a regular basis. He was a lock to make the squad. I was the one fighting for a spot.

Each night before we went to bed, Levern and I played this cynical sort of game based on the lyrics to a popular song at the time.

I would ask Levern, "Will you be here when the morning comes?"

He'd reply: "I'll be here when the morning comes. Will you be here when the morning comes?"

I would come back with, "I'll be here when the morning comes." Then we'd cut off the light and go to sleep.

One afternoon, I came back to the room and Levern's stuff was gone. There was a note on the desk:

"I won't be here when the morning comes."

I was truly shocked. Two white guards made the team over Levern. I don't want to say their names, because it wasn't their fault, although they are examples of how white people who aren't racist still benefit from the racism of the past. But there's absolutely no way those white guys were better than Levern, and everybody knew it.

Levern never played in the NBA. In the first season of the American Basketball Association, he averaged 23.5 points per game, third-best in that league.

And they said he wasn't good enough to be a sub on the Celtics.

Thousands of Levern Tarts got derailed this way before even making it to high school or college teams, let alone the NBA. I've watched plenty of players on the playgrounds, people you never heard of, and said to myself, "Damn, he's a pro." That's one of the reasons I believe segregation was in some ways better than integration. During segregation, you knew the reason you didn't get an opportunity. After integration, they had to invent reasons to exclude us, which made us question ourselves. When it came to basketball, guys started thinking, "What's wrong with me that I can't make it?" They questioned their own ability due to the lies that integration encouraged some white people to tell. I've seen great players literally go crazy because they couldn't reconcile the fact that they never made it to the pros. That's one of the negative effects of integration.

I wonder what they told Levern about why he got cut from the Celtics. He died a few years ago, so I'll never know.

I can't really blame Red, though. Red ended up keeping six Black players, myself included, which I believe was more than any other team. Later in my rookie season, on December 26, 1964, Red put the first all-Black starting five in NBA history on the floor: Russ, K.C., Sam Jones, Tom "Satch" Sanders, and Willie Naulls.

Hooray, right? Not for me. I knew I wasn't getting in the game after that. If Red started five brothers, he couldn't bring in more off the bench. We had a white seven-footer on our team, Mel Counts. Mel was a very good player, we were friendly, and I'm the godfather of his son. But Mel played a lot of minutes that I might have gotten under different circumstances. See, Red had to do things strategically. That was the catch-22 of the first Black starting five, and it hindered my development, which I knew I needed. Other teams had white starters I had killed in college. Not that every white guy in the NBA was lousy, a lot of them could play their butts off. Havlicek, Bob Cousy, Jerry West, Pete Maravich, Larry Bird, the list goes on. Any Black person who said these guys couldn't play was prejudiced. But when I played, white players tried out for twelve spots. We tried out for five or six. We just wanted to be treated fairly. Not better. And it was not fair.

People envision racism as coming from some tobacco-chewing white man with a whip down South. But the North implemented those rules, too. A lot of white people didn't think it was right, but they still enforced those rules and benefited from them, because otherwise they would have been under scrutiny. Where do you think the term "nigger lover" comes from? From treating the niggers fairly.

When I was in high school and my white teammates played in segregated tournaments, it really bothered me. Over time, I came to understand how much some white people had to lose if they pushed too hard against racism, so I was able to forgive. I loved Red for moving the needle on race and standing up for Black players, but he could only push so far.

Red could free the slaves, but he couldn't free them all at one time.

AS MUCH AS I hated not playing, Bill Russell had a major impact on my life. He was very nice to me right from the start. Russ was the first person I knew who called himself Black. Not colored. Not Negro. *Black.* When I was growing up, you only got called Black as an insult, and it came from other African Americans who had been brainwashed into thinking darker skin was ugly. Russ was the first person I knew who embraced his Blackness, years before Afros and raised fists and James Brown's "Say It Loud, I'm Black and I'm Proud." Russ invested in a rubber plant in Liberia, gave his children African names, and boycotted a 1961 preseason game in Louisville after a coffee shop refused to serve him because he was Black. All of this made me feel safe. Not in the physical sense, but psychologically. He was a proud Black man who took no garbage from anyone, and he demanded respect with his dignity and his intellect. Since Black people were often judged collectively, I felt some of the respect given to Russ carry over to me. Nobody was going to discriminate against me with Russ around.

I got to know Russ while we drove in the same car to preseason games up in New England, and I had a lot of time to observe him from my seat on the bench. This man loafed through every single practice, and he hardly broke a sweat in the preseason games. If you sprinted past him in practice, he'd pull your shorts down and laugh. When I first got to the Celtics I thought, *Man, Russ ain't as good as everyone says he is.* Then the first game came around, and he was like Superman coming out of the phone booth.

Russ is well known for having a strange personality. "Strange" is an understatement. He did things like order two entrées at a restaurant, eat one, then not pay the bill. He heard Joe DiMaggio never paid for his dinner, and felt he should receive the same treatment. He never signed autographs, but might offer to shake hands or talk with a fan who wanted a signature. One time Satch asked for his autograph, because he wanted one from every Celtic he played with. Russ wouldn't give it to him, and they got in a big argument in the locker room. The argument bothered Russ, he didn't want to hurt a teammate, but sticking to his beliefs was more important to him. Sometimes you said something to Russ and he acted like you weren't there. Other times, he talked your ear off about some philosophy of his. He was agnostic and sometimes we discussed the concept of God. Russ might not pick up a bottle of water you asked for that was right next to him, but then he would walk a mile to buy you five gallons of water. Once, years later, he flew a player to Georgetown from San Francisco with his own money, trying to help him out. The kid wasn't any good.

See, Russ stood for something. He had the power not to sign autographs or do other things that were easy to do, that people expected us to do. His attitude rolled over into things that other Black people were expected to do, or not do. Russ was in control of his environment. He was one of my role models for demanding freedoms and rebelling against limitations.

Russ also vomited before most games. I'm telling you, the man was different.

RED LIKED SMART players, so he signed lots of them to the Celtics, starting with Russ. I enjoyed interacting with Tommy Heinsohn, who was intelligent and outspoken. Satch used to submerge himself in the whirlpool, and all you could see was his head and his hands holding a book. I loved listening to Satch talk. K.C. was quiet, but when he spoke, it was something that needed to be said. I looked up to Willie Naulls, he was older and talked to me about the politics of the league, including quotas. He was handsome and spoke with a near-whisper that made you draw in close. One day Willie asked me to ride home with him, but didn't say why. When we got to his house, he opened up his closet and gave me what felt like an entire wardrobe. I'm talking mohair coats, three-piece suits, and everything. I wore any old type of clothes back then, and Willie wanted me to look more professional. I think I was still sporting some of Willie's clothes when I got to Georgetown.

Being associated with intelligent people was refreshing. Guys on the Celtics talked about important topics, not just who went to bed with somebody. The level of conversation reflected how the Celtics played on the court. I kept quiet and listened. I knew my place on a championship team. The Celtics had order, and the man on top was Red.

After all those years of interacting with Red in Washington and riding hours in the car with him to Kutsher's, now I had a chance to observe him in his element, running the best basketball team in the world. I studied Red closely. Not because I planned to be a coach; I intended to be a teacher. I just found Red interesting, and my father taught me to observe. Also, I hardly played, so it wasn't like I had to figure out the other team's tendencies. I knew Russ had a tendency to block every shot. So I sat on the bench and studied Red.

The starting point with Red was simple: he ran the whole show. Red drafted and traded for all the players, scouted opponents, and was in total control of the team. After the owner, Walter Brown, died my rookie year, Red also negotiated our contracts and ran a lot of the other business operations. I wouldn't have been surprised if Red flew the team plane. We all knew who was in charge, and it wasn't us. "Your ass will be grass, and I'm the lawn mower," is one of the phrases I got from Red. Some people liked to portray him as a dictator, but that's a misleading and shallow interpretation. Red got input from other people. He was too smart not to be a great listener. He was flexible in how he handled different situations. He didn't have a lot of rules—"don't make rules, make decisions," he advised me. When he made a decision, nobody questioned it. Red was not a person you challenged.

Part of Red's authority came from his toughness. Push never came to shove with Red because he'd punch your lights out first, and this was a guy who stood five foot ten on a good day. Once we won a game in Philadelphia and their crowd was going berserk as we walked off the court. I was walking behind Red. Some guy came out of the stands onto the court, and ran up on Red as we entered the tunnel. Before I could make a move, Red punched him in the face—*bam!*—and knocked the guy down. Red kept walking. I followed behind him with my heart beating through my chest.

As much of an authoritarian as Red was, he knew enough to sometimes look the other way. Once we landed in Los Angeles for a game. We weren't using a team bus, and one teammate, I don't want to say who, got picked up by a couple of women in a car. Red saw him but ducked out of sight, shoved me toward the car, and said, "John, go tell him where practice is gonna be." Red didn't want his player to know that Red knew his focus was on women and not the game. I learned there are some things a coach should not see.

When I was at Georgetown, sometimes I got on the bus late on purpose, because I didn't want certain players to know that I knew they were late. Know what I mean?

Red adapted his actions depending on the situation. That was a big part of his genius. Treating everyone the same is one of the dumbest ideas I ever heard. Red always said, "Don't be predictable. Keep people off guard. Put them on the defensive." Red didn't lose his temper, he used his temper. You never knew when he would explode. He taught me that you argue with refs for the next call. They won't change a call they just made, but they can be convinced to make the next call in your favor. I also noticed that Red sometimes got himself kicked out of the game on purpose, to give his team a lift. He was never out of control.

Red coached each of us differently. Some guys needed to be screamed at, or Red figured he could make an example out of them and they could take it. Russell was not one who would take it. When the team played bad defense, Red would go off on Satch and then mumble, "You too, Russell." Later on, I would curse out Patrick Ewing or Michael Jackson in order to get Reggie Williams's attention. Red was most considerate toward those of us who played the least. He let us know we all had a contribution to make, whether or not it showed up in the box score. We knew Red cared about us. He didn't care anything about statistics, which is a big reason why I don't believe in these analytics that arc in style today. Red didn't need numbers to know who helped the team win games.

But he stayed on us, hard. In practice he liked to say, "What have you done for me lately?" It was not a rhetorical question. "Don't forget about your mortgages and your big cars," he'd say, which was a reminder that he could cut us at any moment. But he never said it in public. Everything was kept in-house. If you took team business outside the locker room, or God forbid to the newspaper, Red flipped out.

Red had a summer camp for kids in Marshfield, Massachusetts, and it was in the players' best interests to accept his invitation to work there as counselors. That was the first time I ever coached a team. I kept quiet on the Celtics, but when I started coaching that kids' team, I was running up and down the sidelines, yelling at the kids to get back on defense. I didn't know Red was watching me. At the end of the camp, he told me he was surprised how much I liked coaching. It meant something to me that he praised me for my level of enthusiasm with those kids. I still had zero intention of being a coach, but it was a glimpse of my future.

When it came to business, Red was the first person I saw get paid by a shoe company. He even put out his own basketball sneaker. It was terrible, but I kept my mouth shut about it. Red had a deal with

General Mills and put a bunch of us in a Wheaties commercial. When we got paid, the check came from Red, not from General Mills—they paid him to produce the whole deal. Red also had an endorsement deal with a cigar company. He got paid, plus all his stogies were free. The man was an entrepreneur.

I unconsciously absorbed all of this, and Red became part of my professional DNA. He was the first person who showed me that there was money to be made off the court in basketball. From sneaker deals to coaching strategies to how to manage people, Red gave me the foundation. I met the man when I was sixteen years old, so I was a Celtic long before I made the team.

Red's wife and children lived in Washington the whole time he was with the Celtics, and he moved back here in his later years. Before he died in 2006, I visited Red every single day in the hospital. Near the end of his life, we were laughing about the time he punched that Philly fan in the face. Red said, "You missed the game where I punched two of those jerks!" I sat at his bedside the day before he died.

In one of his books Red said, "Some people say John is a hostile man. He's a very caring man. He acts the way he does because he does not want people getting too close. He learned that from me and Russell. 'Be in control, put other people on the defensive.'"

As usual, Red was right.

In the playoffs my rookie year, the biggest challenge was Philadelphia and Wilt Chamberlain in the Eastern Division finals. I had broken Wilt's nose in a game earlier that season, totally by accident. I played with scared hustle, just wild running, trying to make a difference and stay in the game. K. C. Jones said they needed to put a bell on me. Wilt's nose healed and he was back at full strength in the playoffs. The series went to seven games and I didn't play one second. Russ only came out for one minute the whole seven games. You can look it up.

Game Seven in the Boston Garden became one of the classic moments in NBA history. With four seconds left, Wilt dunked to bring

Philly within one point, 110–109. Russ made the inbounds pass, but somehow he threw the ball into a guide wire holding up the backboard. The ref called it out of bounds and the Sixers got the ball under our basket with a chance to win. All they had to do was catch and shoot for a chance to end the Celtic dynasty.

Someone called time-out. In the huddle, Russ was mad at himself and said, "Oh, God, I screwed up."

I thought to myself, *You're agnostic until you need some divine intervention, huh?*

Russ guarded Wilt. Philly tried to inbound the ball to Chet Walker, but Havlicek anticipated the pass and deflected it to Sam Jones. The clock ran out and our fans flooded the court. Johnny Most, the Celtics TV announcer with that distinctive voice, went down in history for his call: "Havlicek stole the ball!"

I was happy we won, even though I didn't play. I liked my teammates, and I was thinking about my share of the playoff money. The Celtics were so dominant, when they negotiated your contract, they basically promised you the "playoff share" you got from winning a championship.

As promised, we beat Los Angeles in the finals, four games to one. The series was so easy, I actually played in three games. Jerry West averaged 34 points for the Lakers, but they didn't have much else. Now I had played on championship teams in high school, college, and the NBA.

I LIVED WITH the Furashes my rookie season, which was not an unusual arrangement for young members of the Celtics. They were wonderful people and treated me like a son. In the summer of 1965, Gwen and I got married in Washington, then moved into our own apartment in Boston. The Celtics had the eighth pick in the draft that year, and Red selected Ollie Johnson, a six-foot-seven forward from the University of San Francisco.

Ollie and I were childhood friends. He lived near Benning Road and tore up the city when he played at Spingarn. I used to knock on

Ollie's door all the time, or he'd knock on mine, and we'd head over to Henry T. Blow elementary school to play one-on-one. Ollie averaged 20 points per game in college and made first-team All-American.

When Red picked Ollie, I got a bad feeling in my stomach. Based on the quota system, I knew one of us had to go.

Red couldn't keep more than six Black players. Six was a lot to begin with. I liked and respected Ollie, we grew up together dreaming about playing in college and maybe the NBA. Now that we both had a chance to make it, we weren't competing for one of twelve spots on the team. It was one of six. Five were for Russell, K.C., Satch, Sam Jones, and Willie Naulls. For the last spot, discrimination pitted Ollie and me against each other, like gladiators.

We battled evenly all throughout training camp. It was an extremely stressful experience. Ollie was my man. I revered Red. I also knew that Red was extremely loyal and that his relationship with me would influence the decision. Unconsciously, I was fighting within myself about how the quota system made me feel, and trying to understand the barrier so I could break it down.

The barrier stayed up. Red kept me and cut his first-round draft pick. Ollie never played in the NBA.

In my second season, I played even less than before, and didn't even suit up for some games. Red had publicly announced it would be his last year as coach, so the team was extra motivated to send him out on top. We beat Philadelphia 4–1 in the Eastern Division finals, then faced Los Angeles again in the championship. This time, the Lakers had more than Jerry West. They had the Rabbit. Elgin Baylor spent his whole career with the Lakers, but he had been injured in the 1965 NBA Finals and didn't play. He was back in 1966.

Elgin scored 36 in the first game, West dropped 41, and we trailed in the series 1–0. Before Game Two, Red announced that the next head coach of the Boston Celtics would be . . . Bill Russell. The first Black coach in the NBA.

See, that's why I couldn't stay mad at Red about Levern and Ollie.

We won the next three games, then the Lakers took two, and we held on to win a close one in Game Seven. Red was a champion one last time. I supposedly played five minutes in one of the Finals games. I might as well have brought my newspaper and did the crossword puzzle. But I also knew who I was playing behind, so I dealt with it.

After we returned to Boston, the team gathered to divide up the playoff shares. My salary was about $8,000, and the playoff share was an extra $2,000. We all went into a room. Red and everybody else sat around a long table. Someone said my name and announced that I had half a share.

Half a share?

I was shocked, hurt, then angry. There would be no waiting to speak out this time. The money itself was not the point, although it was a significant amount for Gwen and me. It was the principle of the thing. It went against my nature and what I thought we represented as a team. I told them on the spot: "No thank you. Y'all should just keep this money." I didn't say it in a belligerent manner. I simply told them no thank you, with no further explanation. They started urging me to take it, telling me that I deserved it. They weren't making some sort of conscious effort to stop me from getting the full amount of money. They felt they were giving me something special, given how little I had played. I refused because I respected the organization so much, I suppose I unconsciously wanted them to live up to my concept of what it was.

"I was told that we are all teammates," I said to them. "I'm just as much a member of this team as anybody else. If I'm a member of the team, I deserve a whole share. If I'm not, I'd rather not have any of it. You can keep it."

There was a stunned silence, then some mumbling and murmuring.

"He's right," my man Willie Naulls said.

Another guy chimed in, "Yeah, John has a point."

The team voted again and gave me my full share.

I look back at that moment now and think, how did I have enough nerve to stand up to my heroes like that? I suppose it came from the same place as when I called the nun a white witch, or when I told Slats Gill I wouldn't play in the Olympic trials. All I can think of is heredity, environment, and time.

AFTER RED RETIRED as coach he remained the general manager, and he left me unprotected in the expansion draft that summer. It didn't have anything to do with the playoff money, it was a basketball decision, and not surprising given how little I had played. It didn't change how I felt about Red one bit. I was selected by Chicago, which sent me a contract and a date to report to training camp in the fall.

When I thought about playing for the Bulls, I thought about quotas. How many Black players would they keep? How many spots would I be competing for? Five? Four? Two? I didn't know the people running this team. The money wasn't great, about $8,000 or $9,000 per year. I was attracted to the idea of proving I could play, and my Celtic buddy Larry Siegfried told me this was my shot to make a name for myself. But I could have not played, too. I remembered how Levern and Ollie weren't there when the morning came.

The NBA lifestyle held no appeal for me. Gwen had just given birth to our first son, John Robert Thompson III. I wasn't into partying on the road. Our transportation and accommodations were far from luxurious. We shared hotel rooms and rode to some exhibition games in our own cars. Chicago winters made Boston look like the Bahamas. The Bulls would probably be terrible. And besides all that, Gwen said she wasn't going to Chicago.

I decided I didn't need basketball anymore.

New Orleans tried to get me to jump to the ABA, but I told them no. I always wanted to be some sort of counselor or teacher, so I decided to return home to Washington and work with kids. I got a job working for the United Planning Organization, a poverty program that helped young people coming out of jail or other troubled situations. I had no plan or desire whatsoever to coach.

Basketball had given me a degree from a great university that I never could have attended otherwise. It introduced me to new situations and new people. It taught me about the white man. But as far as I was concerned, in the summer of 1966, I was done with basketball. It was time to begin the rest of my life.

6

THE GAME BEHIND THE GAME

I went to Providence to get a degree. I went to Dr. Anita Hughes to get an education.

Soon after I returned to Washington, I heard about a master's degree program in education at Federal City College, which is now the University of the District of Columbia, and asked a friend how to get in. He said, "There's a lady named Dr. Hughes who runs it, but it's too late for this year, enrollment is closed." I decided to go to an informational meeting anyway, and asked my friend what this Dr. Hughes looked like.

"When you see her, you will know," he said.

I went to the meeting, and as soon as I saw her, I knew. She was a Black lady who carried herself in a very proud way, the type of person who if you saw her walking down the hallway, you'd move aside. You could feel the strength coming out of her. I approached her and asked about applying, but she said registration had been completed and the program was closed. Then she looked at me with a piercing gaze. Dr. Hughes had strong eyes. She didn't know anything about basketball or who I was. She looked at me and said, "Go ahead and register. I have only one other man in the class, and I need a cross section of opinions."

At Providence I learned how to write a lesson plan and supervise children in a classroom. Those were the Xs and Os of teaching. Dr. Hughes taught me how to make an impact on young people within the teaching environment. Teaching is more than just giving students information. A big part of teaching is informal education. Dr. Hughes taught me how to relate to students in a way that would affect their lives outside school.

She was very demanding, in an intellectual sense. She challenged us all the time in class: "What exactly are you saying? Why are you saying that?" She could cut you to pieces, not in an offensive way, but teaching us to think things through. She is the reason I served as a mentor for girls, in a "big sister" program, rather than as a big brother. Dr. Hughes also incorporated our Blackness into the curriculum. One thing I'll never forget her saying is that for a Black person in America, it's not enough to have a Plan A, or even a Plan A and a Plan B. Black folks need to have a Plan C.

I watched Dr. Hughes and thought, *She doesn't apologize for living.*

What I learned with Dr. Hughes overlapped with my job working with troubled youth in the United Planning Organization. Our task was to give these young people work experience with the National Park Service that would help integrate them back into society after they had served time in the criminal justice system. I also directed a 4-H youth program, supervising projects for children. With 4-H we did arts and crafts, built things, camped outside in parks. I can still remember a song we used to sing: "I live-ee in a teeny weeny house-ee, I live-ee on the thirty-first floor . . . ruffles on the petticoat, ten cents more." When people would later call me the big bad bully John Thompson, I wished they could have seen me holding hands in the woods singing Girl Scout songs. On the flip side of that, Dr. Hughes also assigned me to do my practicum in the D.C. jail. She made sure we were exposed to a wide range of life experiences. I didn't like sleeping outside, or coming home with my clothes all smoky from a campfire, but I tremendously enjoyed working with young people.

Growing up, I never used any profanity. My mother would not have tolerated any curse words whatsoever. Like a lot of Black people, I grew up switching my style of speech depending on my environment, but profanity was not part of my street language. In college and with the Celtics, I cursed very seldom, if at all. That changed when I started working with kids coming out of jail. Cussing was the only way to reach some of them. Some of these youngsters had been in shoot-outs with police or other violent situations. One kid in our program later became a hit man. You couldn't be like, "Pardon me, would you please refrain from sitting on that desk?" That ain't gonna work. "Motherfucker, get off that desk!" I didn't speak that way to every kid. I knew better than to fall into the stereotype that every poor Black child is a hoodlum. But for some of them, cussing was a way to connect. They didn't take it in an abusive way, it was just the form of language they understood best. And they knew I cared about them, which was something else I learned from Dr. Hughes.

That was when I began cursing. Now it's habitual, part of my personality. Some of my friends say "motherfucker" is my favorite word. I don't use profanity in places where it would be inappropriate, but I enjoy using it elsewhere. I know I'm wrong. That's what I tell the Blessed Mother when I ask for forgiveness.

One reason I liked working in the youth program is because I had freedom. I wouldn't have functioned well as something like a junior high school teacher, being dictated to by people who want you to follow a formula. I can follow orders, but I think the need for freedom is part of my nature. I'm not somebody who can permit himself to be confined. I had that freedom working for the youth program, and eventually I supervised about thirty people.

I was quite content in my job when the pastor at St. Anthony's High School asked if I would be interested in coaching the basketball team. It was the only coed Catholic high school in the city, with a very low enrollment, and never won many games. The school wasn't trying to build a championship team, it was more like somebody was needed to supervise an after-school gym class. I had never aspired to be a basketball coach, but I did love the relationships that are built working with young people. I suppose that came from my mother being an educator, from being around people like Mr. Trigg who coached me in junior high school, from being around Mr. Jabbo and the others at Boys Club No. 2. I was intrigued by the offer and went to the school building in Northeast Washington to investigate. When they lined up the boys on the team—most of them were white—I thought to myself, "There isn't a kid here taller than six feet." But I also knew I could get players. You can barely walk ten blocks in this city without stumbling over a kid with talent. I decided to take the position and keep working full time in the youth program. I would coach St. Anthony's after my job ended each day.

We finished my first season 12–12. Even before it ended, I was circulating through the playgrounds and Boys Clubs looking for new talent. I had always hung out in those places, since long before I started coaching, because I enjoyed the environment and being around the game. I grew up on those basketball courts, and they felt like home. I didn't think of finding players there as recruiting; I was just living life. My second season we went 28–3 and never looked back.

The way I found Donald Washington was typical. I was driving past Turkey Thicket playground at 12th and Michigan, about three blocks from St. Anthony's, when I saw this boy in a pair of overalls running, jumping, and playing wild. He was awkward, but quick and athletic. I swung around the block and parked to watch some more. He wasn't scoring a lot, but I watched what he did off the ball, like Red taught me, and saw that he played with a lot of effort. I walked over and introduced myself. Donald was in the eighth grade, about six foot four, with hands bigger than mine. I asked if his mom was home, and he said she got off work a little later. "C'mon, let's go wait for her, I'll drive you home." We sat there outside Donald's house until his mother came home. That's how I got one of the best high school players in the country.

Aside from the playgrounds, I knew so many people in Washington, and so many people knew me, there was a natural flow of players in my direction. Once we had some success it just snowballed. Guys like Michael Bennett, Tom Walters, Charles Barrett, Allen Baker, Paul Wagner, John Butler, and Ronald Plummer—almost all of them went on to play in college, not to be pros but to get an education. Then there were the players who would follow me from St. Anthony's to Georgetown: Aaron Long, Greg Brooks, Jonathan Smith, and Merlin Wilson.

I played a full court man-to-man pressure defense because that's what I learned on the Celtics. One day at practice, a young white kid who had just graduated from college and was volunteering to help coach said, "Have you ever thought about using a zone press?" I asked him to show me how it worked. It went on to be one of my trademarks at Georgetown.

Another trademark was the towel. My mother used to wear a towel hanging over one shoulder when she worked in the kitchen. She'd use it to wipe her hands or dry a dish. When I started coaching at St. Anthony's, I draped a white towel over my shoulder during games as a tribute to her. She and my father didn't come to hardly any of the games, but I felt them with me when I wore that towel.

THE LATE SIXTIES was a socially volatile time, and some white people felt threatened by what was happening. Martin Luther King was demanding rights with nonviolent action; the Black Panthers were carrying guns. The world was changing, and some people were frightened by those changes. For example, one of my St. Anthony's teams was in the middle of a winning streak and liked to get fired up before games by counting out our wins in Spanish. I thought it could help them with their grades in Spanish class, too. In the locker room we counted the number of games we had won, then counted one more for the game we were about to play. The players came onto the floor counting and yelling "*ocho*" or whatever the number was. But after we played

Georgetown Prep, I was told that the other team thought we were yelling racial insults, like "Kill those white boys" or something. How does that happen except from fear?

On April 4, 1968, Martin Luther King was assassinated and the city rioted. St. Anthony's administrators didn't know what to do. Looking out the windows of the building the next day, they could see smoke rising from the city. Some of the students were from far-flung areas and traveled home on public transportation. I was at my counseling job and not in the school building. The school kept calling and calling me, at home and at my office. I finally got the message about two or three o'clock in the afternoon and told them to send the kids home.

In the late 1960s, the neighborhood around St. Anthony's was changing from white to Black, and so was the student body. Most of the best players in the neighborhood and in the city were Black. I did have some good white players, like Paul Wagner, who started for me and played for Terry Holland at Davidson. But pretty soon, due to the natural environment, most of my team was Black. Basketball is a poor people's game. You don't see us out there playing polo.

One day the athletic director asked if he could talk to me.

"I think you should have more white players on our team," he said. "And the white players you have now, they should get more playing time."

I wish I could say I was surprised. Here was the same old quota system rearing up.

"That would be extremely unfair," I replied, and explained the reasons why most of our players were Black. "We can't discriminate against a talented Black kid just to appease somebody else." I reminded him that I had attended a Catholic high school and a Catholic university, and then said, "The priests taught me that the end should never justify the means."

What he said next did shock me, and I'll never forget it.

"Who's trying to justify?"

It still angers me to think about it. Not only did this man have the audacity to say that inferior white players should get moved ahead of deserving Black kids, he didn't even try to camouflage it. He was blatant and open with his discrimination. I thought to myself, *I would be furious if my own child lost an opportunity because of him*. I also was angry that we as Black people had accepted it for so long—nobody said anything when St. Anthony's had a white team in a city that was 70 percent Black. Now that a meritocracy had arrived, this man wanted to use his power and position to keep white people on top.

But this time, I had some power of my own. I told the athletic director, not in a mean way, that under no circumstances would I discriminate against deserving Black kids. That was the last I heard of it.

Situations like this started to give the school administrators, all of whom were white, an idea of what sort of person I was.

Another important moment came when one of my players hadn't done some homework on a game day. The teacher kept him after school to finish his work. When it was time for the game, the kid wasn't in the locker room. I went to find him and see what was going on. The teacher in that class was Mary Fenlon, who would become one of the most important members of my staff at Georgetown. She had grown up in Washington and got her high school diploma at St. Anthony's. She became a nun, then left the convent and came back to St. Anthony's to teach English and Latin. She had four or five of my players in her homeroom early on. I observed that she was an excellent teacher, firm but caring, and knew how to hold young people accountable. She wasn't intimidated by the influx of Black people into the neighborhood and the school, she was comfortable with us, and not in a patronizing or pandering way. She dealt with us like people, which is all you can ask for.

The day we started working together, I told Fenlon that if my player's homework wasn't done, he couldn't play in the game. We've been on the same page ever since.

I continued studying for my master's degree while working for the city and coaching my team. When I was about to graduate, Dr. Hughes asked me, "What are you going to do with your degree? How do you plan to utilize your education?" I was a few years into coaching, and that's when I decided to use basketball as an instrument of education. I thought I could intermingle counseling with my coaching. I wanted to help kids win in life, beyond the basketball court.

Some people talk about basketball strategies as if they're coaching the chalk. As if all you need to do to be a good coach is chalk up the right play on the blackboard. This ignores the implementation of the strategy, how you present it to the players, how you get them to believe in it and work at it. You can chalk up all the Xs and Os you want, but those scribbles don't set screens or grab rebounds—people do. Try coaching a person whose mind is heavy because of a problem with his girlfriend or his mother, or the death of a parent. You can't chalk up a play for those situations. Providence taught me the Xs and Os, which was essential. But none of it would have mattered without Dr. Hughes teaching me how to deal with young people. That's why I say a lot of my coaching ability came from people who were not coaches.

Gwen and I had two additions to our household while I coached at St. Anthony's. Our second son, Ronny, was born in 1969, and then we adopted Donald Washington, the player I'd found at the Turkey Thicket playground. Donald's mother had died, and his father had serious legal problems, so we legally adopted him. Gwen had the same passion for teaching and helping young people as I did, and she graduated from the District of Columbia Teachers College, which had been called Miner Teachers College when my mother went there. Gwen is a born educator, one of the best teachers I ever knew, and she spent a lot of time helping Donald and my other players with their schoolwork. A lot of kids on the team were in and out of our house all the time, so it was not a huge stretch when we became Donald's legal guardians.

Donald developed into one of the top recruits in the country. My life changed when Dean Smith, the coach of the University of North Carolina, came to our house to recruit him.

He showed up in what I would learn was typical Dean Smith fashion: jacket and tie, hair perfect, polished manners. I wasn't overly impressed. I felt like he had an aristocratic air. I was probably thinking,

Who is this white boy from down South coming in here? But Gwen was smart enough to observe that Dean knew a lot of details about the classes Donald would take. After Dean left, Gwen said, "This coach knows the professors by name."

Donald chose North Carolina. Dean and I kept in touch, and once I got to know him, he became colorless. That never would have happened if it hadn't been for Gwen, and I thank her for that, because Dean ended up as one of my greatest mentors in basketball. We were definitely an odd couple. Dean liked to eat in restaurants with tablecloths; I'm happy with a fish sandwich. Dean's clothing was immaculate; mine was low budget. Michael Jordan, who played for Dean and is now a friend of mine, likes to joke about how a large Black dude from the city who enjoys profanity became such good friends with a short, prim-and-proper white man from Kansas. Sometimes Dean would say to me, "John, you know we can't get mad at our players and curse them out." I'd reply, "You're right, coach," and keep right on doing it.

HIGH SCHOOL BASKETBALL was bigger locally then than the college or pro game. The king of the city was Morgan Wootten, the coach at DeMatha, a Catholic school in nearby Hyattsville, Maryland. Morgan, who was white, started coaching at DeMatha when I was still playing high school ball at Archbishop Carroll. We never lost to DeMatha—in fact, we gave them a bunch of good whippings. Right after I graduated, my coach, Bob Dwyer, had a falling-out with the administration, and he started sending players out to Morgan. The first guy he sent, John Austin, is one of the best to ever come out of Washington. Austin led DeMatha to its first championship. That was when Morgan's dominance began, when he started getting Black players from the city.

Morgan was a very good coach—smart, well organized, and strategic. He quickly built DeMatha into a national powerhouse. In 1965, his team beat Power Memorial with Lew Alcindor (before he changed his name to Kareem Abdul-Jabbar) and ended their seventy-one-game winning streak. He also was very good at the game behind the game, in terms of working the power structure to his advantage.

Here's what I mean by that. I had a good friend, Harold Dean, who coached at Cardozo in the public school league. They were getting ready to play DeMatha one year and I stopped by his gym. Harold had his players running and drilling and practicing so hard, you could tell they were primed to go.

I told him, "Your kids look great, but you ain't beating DeMatha."

Harold was confused. He was an outstanding coach. "Why not?" Harold asked.

"Because while you're down here sweating in practice, Morgan is eating dinner with the refs at Ledo's."

Ledo's was Morgan's favorite restaurant out in College Park; he ate there after every game. I was messing with Harold, but he got my point. The politics behind the game were almost as important to winning as what happened after the tip-off.

It didn't take long for Morgan to perceive me as a competitive threat. I told you the man was smart. At the end of my second season at St. Anthony's, our team was chosen for a prestigious tournament, the University of Maryland "M Club Classic." These invitation-only tournaments usually determined who was ranked No. 1 at the end of the season, because there were no city or state playoffs. DeMatha had finished the previous six seasons in the No. 1 spot. When Morgan found out we were invited, he used some sort of clause in his contract to force the tournament to rescind our invitation. Basically, Morgan was scared he would lose, so he got us kicked out, and he was astute enough to have obtained the necessary leverage. He won the game before it was even played.

I wasn't surprised, because Dwyer and Red had schooled me about this, but I was still mad. It was a competitive thing. I wasn't in awe of Morgan like a lot of other people. We kicked DeMatha's ass when I was in high school, so I didn't have to genuflect at Morgan's altar. I was a guy who had credentials from their world, from their white schools.

I had studied the white man, meaning I understood their system and what it took athletically and politically to build a winner. I wouldn't be dictated to by somebody with more success than I had been allowed the opportunity to have. A wise man once said the oppressor's most potent weapon is the mind of the oppressed. I wasn't going to act like it was an honor to just be accepted Across the Park. I came to win.

That's why I started to be labeled as a troublemaker.

After Morgan kicked us out of the M Club Classic, things really heated up between us. The newspapers started asking when St. Anthony's would play DeMatha. Morgan only wanted to play us on his terms, in places that he felt would give him an advantage. My position was, you pick one venue, and I pick one. Morgan wanted Georgetown, or the University of Maryland, which was up the street from DeMatha. Okay, my choice is Howard University, the historically Black college. But Morgan wouldn't do a two-game series. He said in the newspaper, "I'll play anyone, provided it's in a healthy, wholesome environment or situation." Oh, you think Howard is unhealthy? I told the newspaper, "Washington becomes more dangerous to Wootten the tougher the competition becomes."

Morgan used his influence to bounce my team from another event, the O'Connell Christmas tournament. Then we got invited to play in the Knights of Columbus tournament out in Cumberland, Maryland. That was a big deal. DeMatha had won it the last six times. The year we got invited, DeMatha wouldn't come.

In 1970, I signed my team up for the summer league at the Jelleff Boys Club, the same league that my Black high school teammates and I had not been allowed to play in. When Jelleff released its schedule, St. Anthony's vs. DeMatha was on it. The whole city wanted to see us compete. We had Donald Washington and some other outstanding players. Morgan had Adrian Dantley, who went on to become a star in the NBA. Everybody got excited when the game rolled around, and the court was packed with a couple thousand people.

DeMatha came out all pumped up, going through their layup line with all this energy. My team came out second, and everybody's jaw dropped. I had gathered a bunch of team managers, kids from the baseball team, male cheerleaders, I might have sent a trombone player out there. None of my regular team was at the game. I didn't even go, I sent one of the junior varsity coaches. We lost 108–26, and I laughed my ass off. Now you know how my kids felt when you kicked us out of those tournaments. If you want to play us, play us in a real game.

See, I didn't idolize Morgan like other people did, I challenged him. Some people started to lie that I was using racist recruiting methods, that I was telling Black kids they shouldn't play for a white coach. They saw me as a nigger who didn't know his place.

The principals of our schools got involved and agreed to a home-and-home series for the 1970–71 season. But when it came time to make the schedule, DeMatha reneged and wanted to play only one game, at a neutral site. The DeMatha principal used to be Wootten's assistant coach, so we knew who called the shots. My principal and I went out to DeMatha for a meeting. It was civil, but I felt some of that Malcolm X bubbling up inside me. I told Morgan, "Where you come to recruit your kids, that's where I live." I didn't say it out of anger or spite. It was just a fact, and it was the reason why I scared them. They never had to deal with a winning Black coach from the city in their sacrosanct Catholic league.

Behind the scenes, I admired Morgan's ability to coach his team and run his program. But he didn't know that, and I didn't want him to know that. I kept him on the defensive. When he used his juice to kick us out of the O'Connell tournament, I'm not certain I wouldn't have done the same thing to him. Morgan was a big part of my coaching education. I studied Morgan and Dean. I got information and instruction from Red. I had conversations with Bill Russell. Later, when people talked about my coaching, very few of them mentioned how I learned to coach. Even Jesus said, "My teaching is not mine."

Truth be told, I didn't think of Morgan as the enemy. He was a very good coach, with an excellent team. We never did play each other. It would have been a great game. All my fussing at Morgan was a competitive thing. I stood my ground.

IN THE SPRING of 1972, an old high school friend named Maurice Lancaster asked if we could have lunch. He was the first Black person to work in the admissions office at Georgetown. When we met, Maurice said Georgetown wanted to hire me as their next basketball coach.

It made no sense to me.

"Mo, they can't be serious," I said. "They wouldn't let me go to school there. How can I be the coach when a few years ago they wouldn't recruit Black players?"

"You can get that job, John," Mo responded. "I know for a fact they want you."

Maurice worked for Charlie Deacon, the dean of admissions, who had some life experiences with Black people. When Martin Luther King was killed and the city burned, Charlie realized that Georgetown had a responsibility to Black people in Washington and helped launch a program to admit more Black students.

Deacon also was a big basketball fan. He knew a successful team would raise the profile of his school. He knew any successful team needed Black players. He knew I was a Black coach who had a lot of Washington's best Black players on my teams.

Are you starting to get the picture?

Georgetown's basketball team had just finished a 3–23 season. Deacon told the university president, Father Robert Henle, that I should be the next coach. Henle instructed Deacon to form a search committee, which was a smoke screen, and made Deacon the chair.

"If you can get John Thompson into the final three candidates," Henle said, "I'll hire him."

That's how I got the job. It was given to me before I even knew about it. Over the twelve years since I had graduated from high school, Georgetown went from not recruiting me because I was Black, to *hiring* me because I was Black. They wanted me to be a bridge Across the Park.

I give the university a lot of credit for recognizing it had to make a change and get some Black people up in here. Georgetown wasn't looking for history professors, though. As progressive as Georgetown was, they still placed Black people in a certain category, consciously or not.

Here's another thing: even though I was very well qualified for the job, my coaching ability was not the main reason I was selected. My ability was secondary to my skin color. These white folks were trying to do the right thing, but I still wasn't judged on the content of my character.

But all that was unknown to me when Deacon came over to our house one night to make his pitch. We talked for three or four hours, and he basically said the job was mine if I wanted it.

I was extremely dubious. But at the same time, I knew I could be successful if Georgetown let me do my thing. I knew that I could get players, and I knew I could win. The opportunity to use basketball as an instrument of higher education was very attractive. The big question was whether Georgetown was serious about basketball and could accept a Black man in charge. That was what I needed to find out. I told Deacon I wouldn't give him a résumé, but I'd meet with the search committee.

My old high school coach, Bob Dwyer, heard the job was open but didn't know it had been offered to me. It came up in a conversation one day, and Dwyer said he'd like to coach Georgetown for a few years, then hand it over to my old teammate George Leftwich. It never crossed Dwyer's mind that I could do the job. He underestimated my abilities, but I let it go.

Then it got really interesting. Morgan Wootten applied for the job. About fifty other people did too, including George Raveling, who was a Black assistant at the University of Maryland, and the future NBA coach Jack Ramsay. But Morgan was the big story, because of how successful he was and the friction between us.

My interview process was a charade. The search committee consisted of two alumni; two former Georgetown athletes, including one basketball player; two faculty members; and Deacon. I thought my interview went poorly. I was nervous and didn't express myself well, but everybody told me I was great. The committee voted 4–3 to make me the top choice. Morgan and Raveling were the other finalists. Morgan was getting information from someone on the committee, and according to Deacon, once Morgan heard I was the top choice, he tried to act as though he never applied. "I don't think the guidelines of the Georgetown basketball program are right for me at this time" is what he told reporters.

Same old Morgan. Our teams may have never played, but in the end I won.

When I went to speak with Father Henle, I asked what his expectations were for the team. He told me, "I'd like to periodically make the NIT, and go to the NCAA tournament once in a while."

"I think we can do that," I replied with a straight face. Inside, I was laughing. That's all y'all want? When you're 3–23, periodically going to the NIT looks like the Promised Land. My goals were much higher than that. I didn't want to be equal to the white man, I wanted to kick his ass.

Next I had to negotiate a contract. My main objective was to obtain all the tools needed to win. I knew I needed a good athletic director. Frank Rienzo was the interim AD, and when we talked, I thought he would do a great job. I asked Georgetown to make him permanent.

Then I needed to create a position that, to my knowledge, did not exist in college basketball at that time: academic coordinator.

Plenty of schools had tutors, but I needed someone to work exclusively with the basketball team. I was convinced that players would not reveal what they did not know to someone they did not know. I asked Mary Fenlon to take the job, and she agreed. She helped me figure out everything that needed to be in the contract for players to succeed academically. The players needed to be housed on campus, in regular dorms. That was important for their informal education. They needed guaranteed entry into the classes of their choice, because their selections were limited by practices and games. They needed flexible meal options, because they might not be able to eat when everyone else did. I said that McDonough Gymnasium needed more lights so we could televise our games. After I got the things I felt were needed to be successful, the dollar figure on my first contract didn't mean anything to me, just like when I started with the Celtics. I took whatever Georgetown offered. Once I won, the money would follow.

One of my friends told me, "Georgetown has no idea who they're getting." That was true. But I respect the hell out of Georgetown because once they did realize who I was, they never asked me to change. They never tried to stop me from being Black.

That's not to say I wouldn't encounter racism within the school. Georgetown was progressive enough to hire me, but at the same time, Georgetown still had a lot of racism within itself. I'm talking about the way some people there thought, what kind of behaviors were tolerated or encouraged, the way opportunities were given or denied. This is a school founded in 1789 with slave labor, whose leaders didn't think to bring in Black students until Washington went up in flames beneath their feet. None of that disappears just because you brought in some niggers to throw a ball through a hoop.

I will always love Georgetown, but I won't let them off the hook, either.

While finalizing my contract, I still had to coach out the season with St. Anthony's. We finished 22–1, which made my record over six years 122–28. In my final game, we beat undefeated St. Peter's from New York City in the Knights of Columbus tournament. The game was played in Georgetown's McDonough Gym, just like my last game at Carroll. We had some great cheerleaders at St. Anthony's, and that day they performed a routine that said, "From '66 to '72, Mr. T did the do!" That brought tears to my eyes.

Next I had to leave my job with the city youth program. On my last day they threw a going-away party, and that's where the legend of the deflated basketball was born.

Over the years, the deflated basketball I kept in my office at

Georgetown came to symbolize my commitment to education. It sent a message to my players that sooner or later, basketball will end and you're going to need a degree. All the reporters loved the deflated basketball. Reporters love metaphors, maybe because it makes them feel literary. The media made that deflated basketball into an almost religious symbol.

But the deflated basketball started as a joke. It was a prank gift from a lady named Blanche Bowman who worked for me at the 4-H cooperative extension. Like, ha ha boss, we're giving you something useless, happy trails. Everyone had a good laugh when Blanche gave me that ball.

I brought it with me to Georgetown to remember the people I used to work with. At first I looked at it and felt depressed, because what good is a ball with no air? Growing up, we didn't have a lot of equipment on the playground, and if the ball went flat, or the guy with the ball had to leave, it would stop the run. The deflated ball in my office was a real downer. Then I started thinking about the thousands and thousands of kids across the country chasing the basketball, focused on the basketball, treating the basketball like the most important thing in the world. This leather object seemed to represent the sum total of their life experiences. But once the air came out of the ball, it felt like the player had no value. I thought, *You never want the sum total of your value to be the eight or nine pounds of air inside a basketball.* That all started with a joke gift from Blanche Bowman.

On March 13, 1972, Georgetown held a press conference to announce my hiring. I was thirty years old. To my knowledge, there were only four other Black coaches at predominantly white colleges: Fred Goss at UC Riverside, Will Robinson at Illinois State, John Staggers at Cal State Hayward, and Bernie Bickerstaff at San Diego. As I stood on the podium next to Father Henle, one of the first questions the reporters asked was whether I planned to bring more Black athletes to Georgetown.

I had barely got the keys to my office, and somebody was already talking about race.

Over the years, whenever I brought up race, a lot of people would say, "There goes John again, playing the race card." Fuck that. Y'all stacked the deck. I played the cards you dealt me.

I told the media I planned to recruit both Black and white players, and that I didn't anticipate having any trouble signing white kids.

"I want to be judged as a person," I said.

Of course, that is not what happened.

7

SEVENTY PERCENT

When I arrived at Georgetown in the fall of 1972, there was another Black man on campus far more famous than me. Everyone called him Pebbles.

Pebbles was born in 1918 and grew up in the neighborhood east of campus, somewhere between 34th and 37th Streets. As a kid, he hung around Georgetown's ball fields, serving as a batboy or waterboy. Students took a liking to him, and he started roaming farther into the campus. I've seen photos of him as a little boy wearing knickers and suspenders, surrounded by a bunch of smiling white students. My mentor Mr. Jabbo knew Pebbles; they were about the same age and played ball together growing up. Mr. Jabbo said Pebbles as a young man was a terrific athlete, with long arms and big hands, who could throw a baseball or football as fast and far as anybody. In the early 1940s, Pebbles got hired by the Georgetown athletic department as an equipment manager. People said he lived in a little room up above one of our gyms. At some point, Pebbles became an alcoholic, and in 1969 he got fired for being drunk on the job. But he didn't leave campus, and after a new athletic director arrived, Pebbles made his way back into the flow of things.

By the time I got to Georgetown, Pebbles was a beloved figure. The common joke among students and faculty was that he ran the university. Walking around at basketball games or other events, Pebbles would dance and shuffle and clown to entertain people. Everybody knew he was an alcoholic, and students liked to slip him liquor. Few people even knew his real name, which was Raymond Medley.

It was immediately obvious to me that most of Georgetown didn't think of Pebbles as a man. They treated him like a pet or a mascot. Not consciously, because everybody would tell you how much they loved ol' Pebs. People showed him a lot of affection, but in the way a family loves its dog. I heard the basketball teams used to rub his head before games for good luck.

There's a campus legend that he got his name by throwing rocks at the first female students admitted to Georgetown. But one of the Black old-timers told me when white students would rub his head, they said his hard, tight curls felt like little rocks. Like pebbles.

When the school was getting ready to hire me, the student paper printed a headline that read PEBBLES IS NOT ALONE.

At first, I was incredibly ashamed of Pebbles. I never publicly criticized him, but hardly anybody else on campus seemed to realize he was treated like a mascot, let alone what that type of treatment meant. I told Mr. Jabbo I didn't like how Pebbles was shucking and jiving, even though he wasn't doing it intentionally. Mr. Jabbo took Pebbles underneath the stands and told him, "This boy Thompson worked real hard to get here, and he's one of ours. He's trying to build something here. Don't you do anything to embarrass him." Pebbles toned down his act after that.

But I felt unsettled about Pebbles. The more I thought about it, I realized he did what he had to do to survive. All of us want whatever privileges life affords us. It's like what happened during slavery with us getting mad at the house nigger. The field niggers didn't have the chance to live inside the house, eat good food, and do easier work. If you'd asked us back then to make a choice between working in the house and doing hard labor in the field, we'd all have been house niggers.

And don't forget, the house niggers were forced into that position. They had no choice but to accept it. That's similar to what happened to Pebbles. He grew up near Georgetown's campus, people took a liking to him, and he survived in the only role in which white society would accept him. He had to be Pebbles to be accepted Across the Park.

To further complicate things, I always got the feeling from Pebbles that when it came to my being on campus, not that he resented my presence, but he would have preferred to be the "one and only." He had a special status, and that changed when I got here. It changed in a lot of ways, because I was a different type of Black man than most white people had encountered. That desire to be the "one and only" happens with a lot of Black people. I can accept it more from Pebbles's generation than today's.

Eventually, I understood that Pebbles was not somebody I disliked or was ashamed of. I resented the school for dealing with him the way they did. I resented the box they put him in. A lot of us were relegated to that position in life. The pitiful thing was that 99 percent of the people who dealt with Pebbles didn't realize how they treated him. They'll read this book and say, "There goes John talking crazy again. We loved Pebbles. We treated him well." But I was trying to break down barriers. I was dealing with the negative perception of Black people that a lot of whites didn't even know they had. I knew a lot of people at Georgetown looked at me and saw Pebbles. Don't forget the headline: PEBBLES IS NOT ALONE.

I'm not certain I wouldn't have been a Pebbles, if I had been in his time and place. What Pebbles did afforded me the opportunity to reach a position to resent it being done.

The students used to have a flea market on campus at the end of the school year and sell their things outside. I bought a photo of Pebbles at one of those sales, which I still have. He's sitting next to a white girl, reaching for a bottle of liquor in her hand. She's tempting him with the bottle. What really hurt me is if you look on Pebbles's other wrist, there's a hospital band on it. The man was being treated for ailments that must have been related to alcoholism, and she's teasing him with some whiskey, like you make a dog jump for a piece of bacon. I'm sure she didn't mean it that way, but that was the box she unconsciously put him in. Certain people put me and my players in that box, too.

Pebbles died in 1982 at Georgetown University Hospital. I named a team award after him, the Raymond Medley Award for Citizenship.

I made sure the name Pebbles was nowhere to be found on that award.

MY FIRST SEASON coaching at Georgetown, in 1972–73, coincided with the first year that freshmen were eligible to play varsity. I needed an immediate infusion of talent, but I recruited my first player, Aaron Long, more for his academic abilities. I had known Aaron since he was a little boy growing up near Benning Road, and he played for me at St. Anthony's. He was a solid six-foot-two guard, and studious. I knew his attention to academics would influence the other kids I planned to bring in, like seeding the clouds to make it rain. Aaron played in only two varsity games at Georgetown, but his effect on the program was bigger than the statistics showed.

After Aaron, I signed three other St. Anthony's kids. Merlin Wilson was a six-foot-nine center who became one of the top rebounders in the country as a freshman. Forward Jonathan Smith and guard Greg Brooks both played a lot of minutes. I will always be grateful to those four St. Anthony's kids who took a chance and followed me to Georgetown, into the unknown. My other two recruits were Mike Stokes, a white guard from Washington who was third on the team in scoring with nine points per game, and Billy Lynn, a big man from Spingarn. As assistant coaches, I hired my college teammate Billy Stein and my high school teammate George Leftwich. Mary Fenlon was the academic coordinator and ran the basketball office. I considered her an assistant coach, and she was probably the first woman in the country working full time with a men's college team.

Some Black folks in Washington tried to get on me about Stein and Fenlon, like, "Why are you hiring these white people?" I hired them because they were extremely capable, but I liked to answer by saying, "I'm going to this white university, so I need some white people to go in front and tell me who's out to get me." Now I had my own natives with the spears.

I also had my guys from No. 2 Boys Club, especially Mr. Jabbo. He came to all our games with Mr. Wyatt and Mr. Butler; we called them my Amen Corner. Jab visited campus often in his station wagon, with the back full of stuff he'd collected from around the city to give to my players. I'm talking loaves of bread, shirts, jeans, transistor radios, table lamps, you name it. I liked to call Mr. Jabbo the biggest beggar in town. He'd pull up outside McDonough after practice and just be handing out stuff. One time he brought some of those high-heeled shoes with fake fish swimming in the heels. I swear, he tried to have my players wear pimp shoes. I told him about NCAA regulations that prohibited extra benefits, but he wouldn't listen. "Buddy, these are my boys," Jab said. "I've been watching over them since they were little." He wasn't about to stop now.

GEORGETOWN WAS NOT accustomed to having Black people around. When I first arrived, one of the guys in the athletic promotions office asked a friend of mine, "How do you talk to John?" I said he should try English.

One day we were emptying out an old file cabinet in the office and found lists of high school players that had marks next to some names. Not grades, but symbols. After studying them for a while, we realized the marks identified all the Black players. That's one reason it was no surprise when we experienced immediate resistance about the Black kids we recruited. Billy Lynn was one example. Billy was originally from the Bronx, and after his mother died, his father sent him to live with an aunt in Washington. That didn't work out, and during his senior year Billy lived by himself in an apartment above a barbershop owned by a friend of mine. Billy cooked his own meals, washed his own clothes, even made some of his own pants from scratch because he was six foot nine and had a hard time buying clothes that fit. He was an artistic person with a talent for making things. When Billy announced he would attend Georgetown, some people made an issue of his grades. But think about his circumstances, about the character and resilience it took to stay in high school while living by himself. This kid was trying to survive, not study for some history test.

From the beginning, I knew Georgetown would need to admit some players with lower marks than the average student. The reason people resisted wasn't because what we did at Georgetown was unusual. All the best college teams admit players with lower qualifications, then and now. They let me into Providence. But I was one of only three Black faces on Providence's team. At Georgetown, which was considered an "elite" university, which was code for most of the students being white and wealthy, I was recruiting poor Black kids for what had been a predominantly white team. Certain people, in and out of the university, didn't think these poor Black kids belonged here.

At the root of it, those people didn't think I belonged at Georgetown, either.

Never mind that some white children of Georgetown alumni got in with inferior grades. Or that plenty of white kids got in only because their fathers were congressmen, or otherwise politically connected, or donated money. Those privileged kids were assumed to belong. Nobody questioned their academic ability, because they looked the part. Even when you'd point out how these rich white kids used their parents' connections or money to get in, many people still said they deserved to be there because "their parents worked hard to give them advantages" or "they come from a good family." As if none of those parents had inherited their money. As if poverty makes you stupid, or not deserving of help.

The bigger question was this: What good is a university that doesn't help disadvantaged people, that educates only those who are already well educated? Is that what Georgetown wanted to be?

Some professors were skeptical of me when I started. One incident still sticks in my mind. A player was having difficulty in a math class, so I asked the professor if I could come see him. Players will give you all kinds of excuses for bad marks, so I needed the professor's side of the story. The man told me to come by his office in the morning. A little while later he called back and said, "I don't want to give anybody the wrong impression, so don't come to my office, I'll come see you." Once he thought about other faculty and students seeing me in his office, that made him uncomfortable. He assumed his peers would think I influenced him to break the rules. Fenlon or Stein could have gone there with no problem, but here I am with a master's degree in counseling and guidance, and he's viewing me just as some guy who coaches basketball. Little did he know I had suspended players for much less than what this player was doing. But stop and think about it. If I had not asked to discuss a struggling kid, then all I care about is playing ball. If I do ask, I'm trying to put the squeeze on a professor. I couldn't win either way.

Fortunately, the administration at Georgetown was supportive, including the university president, Father Henle, and his assistant, Dan Altobello. I worked extremely well with Frank Rienzo, the athletic director. Remember that the admissions director, Charlie Deacon, is the one who had the idea to hire me in the first place. They already had a Community Scholars program in place to bring in more Black students and support them academically and socially, but there were still fewer than one hundred Black students in the entire undergraduate population of more than four thousand. There weren't any basket weaving classes at Georgetown, so athletes had to take the same courses as everybody else. My job was to give them the proper support. By the same token, we didn't bring in a borderline kid and put him in chemistry and calculus. Avoiding those courses should not be considered a bad thing. I didn't take them, either, and I'm the boss.

We like to judge college admissions by standardized tests, but the availability of quality preparation is not standard for all students. American education is extremely unequal, especially for poor kids, a high percentage of whom are Black. A kid from the projects could be extremely intelligent, but if he goes to a neighborhood school with inadequate resources and underpaid teachers, he won't have the same test scores as a more privileged student. It's unfair to put so much emphasis on a standardized test. When I recruited players like Billy Lynn, I looked deeper than just their test scores and grades. I had conversations with their teachers and counselors. Is the boy intelligent? Does he listen? Did outside factors in his life affect his performance in school? How would he perform in a new environment? Then, when I talked to the kid, I tried to gauge his capability and his willingness to do the work. I was looking for brains and ambition. I thought I was qualified to find them, since I was the so-called retarded kid who went on to earn a master's degree.

Now, my belief in a kid's capability to change had a strong correlation to his ability on the court. I wasn't a social worker anymore, I was a basketball coach. Sure, I wanted to help kids, but only the ones who could help me win games. I mean, Billy Lynn was six foot nine and rebounded like crazy. Let's be honest here.

In exchange for the school's trusting my judgment on admitting players, we had to hold up our end of the bargain. The players had to attend every class, complete every assignment, and cut no corners. Our purpose was not for them just to pass. We had to make sure they were educated. Fenlon met with them daily and developed a book to keep track of their schoolwork. All their classes were listed in the book, and each week the players had to write down what grades they had received on various assignments, and sign their name. A lot of kids hated that book, but after they graduated they realized its value, and "Ms. Fenlon's Book" became a famous part of our program.

I also needed Fenlon to be my conscience. She was there to prevent me from becoming what I professed I did not want to be, because when the games came around, all my reverence for education tended to fly out the window. It's easy to care about a math test when you don't have to play Syracuse on Saturday.

The biggest obstacle to education for athletes is time. They have to practice, work out, travel to games, and watch film, all of which reduces the amount of time they have to study. Fenlon took our kids' study time seriously, and we had plenty of arguments. She left the office in tears a few times, but she was a tough, feisty lady who wasn't afraid to buck my system. For example, she would not let freshmen come to practice each day until they had studied for an hour under her supervision. I was mad as hell about that idea, but that's the way it went. I get credit for some educational practices that I fought against.

It didn't take long for Fenlon to become indispensable. Early on, before we got more resources, she answered the phone, opened the mail, kept track of appointments, handled travel arrangements, and more. Over time, she basically became second in command. She was a short lady, with a quick mind and sharp tongue. She was firm with the players, but not in a mean way, although some of them trembled when they had to tell her they had flunked a test. She showed them tough love and had an educator's feel for any difficulties they might be experiencing. Fenlon watched most of our practices from the upstairs balcony and paid close attention to my interactions with the kids. Early on, she saw me chew out a player about something, like a defensive assignment that he missed. After practice she told me, "That boy flunked an exam this week, which might be the reason he's distracted." She was closely attuned to every aspect of how our team functioned, in more of a human than an athletic aspect.

But Mary Fenlon was no pushover. A player came late to the bus during a road trip and she jumped down his throat: "You think we're supposed to wait for you, like you're some sort of king? You think you're a star?" The whole team heard her say that. She had a deep respect for Black kids, but was not afraid to stand up to them. Early on, a player was in her office talking about all the faults his white professors had, and he was characterizing them as prejudiced. Fenlon listened to his whole speech, then said, "Now that you've told me all the problems your teachers have, which might be accurate, what is your problem with these grades?"

I also leaned heavily on Billy Stein. He was in charge of recruiting, and was an excellent judge of talent. He did most of the traveling to figure out which players I should go see. When we went to a game together, we sat separately, because I didn't want my impressions to be influenced by his opinion, and vice versa. After we identified a kid we wanted, Billy's job was to get me into the kid's house. Most of the time, if we could get through the front door and talk to the parents, I closed the deal. I usually focused on the mothers. Fathers talked that macho stuff, but mothers wanted to know their children would be well cared for. Several years after we got to Georgetown, when we were recruiting Ed Hopkins, our first kid out of Baltimore, Billy got me into his house on Hop's birthday, and his mom cooked us fried chicken. When we left, Billy said, "It's over. Hop's mom fed you fried chicken? We got him."

Billy also put together our schedule and was an excellent administrator, levelheaded and no-nonsense. He was great with teaching fundamentals and worked with a lot of our guards. Stein and Fenlon played good cop to my bad cop a lot of times, in terms of reassuring a kid after I cursed them out. Most important, I knew I could trust Billy, and he shared my values. Yes, he was my best friend from college, which meant a lot, but I had a lot of great friends I would never let anywhere near my team. Stein had the type of character and skills I could rely on. If we disagreed, our friendship superseded us being permanently angry at each other, and he still had respect for me as the head coach. In other words, just like at Providence, Billy still threw me the ball.

We did everything we could to help the players fulfill their academic responsibilities. If they didn't, a hammer came down on them. That hammer was swung by me. I didn't put the burden on Georgetown to handle a problem I brought here. I did everything in my power to help kids graduate, including a lot of them who didn't turn out to be good players. But if they didn't take advantage of that opportunity, I put them out. It didn't take but a year or two for Georgetown to see I was serious about getting rid of kids who did not study. After that, they trusted me more with recruiting. I couldn't get everybody in, not by a long shot. I lost a lot of arguments with Charlie Deacon. But at the end of the day, almost every player who stayed four years graduated. Including Billy Lynn. He finished with more than a thousand points scored, the fourth most rebounds in school history, and a double major bachelor's degree in sociology and fine art. Two of his paintings, portraits of my mother and father, are hanging on my wall to this day.

I told people when I got to Georgetown, "You don't have to tell me about the importance of education. My mother and father taught me that."

I ASKED DEAN Smith for a lot of advice during that first season, and our relationship went to a deeper level. We talked on the phone late at night about all kinds of things. He gave me one of the most important pieces of coaching advice I ever received.

"Seventy percent of coaching doesn't have anything to do with basketball," Dean told me. "But that seventy percent affects whether you win or lose."

He was talking about all the little things that go into running a program, from when and where the team ate on the road to what time players got their ankles taped before practice. I had that specific advice in mind as I built the foundation of our program. Today they call it "creating a culture."

I sat in the middle of the bench, like John McLendon. I sat in the back of the team bus, not the front, so I could watch everybody and nobody could watch me. Plus it reminded me of riding the Hound down to Maryland with my father. Our players unloaded their own bags from the bus; the managers didn't do it for them. We required players to clean up after themselves and to thank our managers and trainers, not treat them like servants. I've had NBA trainers tell me that Georgetown players always say thank you when they get up from the table, and the staff at Madison Square Garden said their locker room was cleaner when we left than when we arrived. We wore jackets and ties while traveling, never sweatsuits. We didn't talk loud in restaurants or sit on the backs of sofas in hotel lobbies. I wore glasses, knowing that they represented intelligence and challenged assumptions based on my size and Blackness. None of these things were about playing basketball.

Practice was closed to everyone but the team. Sometimes I had to holler and curse at players to get them where they needed to be, and I didn't want to embarrass them in front of strangers. Sometimes kids were held out of practice because of grades; reporters would have asked where they were. It would have been harmful to expose their weaknesses. You think we put a sign on the door saying my father couldn't read? Our neighbors didn't even know. A lot of my coaching methods could easily have been misinterpreted. That's not paranoia—remember when Spanish numbers turned into "Kill those white boys" back at St. Anthony's? What would they think when I called a kid lazy? I'd say things like "Have you been out all night drinking or something?" or "This guy is killing you in practice, what's gonna happen when you have to guard John Lucas in the game?" I said things to them that could be considered racist. I called them motherfuckers and everything else. Some things I said to them were wrong. I was not trying to permanently damage or abuse anybody, but some outsiders might have interpreted it as that. As loud as I criticized them, I tried to praise them just as loud. I tried to never curse anyone out who didn't know I loved him.

If a kid yawned in my practice, I put him out, like Sametta Wallace Jackson taught me. McDonough Gymnasium had a balcony, and if somebody was talking up there, even if we couldn't hear them, I'd put them out. I wanted total concentration on what we had to do.

We had a room on the balcony with one-way glass. I could look down at the practice court, but they couldn't see me in the window. Sometimes I would pretend not to be around and watch practice without their knowing I was watching. I wanted to see if they worked hard and how they treated the other coaches when I wasn't around. That was a form of watching them off the ball.

The assistant coaches who worked longest with me knew that when we were practicing, they could jump in with comments or instruction, but they better make it quick. I was the head coach, and there was a reason for that. By the same token, I respected my assistants enough to ask their opinion. It wasn't like I was teaching them; they told me what they thought, and I explained everything to the team. They made suggestions, and I made decisions.

We spent a lot of time at practice talking about things that had nothing to do with basketball. This is when my philosophy about using the game as an instrument to teach came to fruition. Now I truly understood that my classroom was the court. Sometimes we talked for an hour without touching a ball about history or current events. When a serial killer was targeting black children in Atlanta and not enough fuss was made in the media, I explained to the team that we would wear green ribbons on our uniforms to help draw attention to the situation. Other times, we talked about the best way to ask a girl out on a date.

When the balls did roll out, we practiced until we got it right. We had some long practices, probably too long, past three hours sometimes. We practiced on Christmas Day or New Year's Eve, which didn't bother me one bit. I used to tell my high school team at St. Anthony's, "Merry Christmas to all, and to all wall to wall," and they'd sprint from one end of the gym to the other. I was inconsiderate on some holidays, but I knew we had to work to be great. I ran them a lot, because we needed stamina to press and trap the whole game. What people call "suicides" today I called wind sprints: run from the baseline to the free throw line and back, then midcourt and back, the other free throw line and back, and finally the length of the court and back to the starting point. The whole team had to finish within a certain time, and if one guy was slow, everybody ran it again. Managers stood at each line to make sure nobody took any shortcuts. We ran a lot of those every practice.

To tell you the truth, there weren't many places I preferred to be than the gym, and there weren't many people I enjoyed being around more than my team. Long practices were not a punishment for me. They probably felt that way to some of the players.

From the jump, I made it clear to my players there would be no pampering or kissing their ass. I told them I would be fair. I'll jump over any hurdle if I see you're going to work. But I'm not going to waste my time if you won't do what you're supposed to do. For example, if players were late to the bus, we left them behind. There was a player named

Mark Edwards who was already at Georgetown when I arrived. Early on, I left Mark at the Providence airport, and he had to take an hour-long cab ride to the Holy Cross game in Worcester, Massachusetts. He wasn't the only player I left someplace, but he was the first. That let them know, this is how it's going to be.

I also was known to follow a kid or two. Jonathan Smith left campus early one morning and caught a bus someplace. I made a point of knowing all the blue-collar workers on campus, the security guards, cafeteria workers, and custodians. They told me things people did not expect me to know. I used to tell my players, "Y'all don't even speak to all the people who work here. But back in slavery times, these were the people who would know you were about to get sold down to Mississippi. People talk openly around them, and they pay attention to everything." That's how I figured out where Jonathan had gone. When he was riding back to school on the city bus, he looked out the window and saw me looking right back at him. That'll make a kid think twice.

All the things I built the program on provided the type of informal education that can be just as useful as a history or economics class. The principles of our program were part of my nature, based on how my parents raised me and what I had absorbed from people like Sametta Wallace Jackson, Dr. Anita Hughes, and Red Auerbach. I responded to heredity, environment, and time.

Regardless of what I did with the seventy percent, though, a team could die from the other thirty. We finished my first year at Georgetown 12–14. It was the only losing season of my life.

8

"MY MORTGAGE"

In the fall of 1973, a few weeks before the start of my second season, my father got sick and could barely walk. I brought him up to Georgetown to bathe him in our big walk-in showers. He died a few weeks later.

You always feel you could have done more for the people you love. Could I have spent more time with him, shown more gratitude, given him more money? He only got to see me coach a few games at Georgetown. I was comforted by the knowledge that my father was proud of me. His approval meant more to me than any championship. He didn't define his love for me by the type of job I had, or whether my teams won. My father's death made me determined not to forget the world he grew up in, and how relentlessly he worked for me to get out of it. For *me* to get out, not him. My father never did learn to read.

I started smoking a pipe after he died, as a way to remember him. It also was me telling myself, "I'm the man of the family now." By that time, I had fully absorbed my father's lesson to study the white man, to learn how his system worked. Now, I was about to make the white man's system conform to me.

YEAR TWO DIDN'T begin well. The word was out on our leading rebounder, Merlin Wilson, and he had some difficulty adjusting to the extra attention. Another starter, Mark Gallagher, had a back injury that eventually ended his playing career. Mike McDermott, a freshman, also got hurt—he was a tough white kid from upstate New York. My first few seasons I had several white recruits. I had no problem getting white players until people started claiming I was a racist.

Our team was young and inexperienced. The upperclassmen tried hard, but let's not forget there's a reason Georgetown went 3–23 before I arrived. Early in the season, we upset heavily favored St. John's in overtime, but we got blown out by Lefty Driesell's Maryland team, which was ranked fourth in the nation and had three future pros in John Lucas, Len Elmore, and Tom McMillen. Lefty had brought big-time college basketball back to the Washington area with his "UCLA of the East" motto, and when I first came to Georgetown, he whipped us good every year. We got killed by second-ranked Notre Dame and their star forward Adrian Dantley. Halfway through the season, when our record fell to 2–7, a column was published in the student newspaper the *Hoya*. It foreshadowed what I would deal with my whole career.

This young white writer said my kids had lots of physical talent but were "poorly drilled," "careless," and "don't know what they are doing." He said we had "concentration lapses," were "unprepared," and that "mental laziness has probably cost the Hoyas four games so far this season." He said the players had to bring "their minds as well as their bodies" to the game, and that I should bench the young players—the Black kids—in favor of "smarter" players.

The writer didn't call us dumb niggers, but that's clearly what he thought.

I felt the sentiment behind the article on campus. Not from everyone, because plenty of white people supported us, and the university president, Father Henle, was strongly in my corner. But it also was clear what more than a few white people thought: *These Black kids and their Black coach are too dumb to succeed at Georgetown. They can run fast and jump high with their "quick" and "agile" Black bodies, but they can't think.*

These are the same things they've said about us since they brought us to this country. The same things they're still saying. What made the problem worse is that if you asked the guy who wrote that column if it was racist, he'd deny it to his grave. Some of you reading this right now are coming up with rationalizations for why it was okay.

Here's the reality: I had a bunch of nineteen- and twenty-year-olds trying to learn how to win games in a difficult environment. My practices were extremely detailed and demanding, what one of my players described as "a slight version of hell," but our kids still made a lot of mistakes. I'd like to see that writer try to make the correct play in front of twelve thousand screaming fans at Maryland's Cole Field House with Lucas, McMillen, and Elmore in his face. I made mistakes, too, in terms of certain strategies or decisions. None of this had anything to do with concentration or mental laziness. What I did in my second season at Georgetown is what I did to win a national championship ten years later, what I had been taught by Red Auerbach, Dean Smith, and John McLendon. But certain people stopped their analytic process at "mental laziness."

Who's really lazy here?

I don't want to suggest that only white people opposed what I was doing. Some Black people did too. Not because of my complexion, but because they wanted acceptance from white people and thought some things I said and did would threaten that acceptance. The first time I put five Black players on the floor, it was a Black friend who questioned my action and told me to be careful. Some Black people came out later and supported me, like, "You tell 'em, Big John! That's what we do!" But in the early days they left me in the fire by myself.

We finished 13–13 my second season, which was the last time one of my teams didn't qualify for the postseason. But even when I became successful, very few people said we won because we were smart. Most said we won because we were aggressive, athletic, tough, or intimidating, and that was when they were being nice. Yes, we were all those things, but the foundation of everything was strategic. All the athleticism in the world wouldn't have worked without strategies like switching defenses to confuse the opponent, pressing when we missed baskets, closing off passing lanes in a half court zone trap, or running a primary and then secondary fast break. Syracuse coach Jim Boeheim is famous for his zone defense, and I can testify that it was outstanding, but Boeheim himself said our 1-3-1 with Patrick Ewing in the middle was the best zone he ever saw. Yet people still believed all Georgetown did was bump, grab, and hold. This connects back to why we always wore jackets and ties in public, and why I made eyeglasses part of my identity, and why I was so impressed by my Uncle Lewis. We had to work twice as hard to show people we were half as intelligent as we really were.

MY FRIENDS FROM Black Washington thought I had the world at my feet Across the Park, with all the money and resources I could want. That was not true at all when we started. Georgetown had a deal with Converse, but the school paid for all our shoes and other gear. I used my own projector for film sessions. Stein, Leftwich, Fenlon, and I walked up and down M Street asking businesses to buy radio ads or program ads for our games. We didn't have a clue about how to compete with the teams we ended up competing with. Everybody on the staff worked extremely hard—it was nothing for us to arrive at seven in the morning and stay until eight or nine at night. One time we were in the office and Fenlon said she was hungry and needed to go get something to eat. I said, "Have you talked to a doctor about your problem?" After that, she'd say she was going to the bathroom, then run out to grab a sandwich. We imposed a lot of expectations on our players, but we also imposed them on ourselves.

We played our home games in McDonough Gymnasium, which seated about four thousand people. It was a fairly typical venue for the level of program Georgetown had at that time, with bleachers, an upper balcony, and windows high up on the walls. All the athletic teams and offices were in McDonough, and we practiced there too. I had to negotiate for court time with the volleyball and women's basketball teams. Sometimes the volleyball coaches got upset because I locked their team out and stayed past our allotted time. Our basketball offices were on the second floor of McDonough, next to an old handball court that we turned into our locker room. I wanted the locker room nearby so our staff would know when the players were coming and going. That was more conducive to building relationships with the players. I made sure they didn't put any names on the office doors, not even "Georgetown Basketball." I didn't want anybody dropping by. Those who needed to be there knew where I was. I hung a wind chime on the door so if anybody came in, we heard them. You could say this was an early manifestation of my paranoia, which came from things I had seen and experienced as well as from my knowledge of the history of our country. Some memories never die. I have a bell on the door of my house to this day.

One guy who worked at Georgetown got upset because he couldn't walk into my office unannounced anymore. I told him, "Yeah, and y'all used to win three games in a season, too."

Inside our unmarked metal door, the first room was a reception area, where Fenlon sat. Behind her was a hallway leading to the assistants' offices. My office was at the end of the hallway, for privacy. It was big enough to have meetings with the whole team. At the rear of my office was a back door that opened into the main McDonough hallway. From the outside that back door was unmarked, with no windows. I told players if they had a problem, if they failed a test or got a girl pregnant, they'd better tell me before someone else did. Whenever it was getting on toward evening and I heard a *tap tap tap* on the back door of my office, I knew it was a player with a problem. They never brought problems through the front door.

For me, coaching had a lot in common with raising children. The players were still developing, physically, emotionally, academically, and psychologically. We housed them, fed them, and spent the majority of our time with them. That sounds like parenting to me. But I always told my players I did not want to be their father. A lot of them have called me a father figure over the years, which I consider a compliment, but I think your father has a special and unique place. That's not what I am. I had no desire to be anything other than a coach, and I made it clear to my players that I never wanted to infringe upon or replace their parents. A father-son relationship did develop with some kids, but it wasn't something I sought. It happened. Guys like Allen Iverson, Victor Page, Patrick Ewing, Lonnie Duren, Gene Smith, Mark Tillman, Mark Thompson, Steve Martin, Charles Smith . . . I could go on and on. I love those guys to pieces. Some of my former players call me up and say, "Hey Pops," and it makes me feel good. But just as many guys say I did them wrong, and they may have good reason. That can happen when you are trying to teach somebody. When Sametta Wallace Jackson said I had to stay back a grade, I was angry with her at first. I have to accept that some of my players might still be angry with me. My goal was not to get approval from my players at the risk of changing what I thought was right, which sometimes was not right. There's a group of guys out there who sincerely don't like me and hope they never see me again. I feel the same way about some of them, too.

IN 1974–75, MY third season, Merlin Wilson had a mysterious back or shoulder ailment that nobody could figure out. It hurt to lift his arms over his head, which was a problem for one of the top rebounders in the country. We sent him to the best doctors, and he still didn't get better. Two of my other starters, Jonathan Smith and Larry Long, had academic issues and I made them sit out some games. I didn't talk about any of this with anybody outside our program.

College players have their names in the newspaper, so people want to treat them like adults, but I always believed they needed to be protected. First of all, their problems weren't anybody else's business. In many cases, revealing their problems publicly could have made them worse. Lawyers and doctors aren't the only ones who shouldn't reveal everything about the people they work with. Merlin wanted to be a pro, and it would have hurt his NBA chances to reveal he had a health problem nobody could solve, especially since in the end we did solve it. I had no reason to embarrass Jonathan and Larry. When we became successful and everybody wanted to write about Georgetown basketball, much of the media interpreted my protecting our players in negative ways. I didn't feel the need to explain myself, or to apologize for caring about the well-being of the kids on my team. I had to absorb a lot of my players' mistakes as mine.

We had a freshman that year named Derrick Jackson, from Wheaton, Illinois. Derrick was not highly recruited out of high school, but a Georgetown alumnus kept calling and calling the office about this kid who the Texas Rangers drafted to play baseball but was better at basketball. After about a dozen calls, I broke down and went to see Derrick play. He was a six-foot-one guard with a quick-release jump shot, and he could get to the basket, too. I saw him score 20 points in the second half of a loss and thought he could develop into a good player. Derrick's father was pastor of a church, and when Derrick got to campus he carried a Bible everywhere he went. He progressed more quickly than I had anticipated, and as the season got under way in 1974 he contributed about ten points per game off the bench. But I could see that Derrick was incredibly lonely, and it reminded me of how I felt up at Providence. Most of the rest of the team was from the Washington area, but Derrick was far from home for the first time in his life. When Christmastime came, we had games to prepare for, and Derrick was stuck on our deserted campus while most of his teammates could visit family nearby. I tried to think of some way to cheer Derrick up, and I had the idea to take him to the movies with my sons. Buying him a movie ticket and popcorn might have been an NCAA violation, but I felt that Derrick's well-being was worth it. After our season ended, I let Derrick play on the baseball team, and I took Stein and Fenlon to

When John Thompson stood on the Georgetown sideline, leading the Hoyas past obstacles physical and psychological, few knew that what would become his iconic towel was inspired by the need to keep his family close: "My mother used to wear a towel hanging over one shoulder when she worked in the kitchen. She'd use it to wipe her hands or dry a dish. I draped a white towel over my shoulder during games as a tribute to her. She and my father didn't come to hardly any of the games, but I felt them with me when I wore that towel."

COURTESY OF THE THOMPSON FAMILY

Thompson's father, John Robert Thompson Senior, woke up at five o'clock every day without an alarm clock to go to work in a tile factory. Although he could not read or write, "my father taught me more about life than someone with a doctorate," Thompson said.

COURTESY OF THE THOMPSON FAMILY

Segregation prevented Anna Alexander Thompson from using her college teaching degree, so she cleaned white folks' houses to help support her family and made sure her four children were educated. She told John, her youngest child, "Always speak your mind."

PHOTO TAKEN BY GORDON PARKS. © LIBRARY OF CONGRESS, PRINTS & PHOTOGRAPHS DIVISION, FSA/OWI COLLECTION, LC-USF34-013368-C

John Thompson (*below, at age six*) enjoyed an idyllic childhood in the Frederick Douglass housing projects (*above*) in the Anacostia section of southeast Washington, D.C., making toys from scraps and gathering berries in nearby woods. "I had no idea we were living under segregation and poverty, because my parents kept food on the table and clothes on our backs. . . . My parents made sure I had everything I wanted. But I also knew what not to want."

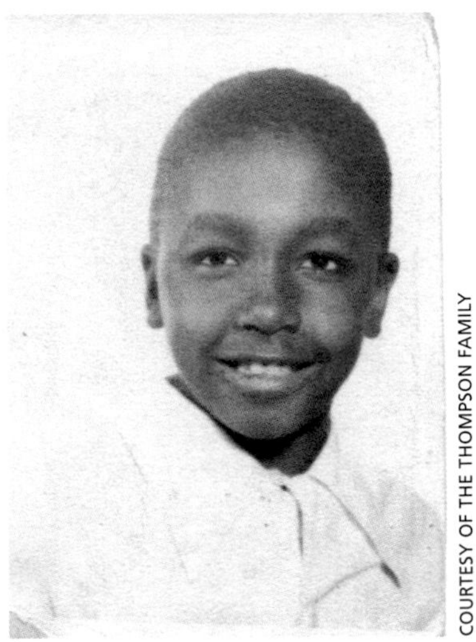

COURTESY OF THE THOMPSON FAMILY

COURTESY OF THE THOMPSON FAMILY

By the time John reached middle school (*above, with his father*), he was over six feet tall. Thompson never found out how his parents were able to surprise him with his own car to take to Providence College, where the six-foot-ten center was an All-American and won the NIT championship in 1963.

© PROVIDENCE COLLEGE

Thompson (*back row, No. 18*) was drafted by the Boston Celtics and their legendary coach Red Auerbach (*front row, with ball*), who had mentored Thompson since high school. “I own two NBA championship rings,” Thompson said. “But I didn’t get to play for the Celtics, because Bill Russell (*front row, No. 6*) never came out of the damn game.”

Thompson maintained a loving relationship with Auerbach until Red’s death in 2006. Red’s lessons about basketball and life were part of Thompson’s professional DNA, especially his advice to always watch people “off the ball.”

"I used basketball as an instrument to teach. My classroom was the court."

© GEORGETOWN UNIVERSITY

The point guard Michael Jackson helped Georgetown win a national championship and played in the NBA, but his post-basketball success, such as assembling the *Inside the NBA* television show, made him the perfect example of Thompson's saying that "more money is made sitting down than standing up."

© MITCHELL LAYTON / GETTY IMAGES SPORT / GETTY IMAGES

Even when his coaching days were over, Thompson never stopped teaching and loving the Hoyas. Thompson celebrates a one-point Hoyas win in 2016, with the team's longtime trainer, Lorry Michel, in the background.

© THE WASHINGTON POST / THE WASHINGTON POST / GETTY IMAGES

Thompson often took his sons John (*left at top and below*) and Ronny (*right at top and below*) to practices and games. John Thompson III would eventually coach the Hoyas for thirteen seasons, winning three Big East championships and making the Final Four in 2007.

© SIMON BRUTY / SPORTS ILLUSTRATED / GETTY IMAGES

watch him play once or twice. Some people think baseball is boring, but I love it, and I enjoyed watching Derrick in center field.

Two other freshmen on that team were Craig Esherick and Mike Riley. Craig was a six-foot-three white guard from Silver Spring, Maryland. He was intellectually oriented, and he could shoot the lights out from long distance. Mike was a five-foot-eight defensive specialist I recruited off a navy ship. I had seen Riley play for Cardozo High School and lock up DeMatha's point guard so bad, the kid stopped bringing the ball up the floor. But Riley enlisted in the navy out of high school and fell off the radar. A year or two later some random guy stopped by campus and told me, "I heard you were recruiting Mike Riley once upon a time. I served with him in the navy and I just wanted to say he's one of the best people I've ever been around." I sent Stein and Fenlon down to his navy ship in Charleston, South Carolina, to find him, the captain invited them to eat dinner with him, and Mike agreed to join our team. Mike played defense like nobody I had ever seen; he and Gene Smith were the best two on-ball defenders I ever had. Mike was a genius at taking charges and would have been happy never to set foot on the offensive side of the court. Just play defense, take the ball from the other team, give it back, then take it again. When Riley got in the game, the student section knew what was about to happen. As soon as he made the steal, the students yelled, "Got it!"

We started the season 3–0 before Lefty's fourth-ranked Maryland team blew us out. We lost to Dartmouth in a Christmas tournament up in Rochester—I could have cried after that one. Then, with Merlin hurting, plus Jonathan and Larry in and out of the lineup for academic problems, we lost six straight games to drop our record to 8–8. I didn't make any excuses publicly, and tried to keep a calm front for the team, but at home I had trouble sleeping. I had never lost six games in a row in my whole life.

In early February 1975, Dickinson College came to our gym. They were a Division III team that we killed every year, but the atmosphere was tense because of the losing streak. During the game, I think during a time-out, somebody threw a bedsheet through one of the gym windows, where it dangled briefly before security guards pulled it down. The sheet had a sign painted on it: THOMPSON THE NIGGER FLOP MUST GO.

My whole team saw it. My wife and children were at the game and they saw it too. My first reaction was that we should not make it a big deal. But there was a professor on campus, Father Ed Glenn, who was the official scorekeeper for that game. Father Glenn always supported me, and I remember him saying, "This needs to be told." We beat Dickinson as appropriately as we should have, 102–60, then went about dealing with the sign.

The sign was hurtful, and I told reporters so after the game. I didn't reveal that the sign was nothing new for us. We had been receiving a large amount of racist hate mail ever since I got to Georgetown. Fenlon threw most of it away without even showing it to me, but the knowledge of its existence remained, and I had to operate under those conditions. That bedsheet was far from the first time somebody called me a nigger coach. I didn't make a big deal out of any of it. As a person of some significance, I have two ways to make somebody else important. I can make them my friend, or I can make them my enemy. The way to weaken these people is to ignore them. That could be hard sometimes. One morning we came to work and someone had smashed a hole through the door to our office, probably with some sort of pole. The door was metal, so it took a lot of force to smash that big a hole. It had to be an inside job, because you couldn't get to our office on the second floor of McDonough without passing through several other doors that were supposed to be locked. Nothing inside the office was stolen or vandalized. It felt as if somebody was trying to send us a message, like, "We can get you if we want to." This was something else we did not announce to the media. So a banner calling me a nigger flop wasn't much of a departure from business as usual at that time.

The school administration was extremely upset, as it should have been. What happened did not reflect well on Georgetown. Administrators were unable to find whoever made the sign, but Father Henle made a strong public statement that my job was safe, and my players insisted on speaking to the media about it. They called a news conference, and a freshman who had come from St. Anthony's, Felix Yeoman, read a long statement the team had prepared. It described how I had kept various problems hidden, even from the rest of the team, which explained why we were losing. "All of us on the team know of personal instances where Mr. Thompson has protected us from public criticism and shouldered the blame himself," Felix read. The statement touched me, because my guys were refusing to roll over. Still, I made sure to run them just as hard the next practice. Harder, even. We had to win.

Our next game was three days later, at home against Fairleigh Dickinson. While my team warmed up, my sister Roberta walked up to me and asked, "Where did they throw that sign in?"

I pointed up to the window and asked, "Why do you want to know?"

"If a sign comes in here tonight, there's gonna be more sports than basketball going on," Roberta said. She opened her purse so I could see a pistol tucked inside.

We blew out Fairleigh Dickinson by 35 points. Then we beat St. Joseph's by 19, Boston College in double overtime, St. Francis by 19, and Manhattan by 28. In total, we won seven of our last eight regular season games to qualify for my first postseason conference tournament.

A lot of people claimed the sign motivated us to save our season and turn the program around. I refuse to even acknowledge that. We won doing the same things we had been doing all season. Merlin's health got better. Jonathan and Larry got their act together in the classroom. Billy Lynn stepped up with some strong games. All seven of our victories were at home. The biggest factor might have been that Derrick Jackson became a great player, and our best scorer. None of this had a damn thing to do with that sign. We didn't need racism to motivate us. The people who made that sign, and all the people who agreed with it, they wanted credit for making us successful: "See, we got them to play better." No, you didn't get shit. I had won all my life. The people who made that banner, the people who said Georgetown had too many Black players, whoever busted a hole in my door—they're the ones who went 3–23.

In slavery, they had a guy called the pusher. The pusher was the best worker, and they'd put him at the front of the line in the field so everybody else had to keep up with him. The people who attacked us, they're not the pusher of me. We made our first postseason tournament because we worked. That's it.

GEORGETOWN WAS AFFILIATED with the East Coast Athletic Conference back then, and the ECAC South Region tournament was at West Virginia's arena in Morgantown. In the first round, we beat George Washington by seven, which was sweet because they had nipped us two weeks earlier. In the finals, we played West Virginia in what was a home game for them. They had fourteen thousand fans there; we might have had a hundred. Bob Huggins, who coaches West Virginia now, was a player on that team. With a few seconds left in the game we were down one point. I told Mike Riley to foul and put West Virginia on the line. They missed the free throw, we got the rebound, and I called time-out. I drew up a play to make a long pass to Derrick in front of our bench. We threw it all the way upcourt, and Derrick hit a twenty-footer from the corner as time ran out to win the game and give us an automatic bid to the NCAA tournament. Huggins caught Derrick's game-winning shot after it fell through the net.

That's when I started calling Derrick Jackson "my mortgage." This guy almost didn't play college basketball, and he was responsible for the shot that put Georgetown on the map. He didn't need any racist banner to do it, either.

For Georgetown's first NCAA tournament game in thirty-two years, we got sent to Tuscaloosa, Alabama, to play Central Michigan in the first round. The score was tied at 75 with six seconds left. I ran a play that got Jonathan Smith open for a long jump shot. Jonathan rose up and let it fly, and as he came back down, a Central Michigan player undercut him. The buzzer sounded, they both fell down, and the referee blew his whistle. I was ready for Jonathan to go to the free throw line and win the game.

The ref pointed at Jonathan and called him for an offensive foul.

How the hell can a jump shooter commit an offensive foul, especially against a defender who slides in underneath him? At the very least, it's a no-call, which would have been terrible but not fatal. But there were zeroes on the clock when the kid from CMU walked to the free throw line with a grin on his face. He made both shots and ended our season. I didn't care that Georgetown had made the tournament for the first time in thirty-two years. I didn't feel grateful to have made it that far in my third season. I knew we had earned the right to win the game and play Kentucky in the second round. Later, the video proved I was right.

Here's the thing about that call. The ref who cost us the game was a white man named Reggie Copeland, born in 1929 in Mobile, Alabama. Copeland lived his life with Jim Crow as the law of the land. He refereed in the then-segregated Southeastern Conference, which was ruled by the Kentucky legend Adolph Rupp, who only started signing Black players after they beat him in the national championship. What did Copeland think about a Black team from up north, with a big Black coach hollering on the sideline? What did he think about us having Fenlon, a young white woman, on our bench? Why did we get called for twenty-two fouls and Central Michigan only twelve? It's impossible for me to know. It's also impossible for me not to wonder if Copeland was a racist who stole the game from us because we were Black. There's no evidence of that, but I have to ask the question because I'm haunted by my past. Any intelligent person would ask the question, because it's this huge, unreachable mystery so many of us have to endure. It's an itch we can never scratch. The whole problem reminds me of the lyrics to the great Syl Johnson song: *Something is holding me back / Is it because I'm Black?*

Was that call made because I was Black? I thought it was. I thought a lot of bad calls later in my career were because I was Black, too. I'm sure all the time that I thought it was, it wasn't. But I'll tell you what—most of the time it was.

DEAN SMITH HELPED me through a lot of things. He had a deep understanding of the challenges and pressures I was facing, on and off the court. From a basketball perspective, the range of his coaching ability was extraordinary. Most of us get a reputation for a specific area that we emphasize, but Dean's North Carolina teams excelled on offense, defense, and everything in between. Every little thing he did had thought behind it, down to how towels were handed out in the locker room. He started a lot of trends that are now standard at all levels of basketball, like players on the bench standing up and clapping for a good play, or the guy who scores pointing in acknowledgment at the teammate who gives him the assist. Dean and I were watching a game once, and the coach looked at his player who made a mistake and tapped his temple. Dean told me, "Don't ever do that, because you're telling the whole arena the boy is stupid." He cared a lot about the perception of his players, and about their feelings. He was a caring person in general. When we traveled someplace, he was concerned with whether my room was comfortable and what I had to eat. One day Dean, whose clothes were always immaculate, pulled me aside and looked inside my suit jacket. He literally opened my jacket, looked inside, and said, "John, you have to buy better clothes." I didn't understand and asked what he was talking about. I was perfectly happy with whatever I found at the discount store. "You can't buy a coat that doesn't have a full lining," Dean said. Another time I visited him in Chapel Hill and rented a regular car at the airport. When I got to campus, Dean made me take it back and get a nicer one. He was teaching me how to best represent myself, and represent Georgetown as well.

Red taught me to watch players off the ball, to observe what they do when they're not getting the credit and the glory. Dean Smith was fantastic off the ball.

There was a point where my team was playing poorly and I felt I was doing a lousy job. I called Dean to vent about all the things I was failing to teach my players to do. Dean listened quietly and finally said, "You'll be all right."

I was looking for more than a pat on the back. "I'll be all right?" I said. "What do you mean, I'll be all right?"

Dean said, "As long as you blame yourself and not those kids, you'll be all right."

That was one of the most valuable things he ever told me, because when you blame the kids, you're saying they're the problem. When you blame yourself, you keep searching for the answer. Sometimes people forget that college athletes are part of a school. These are not perfect young people. We have to work with them and educate them. We wouldn't call it a school if they came here perfect.

These are just a few of the things I learned from Dean. Not only did he become colorless to me, he became my mentor, which was not an easy thing for me to accept. Maybe it was paranoia on my part, but sometimes when white folks were talking to us, it seemed like they needed to be in the teaching position, with Black people needing to be taught. I never got that feeling from Dean, even when he told me things like "Buy better clothes." Dean was extremely sensitive to the position Black people were confined to in American society. Some of the injustices that Malcolm X questioned, Dean questioned privately to me. He wasn't a rabble-rouser or speechmaker, but behind the scenes he opened a lot of doors for me to get in places no Black coach had gone before. Dean was directly responsible for getting me on committees in the National Association of Basketball Coaches, because he recognized the need in the organization for a Black coach with a strong voice, and he saw other Black coaches doing things that didn't advance racial equality. He told me, "I need to get you on this committee because someone has to push back." Then we'd both be in the committee meeting, and another Black coach in the room would say something like we didn't need to consider players from historically

Black schools for the Olympic team, because they were undisciplined. These Black guys were taking on the characteristics of the oppressor, trying to gain approval or get ahead in some way. Dean would kick me under the table, like, "See, what did I tell you?" He never looked at me when it happened, just gave me that silent kick. By 1976, thanks to Dean, I was the youngest coach on the NABC board of directors, which played a significant role in rule changes, setting academic policies, Olympic team selection, and running the NCAA tournament. In a few more years, I became the first Black president of the NABC.

I made another white friend around that time who would play an important role in my life. I was walking through the gym and saw a flyer for an upcoming meeting of the Fellowship of Christian Athletes. They were starting a Georgetown chapter, and the flyer invited people to come and join. Despite having to sit in the back of the church as a boy, I'm still Catholic. I'm able to separate the actions of those priests from the teachings of Jesus. I have always depended on the Blessed Mother, I lean on her and pray to her when I'm afraid or unsure. My favorite color is blue because of its connection to the Blessed Mother. After I run around calling people all sorts of names, I ask the Blessed Mother to forgive me. Like Tom T. Hall says in one of my favorite country songs: "Me and Jesus got our own thing goin'."

I thought the Fellowship of Christian Athletes was a worthwhile endeavor, so I went by the classroom on a Sunday night to see what the first meeting would be like. The only person there was the kid who organized it, an eighteen-year-old freshman named Jack DeGioia, who played football and ran track. Nobody else showed up, but I stayed and talked with Jack. He was not a big-time athlete, but he was extremely smart and sensitive to the experiences of other people. We had a good conversation, mostly about God and education, which are two things we both care a lot about, so I kept coming back to the meetings. For a long time, it was just us two, which was fine with me.

Little did I know that Jack would become my boss. He became dean of student affairs in the 1990s, with oversight of the athletic department, then became associate vice president of the university. In 2001, Jack became the first Georgetown president who was not a priest, and probably the first layman to lead a Jesuit school. He has been extremely sympathetic to my views, and has insisted that I remain closely involved with the university. I love Jack, and it all started with us alone in a classroom, talking about things we had in common.

IN 1976, DEAN asked me to be one of his assistant coaches for the United States Olympic basketball team. I was blown away. That's when I knew he loved me, because Dean made no compromises with the game. He was not nice when it was time to win. Plus Dean knew every coach in the country and could have chosen anybody. I have gone through life being selective about who I would like to give me their approval, and Dean was one of the few. I would never be an assistant coach for anybody but Dean Smith.

After he chose me, Dean came to Washington and asked me to go to dinner with him at the Watergate Hotel. I was a McDonald's guy, I wasn't into sitting down at fancy tables with heavy silverware. But Dean wanted to interview someone for the Olympic support staff and said I should be there. Dean started asking the guy how it was to work for this or that coach. The guy kept saying, "He was a great coach, but . . ." and then came the real meat of the discussion. Every time he said "but," Dean kicked me under the table. I sat there with a straight face. I like to talk, but I know when to shut up, too. The guy kept bad-mouthing people he worked for. Dean taught me that if someone was disloyal to his old boss, he would do the same thing to you.

The Olympic Games were held in Montreal that year, and the entire experience was a thrill. I always enjoyed the relationships with players, and at the Olympics I got to meet a bunch of guys I'd only read about in the newspaper. This is when the rest of the world brought professionals to the Olympics, and the United States still used college kids.

There was a lot of controversy about American players who didn't try out for the team because they were protecting their NBA futures. Then people complained about the guys who did get picked. I thought the criticism was tremendously unfair. The guys who opted out had millions of dollars on the line, and the kids who did play were risking something to represent their country. Besides, we had a strong group: Kenny Carr from North Carolina State, Adrian Dantley from Notre Dame, Scott May and Quinn Buckner from Indiana, Ernie Grunfeld from Tennessee. Four Carolina players made the team, including Walter Davis, Phil Ford, and Mitch Kupchak. I got to know May, Ford, and Buckner pretty well. I learned to like Indiana coach Bobby Knight from hearing what Quinn Buckner thought of him. Quinn respected Bobby and thought he was a good coach. I shared a dorm room with Bill Gutheridge, Dean's assistant at Carolina, and we got along great. I loved collecting Olympic pins and trading them in the Olympic Village, and meeting people from all over the world.

In the previous Olympics, the Soviet Union had beaten the U.S. in a rigged gold medal game. They played the final seconds over three times, until the Russians could make a last-second basket. We wanted to avenge that defeat, but the Russians lost to Yugoslavia and we didn't get to play them. Still, some of the games were close. We were competing against grown men, pros who had been playing together for years. We beat Puerto Rico by only one point and Czechoslovakia by five. A few hours before the gold medal game against Yugoslavia, Dean asked me to give a speech to the team.

I didn't prepare anything. I just spoke my mind, like I had been doing since I spoke to my classmates at Providence. I started by reminding our team about all the criticism they took from so many people back home. This was my time to let out the anger I had been holding in about those comments. I tried to convey what a tremendous honor it would be to win a gold medal for our country. As I spoke, I was remembering my own Olympic tryout experience, and how badly I wanted a fair chance to just compete for a spot on the team. Not even *get* a spot, just compete fairly for one. I spoke for just a few minutes, but by the end there were tears on my face. I told our team, "God, I wish I could have the opportunity you all have today."

We blew Yugoslavia out, 95–74. Not because of my speech, although it might have helped a little. Dean deserved all the credit.

Now I had an Olympic gold medal. There was only one championship left for me to win.

9

BAY BAY, BIG SKY, AND THE BIG EAST

I returned from the Olympics in the fall of 1976 to some fresh faces on campus, starting with a new president, Father Timothy Healy. He would run Georgetown for the next thirteen years, and we developed an outstanding relationship. I called him the Big Irishman. He called me the Boss. But the most important newcomers were two freshmen on my team, Craig Shelton and John Duren.

Shelton was a strong, high-jumping power forward nicknamed Big Sky, one of the most highly recruited players in Washington. When he was in the post, the ball was like a weapon in his hand. Duren was a big, smart point guard everybody called Bay Bay. They had both played at Dunbar, my mother's old school, and led the team to a 29–0 record their senior year. Dunbar was up the street from Boys Club No. 2. I had known Bay Bay and his older brother Lonnie since they were too little to cross Third Street by themselves, and I offered both of them scholarships.

Dunbar had a Black coach named Joe Dean Davidson, who helped me sign Big Sky and Bay Bay against some stiff competition. Craig Shelton could have gone to any college in the country. Some people thought I had a recruiting advantage in these types of situations because I was Black, but at that time there was a perception among a lot of our people that blue-chip recruits should play for white coaches at established programs. No Black coach had yet won anything significant. The dynamic was similar to when I came out of high school, and my mentors like Mr. Jabbo and Red sent me to Providence, not to a Tennessee State or a Winston-Salem. I appreciated that Joe Dean wasn't afraid to let his players sign with a Black coach.

Derrick Jackson was a junior in 1976–77, our leading scorer, and still paying my mortgage. Sophomore forward Al Dutch was an important scorer and rebounder I signed from my old high school, Archbishop Carroll. Steve Martin, a six-foot-four sophomore from New Orleans, moved from guard to forward because we had Derrick and Mike Riley in the backcourt. He adapted to play a bruising style and I nicknamed him the Beast. At center we had Ed Hopkins and Tom Scates. When we added Big Sky and Bay Bay to this nucleus, it brought Georgetown basketball to a new level.

I never paid any kid a dime to come to Georgetown. First and foremost, it was against the rules. I didn't care that other people did it. Illegal payments weren't any shock to me, because colleges had offered me money when I was coming out of high school. But paying for players also went against my nature, and against my belief in college basketball as an instrument of higher education. It always bothered me when people rationalized paying players by saying they otherwise got nothing. Ask someone with student loans how much free tuition, room, board, and books are worth.

Not that recruits didn't ask me for money. Their coaches or parents usually implied something or said something cute, almost like throwing out a fishing line to see if I would nibble. A few kids asked me flat out, "What are you gonna do for me?" I'd just say "That's not going to happen" and leave it at that. A lot of kids who asked for money signed with schools we played against every year. It would have been stupid for me to pay players, because I was so closely scrutinized, especially once I started winning big and challenging the NCAA. I'm not so holy that I never broke a single rule, especially since some rules were silly or wrong. I bought that movie ticket for Derrick Jackson. I said hello to kids I bumped into at summer league games. But Georgetown was never accused of any NCAA violations whatsoever. The NCAA never even made an inquiry. There was nothing for them to inquire about. I'd rather come in second doing it the right way than win by cheating.

I recruited all my players the same way, from the unknowns to Patrick Ewing and Alonzo Mourning. Take Steve Martin, for example. He was All-State in Louisiana and had plenty of other scholarship offers. When he got to campus, the first place I took him was the library, and I told him, "If you come to Georgetown, this is where you should plan to spend most of your time." I set up an appointment with the dean of the business school, who talked with Steve for forty-five minutes. Then I took him out to eat at the Rib Pit on 14th Street, a tiny joint with the best ribs in the city. They knew me well in there. The owner told Steve, "If you come to Georgetown, you can eat here for free whenever you want." I stopped that conversation quick, because it was the kind of NCAA violation I took seriously. We got our ribs to go, in the paper bags that the grease soaks through, and went outside to eat in the car. I told Steve what I told every kid I ever recruited:

"I've heard a whole lot of good things about you, and would love for you to come to Georgetown. But if you do play for me, I can't guarantee that you will be in the starting lineup, or even play one minute in a game. The only thing I will guarantee is that if you stay here for four years, and do what you're supposed to do, you will walk out of here with a degree."

That was a surprise to most kids who had been promised the world by other coaches. But I didn't consider it some kind of religious observance. I believed it was the right thing to do. I was just going from A to Z, doing what came naturally. For players with a certain type of character, my recruiting pitch was an attraction in spite of itself.

Bay Bay became a leader right away. In addition to his talent, which was extraordinary, he had a terrific sense of humor. One day the kids screwed something up at practice and I lined them up to run. In many of those situations I didn't yell, I just swiped my index finger from right to left, and everybody knew what that finger meant. The players lined up on the baseline, and when the whistle blew, Bay Bay hollered out, "Police! The police coming!" He took it back to the neighborhood where we grew up running from the cops even though we hadn't done anything wrong. Everybody in the gym busted out laughing, and nobody laughed harder than me. That was one of the small ways Bay Bay orchestrated the team. He was a pure point guard who controlled the flow, not only on the court but emotionally. He could score on anybody, but he was unselfish and always made the right decision for the team. If he saw things were not going well, then he took it upon himself to score. Bay Bay became the starting point guard midway through his freshman year, and he basically never came out of the game after that.

My focus and intensity were always high, so I don't want to say they increased at this point, but they manifested themselves in different ways. My practices got sharper after watching Dean coach the Olympic team. I believe that genius borrows nobly. It was not unusual for me to watch film in the basketball office until one in the morning. I told the players, "The guy who gets up at six and starts walking will always beat the guy who gets up at noon and starts running." We installed a greater variety of pressure defenses: full court man, 2-2-1 full court press, half court trap, run and jump. We fast-breaked after made baskets, like the Celtics. I had a manager film nothing but the bench for a whole game so the kids could see their reactions to good and bad plays. We lined up chairs on the sideline during scrimmages and practiced standing up and clapping when players came out of the game. Everything had a reason and purpose.

One day we were at practice and someone did something silly like throw the ball off the back of another kid's head. I blew my whistle.

"I am going to win a national championship," I told my team. "You can either be here, or not be here."

We went 19–9 in 1976–77 and should have made the NCAA tournament again, but ahead of the ECAC tournament Ed Hopkins injured his ankle and we lost to Old Dominion. We went to the NIT instead. The next season, with Derrick Jackson as a senior and Bay Bay and Big Sky as sophomores, we were 21–5 going into the ECAC tournament, ranked eighteenth in the country, and determined to get back to the NCAAs.

The morning of our opening ECAC game against Virginia Commonwealth, Craig Esherick came to see me. Craig was Derrick Jackson's roommate. He told me Derrick was really sick. I rushed over and found Derrick in terrible pain, spitting up blood. He had a Bible open next to him and was trying to heal himself through prayer. We forced him to go to the hospital, where they found a bleeding ulcer that Derrick had been hiding from me. The kid wanted to play so badly, he almost died. We lost to VCU that day and made another trip to the NIT in 1978.

Remember how when I was hired the president said he'd be happy periodically going to the NIT? Nobody was happy now.

We were supposed to play Lefty Driesell's Maryland team in the first round of the NIT. At that point, I had been at Georgetown six seasons, we had played Maryland five times, and they'd beaten us all five. At first Maryland annually blew us out by twenty and thirty points, but Bay Bay and Big Sky evened the scales, and Lefty knew it. Lefty was his own worst enemy, because he made all of us raise our game to beat him. He showed me a lot about how to market a team and raise the profile of a program, and had the most influence on me learning how to graduate from a high school mentality to being successful in college. I had a competitive dislike of Lefty, but my friend George Raveling was his assistant coach, and he told me hilarious stories about some things Lefty did in the office or said to parents on the recruiting trail. Lefty definitely gave me something to aspire to on the national level.

When the NIT people matched us up in the first round, Lefty tried to bogart them into scheduling the game at his home arena. Frank Rienzo blocked that move, so Lefty pulled out of the whole tournament. That's when I knew I had him. He didn't mind coming into our gym and kicking our ass when we were nobody, but once we got good, he was like, "Where are we going to play?" Still, I respected Lefty's game behind the game. Once my team got good, I stopped playing George Washington and American. I had little to gain and a lot to lose by scheduling them. Eventually I stopped scheduling Maryland, too, when we became one of the best teams in the country. I became very political with my schedule. Wes Unseld showed up at my office one day, unannounced, and offered me $20,000 to play Maryland at the Capital Centre. Wes had a Hall of Fame playing career for the Washington NBA team when they were called the Bullets, then worked for the team as head coach, vice president, and general manager. Wes was uncomfortable making the offer, and even told me he didn't like the idea of being sent to pay me money, but he had been sent by his bosses, who also owned the Capital Centre. They knew a Georgetown-Maryland game would make big money and tried to bribe me to do it. I said no.

After Lefty backed out of the NIT, we beat Virginia instead, when Mike Riley drew an offensive foul on a Virginia inbounds play and sank two free throws in overtime. In the NIT semifinals, we went to overtime again, but we lost to North Carolina State by one point on a forty-foot prayer at the buzzer.

After that game, we didn't return to the NIT for a long time. The kid who put us over the top was another diamond in the rough.

I got a call from Clarence "Big House" Gaines, the coach at Winston-Salem State in North Carolina, one of the Black coaching legends my friends used to talk about under the tree at the playground. I admired Big House and appreciated that we had become friends. He always called me "boy," and I loved it.

"Boy," Big House said over the phone, "there's a kid down here in Gastonia you should try to get on. His name is Eric Floyd, but they call him Sleepy."

Sleepy was from the same town as the future Hall of Famer James Worthy, who was headed to play for Dean Smith at North Carolina. Worthy's greatness meant that Sleepy was overlooked by many recruiters, but those were the kind of kids that built our program. I loved finding players in the nooks and crannies, like Mike Riley in the navy or the baseball player Derrick Jackson. Dean used to laugh when I called McDonald's All-American types "hamburger heroes." We signed another player in Sleepy's class, six-foot-nine Ed Spriggs, who was working for the post office and playing in a rec league. I'm not saying we got the leftovers, because we also signed Eric Smith that year, who was one of the most highly recruited players out of Washington. But we found outstanding players who were not acknowledged as such.

If Big House told me to look at a kid, I looked. What I saw in Sleepy was a future pro. He wanted to go to Maryland, but Lefty gave his spot to a big-name kid named Reggie Jackson, so Sleepy signed with us. I also got two other important players, Mike Hancock and Ron Blaylock. Along with Sleepy, Spriggs, and Eric, they did a whole lot for our program.

When informal pickup games started in the fall of 1978, Sleepy killed everybody who guarded him. He was such a phenomenal scorer, if he missed shots, he thought it was the rim and not him. "Something's wrong with these rims, coach," Sleepy said to me on more than once occasion. And he was serious when he said it. I believed in taking things slow, so I didn't put him in the starting lineup until the third game of the season. That just happened to be against Maryland, ranked nineteenth in the country, with Buck Williams and Albert King. Before the game, I reminded Sleepy how Maryland didn't want him and Reggie Jackson was supposed to be way better than him. Sleepy dropped 28 points and I finally beat Lefty, 68–65.

Two games later we beat Indiana and cracked the Top 20 rankings, where we stayed all season. In the ECAC finals, Bay Bay led us to a victory over sixth-ranked Syracuse, and we were back in the NCAA tournament. We lost in the first round to Rutgers, but that season was a major turning point. My leading scorer was Sleepy, followed by Big Sky and Bay Bay, who were coming back for their senior year. We were on the rise.

As we became more successful, things got more complex. Nobody cared when we were struggling to win the ECAC tournament. But once we started cracking the national rankings and going to the NCAAs, things changed. The seventy percent that Dean taught me about expanded to include more challenging things.

We needed depth and muscle at the forward position, and I was recruiting Rick Weber, a six-foot-seven forward from southern Maryland. Weber seemed ready to commit. Then I was told that my old high school coach, Bob Dwyer from Archbishop Carroll, told Weber that the only reason I was recruiting him was because he was white. Dwyer told Weber that I didn't think he was good enough to play at Georgetown but wanted a few white players around for appearances' sake.

What Dwyer said hurt me deeply. I had admired and respected that man and always considered him more than just my coach. It felt like a sucker punch from a mentor. I remembered how he wanted the Georgetown job and didn't even think that I could be considered for it. What Dwyer said convinced me that some white people will accept a relationship with Blacks only if they are in the superior or teaching role. They feel they're going to heaven for teaching you, but once a Black person moves into a role of authority, they can't acknowledge that new relationship.

Weber chose another school, and I never spoke to Dwyer again. When Carroll had a reunion for our undefeated championship teams, I declined to attend. I may have been wrong for that, but I didn't want to be associated with anything Dwyer could receive credit for. He sent me a letter near the end of his life, trying to bury the hatchet, but I did not respond. That's one of the things I hope Jesus forgives me for.

The Weber situation happened again with a kid named Jeff Bullis. The *Washington Post* reported that James Madison head coach Lou Campanelli told Bullis he would only be a white token on my team. Bullis came to Georgetown anyway and gave us good minutes off the bench, for an outstanding team that made a deep NCAA tournament run. Little did these people know that I had already refused to use white tokens when I was coaching at St. Anthony's High School. I had no reason to start at Georgetown.

I faced another conundrum with Black officials. There were very few of them in the 1970s, and I advocated for more, because I believed they deserved an opportunity to move ahead in that profession. The fact there were so few, when so many of us excelled on the court, indicated that some barriers must exist. But here's the thing: when Black officials did work my games, I started to think they wanted to prove they wouldn't favor a Black coach. It seemed they made every close call against me, and some that weren't so close, too. I don't think it was necessarily a conscious decision on their part. Imagine what kind of scrutiny these Black refs were under, from their supervisors and others who controlled their careers, when it came to officiating my games. There's no way they could not have reacted, on some level, to the fact that a lot of people thought Black refs would conspire to help a Black coach. It got to the point where I hated to have them officiate my games. A lot of young coaches today tell me the same thing. When I was coaching, the Black ref Jimmy Howell was one of the best officials I had ever seen, but I didn't want to see Jimmy at my game. Once a Black ref cost us a game with an absolutely horrible call at the buzzer. I busted into the refs' dressing room and went the hell off, called the guy a "handkerchief-head nigger," which was wrong of me to say. Later, when I thought about it, I regretted how the white system had two Black men fighting over some type of psychological double-reverse mind trick. I shouldn't have come at my brother that way. But he did make a terrible call.

Let me say something here about the word "nigger." Some people want us to say "n-word" now, which is some of the biggest bullshit I ever heard. If we're not supposed to use words that were once used to demean us, then we couldn't call ourselves "black." When I was growing up, if somebody called you black, they sure didn't mean you were beautiful. And if someone says "n-word," you immediately spell the rest in your mind, and what's in your mind is what bothers you. So what's the difference between saying "n-word" and "nigger" or "nigga"? The word is part of our history, and I don't see any good reason to deny that. But we go through all these games to hide our guilt or shame about some things.

As more attention was focused on our program, I made a decision to keep my family life completely private. There are certain things you save for yourself, certain experiences that you cherish and don't want other people involved in, even with this book. Gwen and I had three children by then—our daughter, Tiffany, was born in 1975. Crazy people smashed a hole through my office door and sent racist hate mail. If people couldn't get to me, what might they do to my wife and children? People who can't hurt you try to hurt the ones you love. Even without any physical harm, what might they say to my family, based on their hang-ups about me? In politics, I saw people attack the children of elected officials, they made the children responsible for the actions of their parents. I wondered whether my kids' teachers, or others they might encounter in life who might disagree with the things I said, would take something from my children that they wouldn't even know was being taken from them.

I didn't want to put that on my family.

Gwen and the kids came to most of our home games and sat on the baseline under our basket, but I kept them as far as possible from the media. Coaching took up an extreme amount of my time, and Gwen did a fantastic job raising Tiffany, Ronny, and John when I was gone. When I came home, Tiffany liked to fall asleep on my chest while I watched film or made phone calls. She also made a conscious decision not to play basketball, because she wanted me to just be her father. John and Ronny wanted to play, so I took them to Boys Club No. 2 for games when they were young. It was not unusual for me to bring them to practice, where I might tote Ronny with one hand and blow my whistle with the other. Once John came up to me at practice and said, "Daddy, they're staying in the lane longer than three seconds." He wasn't yet ten years old. I gave John a whistle and told him to blow it whenever he saw players in the lane too long. After John blew his whistle for about the fourth time, our center, Tom Scates, gave little John the meanest look you ever saw.

People began to take note of my public personality. Before we won, they didn't care how I acted. The observations that people now made were always connected to my size. I'm a large person, with a loud voice. I felt strongly about my profession. I yelled a lot, even when I wasn't angry. When I hollered at a kid or argued a referee's call, it was perceived differently than if a small coach, or a white coach, did the same thing. Sometimes I did get angry and lose my temper. That was something few white people had seen from a Black man in public, but I didn't think I should be held to a different standard than white coaches. Mary Fenlon told me, "When you get angry, people don't hear what you're saying. They hear how you are saying it." They also saw it coming from a six-foot-ten person with dark skin. That's how a certain aspect of my reputation began.

But another time when I was fussing or arguing about something, Fenlon told me, "You wear your Blackness well." I considered that a great compliment.

I'M FORTUNATE THAT my greatest players who came to Georgetown say nice things about me, and I adore those guys. I also loved a lot more guys whose names nobody knew. One of the unknown players I have a great relationship with is Lonnie Duren, Bay Bay's older brother. Lonnie is Tiffany's godfather, and the only one of my players to have that role in my family.

Lonnie wasn't a great player in high school, but when he was a kid I always enjoyed being around him, so I gave him a scholarship and he graduated with a Georgetown diploma. Even though Lonnie didn't hardly play, he had an important role. For example, we picked up one of his expressions and said it when we left the locker room before games: "Forty hard minutes!" Lonnie would be at the end of our bench trash-talking the other team so bad, he sweated through his uniform as if he had played. He gave us forty hard minutes from the bench.

In the 1970s we had a good crosstown rivalry with George Washington. During one game, one of the GW players cheap-shotted big Tom Scates, hit him from behind and tried to hurt him. The refs broke it up and there was a lot of confusion on the court. Instead of going directly to his bench, the GW player took the long way back and walked in front of our sideline.

Lonnie was sitting way down there in his usual spot. Everybody's attention was on Scates and the refs. Lonnie scoped out the GW aggressor coming toward our bench. When the guy walked in front of Lonnie—*pow!* Lonnie popped him right in the face.

I ran over and started gesturing all wild, pointing in Lonnie's face, yelling and cussing. But the whole time I told him under my breath, "Nice job, Lonnie. That's how we protect our teammates."

In those days I had them sumbitches you didn't fuck with. We didn't start any fights, but we wouldn't back down from them, either. I never told any player to fight somebody, but I never wanted anybody who didn't know when he should fight. Most of my players had to fight all their lives for what they got, metaphorically speaking. They weren't going to let anybody punk them. We played extremely organized and controlled basketball, but with an edge. We came after you, and we never backed down.

Fast-forward thirty years. Lonnie is the director of Boys Club No. 2 and lives right next door to the club in the Sursum Corda cooperative, a tenant-owned, publicly subsidized town house complex. Sursum Corda is Latin for "lift up your hearts." The neighborhood was founded by a Georgetown graduate in the 1960s who wanted to help poor people, but you know how that goes, and over the years it became full of drugs and crime. After drug dealers killed a fourteen-year-old girl in Sursum Corda, the city decided to redevelop the property and tried to use eminent domain to push all the poor people out. That part of the city was gentrifying, it's only a few blocks from the U.S. Capitol, and the property was worth millions. As the city tried to take over, Lonnie got himself elected to chairman of the Sursum Corda co-op board, then began negotiating to make sure the residents who lived there for decades didn't get taken advantage of. I should mention that my nickname for Lonnie is Columbo, after that TV detective who looked disheveled and slow but was smarter than everybody. If you saw Lonnie on the street you might think he didn't have a job, much less a Georgetown degree. Anyway, the negotiations between Lonnie's co-op board, the city, and the developers went on for years. The little boy who couldn't cross Third and K was holding the city hostage. One of the people who helped him was his old teammate Felix Yeoman, who had a MBA in finance. Finally, in 2018, Lonnie and Felix got the deal they wanted. The Toll Brothers real estate company bought Sursum Corda for $63 million. You read that right: *sixty-three million dollars*. Seventeen percent of the development was set aside for affordable housing. All the longtime residents were guaranteed the right to return there with subsidized rent, or take their subsidy elsewhere.

For a Washington native like me, who grew up in the projects, who studied the white man's game behind the game, what Lonnie and Felix did makes me incredibly proud. They didn't make the All-American team. Lonnie didn't even play in the games. But they did a lot more than some guys who went pro. Lonnie fought for years to get what his people deserved. That's what I mean about our guys knowing when to fight. I'm as proud of what Lonnie accomplished as I am of what Patrick Ewing did in the NBA. Some people make the mistake of defining my coaching by my great players. What Lonnie and Felix did with Sursum Corda? *That's* Georgetown basketball.

MY OLD FRIEND Dave Gavitt had succeeded Joe Mullaney as head coach at Providence, then became the school's athletic director. In the late 1970s, Dave started talking about forming a new basketball conference. I didn't like the idea. My team was already good as an independent. I had the freedom to make my own schedule and set up my own deals. What did I need a conference for? I thought it would be another entity telling me what to do. But Dave saw the future of college basketball in terms of the importance of television, the politics of how conferences would influence the game, and the money that would be made. I was blind to all that, but Dave's vision was extraordinary. He wanted to gather teams from all the biggest northeastern markets, from Boston through Connecticut, New York, and New Jersey and on down to Philadelphia and Washington. He understood how attractive those markets would be for television. He also recognized that a big-time conference would help us retain a lot of eastern talent that left for other parts of the country because the UCLAs and North Carolinas and Indianas were on TV all the time. I trusted Dave, and so did Frank Rienzo. In the summer of 1979, we started the Big East conference with Georgetown, Syracuse, Providence, St. John's, Boston College, Seton Hall, and Connecticut. Villanova joined the following year, and Pittsburgh in 1982.

Dave told all of us we had to move out of our little gyms, because to compete with the Big Ten and the ACC we needed the whole show: arenas, cheerleaders, bands, mascots, the whole nine yards. Our team finally moved out of McDonough, which could no longer fit all our fans. Our home arena became the Capital Centre in Landover, Maryland, a forty-five minute drive from campus. That was great for television and revenue, but it made life harder for our team. Now every game was like an away game for us in terms of logistics. We didn't practice there, so it was hard for players to get a feel for the rims. We couldn't do shoot-around there. To get kids out of class I had to fight with Fenlon and the teachers. And traveling to and from the Capital Centre took an extra two hours out of their day. But those negatives were more than balanced out by the positives. Dean always told me that playing on television was a major key to success, and now we were on TV all the time. ESPN was new and broadcast a lot of our games. We also had coaches with engaging personalities: Lou Carnesecca at St. John's, Rollie Massimino at Villanova, the Black guy at Georgetown. Jim Boeheim at Syracuse had a bland demeanor, which became distinctive in itself compared with the rest of us excitable guys. The whole mix made for great television. Not to mention that all these guys were outstanding coaches with talented players.

In 1979–80, the first Big East season, our conference had three teams consistently ranked in the Top 20: us, Syracuse, and St. John's. We won so many close games, people started calling us the Heart Attack Hoyas. At Boston College, live on ESPN, Eric Smith played great in the clutch and we came back from eight points down with a minute left—with no shot clock or three-point line—to win in overtime. We beat Maryland again, 83–71, and I had a big blowup with Lefty. The ref called a crazy technical foul on one of my kids for hanging on the rim after a dunk. I'm out there dealing with those idiots and one of the Maryland players, Ernie Graham, patted me on the head. Ernie and I had a great relationship, I recruited him hard out of Dunbar Baltimore, but that pat was disrespectful and got me revved up. When Lefty came over and added his two cents, I gave Lefty twenty dollars' worth of cussing, which was a mistake on my part. I did not shake his hand after the game.

Syracuse was playing their last season in the Manley Field House before moving into the Carrier Dome. When we went up to play them in February, they had won fifty-seven straight home games. People hyped the matchup because it was the final game in Manley. Syracuse had Louis Orr, Roosevelt Bouie, and Danny Schayes. They were ranked second in the country and acted like they were going to kick our ass. They were up 14 points at halftime, but then Big Sky went to work, and with five seconds left Sleepy hit two free throws to give us a 52–50 victory.

At the postgame press conference I said, "Manley Field House is officially closed. May it rest in peace."

People still talk about that quote. It wasn't premeditated. I was just going from A to Z, doing what came naturally. Some people believe that remark created our Syracuse rivalry, but it actually began before then. At a tournament in 1974, one of their best players, Rudy Hackett, stood outside our locker room door as we walked in and tried to stare us down with a tough-guy look on his face. That was the best thing he could have done, because my kids didn't play that. When we got into the locker room it was like, "You see what this motherfucker Hackett just did?" and we went out and upset them. But putting that stake through Syracuse's heart in the last game at Manley Field House definitely added fuel to the fire. Over the years, Georgetown and Syracuse came to hate each other.

One of Dave Gavitt's most brilliant ideas was holding the Big East conference tournament in Madison Square Garden. There's no city like New York, and having so many good teams there at one time created an electric atmosphere. In the first Big East tournament, we beat Syracuse in the finals, 87–81, and Bay Bay was named the first Big East MVP. We earned a third seed in the NCAA tournament, which then had forty-eight teams. In our first game, we beat an Iona team coached by Jim Valvano. That was my first NCAA tournament victory, and Georgetown's first since 1943.

But I was far from satisfied, especially since our next opponent was Maryland. Beforehand, I apologized in the newspapers for what I had said to Lefty during the previous game, and I said publicly that my behavior had been wrong. It came from competitiveness, not hatred or disrespect. I had a lot of admiration for Lefty that he didn't know about. After we both retired, I advocated for him to get into the Hall of Fame, and when he was inducted, he asked me to introduce him. But when we were playing each other, I needed to cultivate a competitive dislike of Lefty. I needed to kick his ass.

Another thing I did before the Maryland game was pull my seniors John Duren and Craig Shelton aside to privately thank them for everything they had done for the program. When they got here, Georgetown was periodically going to the NIT. Now we were consistently in the national picture, and I knew we were on our way to something special. A lot of other guys contributed significantly to our success up to that point, too many to name here, but Bay Bay and Big Sky led the way. I wanted them to know how much I appreciated them. Bay Bay might be the best point guard who ever played here, if I had to choose between him and Michael Jackson I'd have to blindfold myself. Big Sky is the best power forward I ever had, bar none. They weren't scared of playing for a Black coach, and they opened a door for Georgetown basketball. It's not a coincidence that they were my first two players to make the NBA.

We beat Maryland again, 74–68. Eric Smith held Albert King to 6 for 18 shooting from the field, and even though the great Buck Williams had 18 points and 15 rebounds for Maryland, it wasn't enough. After the game, I got a call from Mr. Wyatt at the Boys Club. "Hey baby," he said, "the Buck stops here."

In the Elite Eight our opponent was Iowa, coached by Lute Olsen. We were up ten points with eleven minutes left, headed to the Final Four. Sleepy was cooking, on his way to 31 points. Then Iowa went on an unbelievable streak and absolutely shot the lights out. They scored on fifteen of their final sixteen possessions and made all fifteen of their free throws in the second half. We battled them shot for shot, and the score was tied in the final minute. With five seconds left, Iowa made a layup to go up by two, and to make matters worse, Big Sky was called for a foul on the play. It was a terrible call, by a Black ref. Iowa hit the free throw to go up three. That was the nail in the coffin, because there was no three-point line then in college basketball. We made a layup on the other end and missed the Final Four by one point.

I don't think I had ever felt pain like that loss before. I couldn't fault our kids, though. Our team played well, but Iowa played an incredible game and deserved to win. When you enter the battlefield, sometimes you get shot. As terrible as I felt, I also felt more determined. I borrowed a line from General Douglas MacArthur and declared publicly, "I shall return."

In eight years, we built Georgetown from nothing into a national contender. All we needed was one more piece to reach the mountaintop.

10

PATRICK

Billy Stein and I went up to Boston to watch a high school kid named Paul Little play some sort of championship game at the Boston Garden. Billy and I sat at the scorer's table. Early in the game, another kid, a tall sophomore, blocked a shot and then threw an outlet pass. They ran the fast break and missed the layup, but the tall kid flew in out of nowhere and tapped the ball in. I had no idea who he was but I thought, *Man, this kid can run.*

I started watching him off the ball, and pretty soon I forgot all about Paul Little. This tall kid was always in the right place. He gave a hundred percent effort and was extremely competitive. In the second quarter I turned to Billy and said, "Get me that boy right there and we'll win the national championship." That boy was Patrick Ewing.

By the time he was a senior at Cambridge Rindge and Latin School, Patrick was seven feet tall and the No. 1 player in the country. His coach, Mike Jarvis, set up a recruiting process in which colleges that wanted Patrick had to promise all sorts of special help. Patrick was born in Jamaica and didn't come to the United States until he was twelve years old, so his reading was not as strong as it could have been. Jarvis, a Black coach with experience at the college level, asked for untimed tests, tutors, tape recordings of lectures, and more. I understood what Jarvis was doing. He wanted to make sure Patrick was not exploited. But I thought the process exposed too much of Patrick's personal business, and I worried about how the requirements would be interpreted. In my opinion, much of what they were saying about Patrick should not have been revealed to the media, because it created the false impression that Patrick couldn't read.

Jarvis cut down the list of colleges to sixteen, including us, North Carolina, and two Boston schools. I went up there with Stein and Mary Fenlon to make our recruiting presentation. Across the table were Jarvis, Patrick, his parents, and some academic people from his school. I did what I normally did, which was sell the attributes of Georgetown from an academic and career perspective. I told them we would not provide untimed tests and those other things, but Patrick would have access to the same help as any other member of the team, and if he worked hard he would graduate. I did not promise he would start, or even play. Some other schools were offering him illegal payments, but none of Patrick's people even hinted about money, so I thought we had a chance.

What I remember most is his mother, Dorothy, sitting there watching me. She didn't say a word, just stared at me the whole time and barely even blinked. I'm talking with the other people but wondering what she was thinking about. My father always told me to keep an eye on the person who doesn't say anything, because they're listening the closest. Now I'm nervous. When I finished talking, Mrs. Ewing asked me what Patrick's social life would be like at Georgetown, since it was predominantly white. I said, "Mrs. Ewing, the city of Washington is seventy percent Black. I can help your son with school and with basketball, but if he can't find somebody to socialize with in Washington, he's got a problem I can't solve."

Mrs. Ewing looked at me and said, "Funny man, funny man." I thought to myself, *Uh-oh, what does that mean?*

Mrs. Ewing had immigrated to Boston from Jamaica by herself. She worked in the kitchen at Massachusetts General Hospital to earn enough money to bring over her husband, Carl, and their seven children. They came by ones and twos. Mrs. Ewing kept her job at the hospital, and Mr. Ewing worked in a factory making rubber hoses. They did not come here for their children to do that type of job. They valued education above all else. Patrick took an official recruiting trip to Georgetown.

When he got here, it was an unseasonably warm fall day. He asked if the temperature was always this pleasant, because it reminded him of Jamaica. "Oh, absolutely, it's very warm here," I told him. When we ate breakfast, the boy ordered a whole pitcher of orange juice. Fenlon was about to jump down his throat, she never let the players have more than two glasses of anything. I kicked her under the table and shot her a look that said *Let it go!* But Patrick later said the real reason he chose Georgetown had nothing to do with orange juice. He was impressed by how I spoke and carried myself, thought I was intelligent, and saw me as someone he could emulate. I consider that an incredible compliment.

A few months later, Patrick called a press conference at Satch Sanders's restaurant in Boston to announce his decision, and the place was packed with locals. When he said, "After considering all the facts, I've decided to attend Georgetown University," half the room walked out. Imagine doing that to a teenager. Nobody realized it then, but for a lot of people, Patrick's announcement was the moment Georgetown became the villains of college basketball.

When it came time to sign the letter of intent, I went back up to Boston with my assistant coach Norman Washington. The letter of intent was a binding contract to guarantee we would offer Patrick a scholarship, and he would play only for us. Until that letter was signed, anything could happen.

I made some small talk and then said, "Well, we have this letter for you to sign." Mrs. Ewing said, "Sign? You sign for land, not for people." It felt like my heart stopped. Then she smiled and told her husband to sign it. I had learned from my friend George Raveling that as soon as you make the sale, get the hell out of Dodge. Don't hang around and wait for things to go wrong. As soon as that pen came off the paper I said, "Mrs. Ewing, I know y'all are busy and I have a flight to catch, so I'm going to get on back home," and I was out of there.

I was headed to another city and Norman was taking the letter back to school. We had the letter in a Samsonite briefcase, and back then they had these advertisements saying Samsonite is indestructible. When Norman was about to board his flight I told him, "If the plane crashes, throw the fucking briefcase out the window."

Not long after Patrick signed, a Boston newspaper published a big story about the academic help Jarvis asked for, basically saying Patrick shouldn't have been admitted. The national media acted outraged that prestigious Georgetown University recruited Patrick because of his basketball talent. It was the biggest crock of bull I ever heard. Everybody knew that colleges had been letting athletes in with lower grades forever. Why make it an issue now? Why go after Patrick, who was actually a solid student whose progress had been limited due to his having come here from another country? Because they thought, consciously or not, that he was a nigger who didn't know his place. That newspaper story created a racist lie about Patrick being stupid that he never escaped, not even after he graduated in four years with a bachelor's degree in fine art. Patrick didn't let it bother him. I was more hurt than he was. But then I said to myself, "I signed the best player in the country," and got back to work.

It was cold when Patrick enrolled on campus in the fall of 1981, and he asked me why I had pretended the weather in Washington was warm. I told him, "You're here now, so don't worry about it." The bottomless orange juice dried up, too. I knew how to recruit, but I knew when to draw the line, too: his first day on campus.

When we got into practice, Patrick's teammates were pushing him around and Patrick just smiled and kept playing. I thought, *This kid ain't as ferocious as they said.* I almost thought he was soft and we'd have to toughen him up. Then in our first game, against an international team, somebody shoved him one too many times. Patrick turned around and socked him. See, off the court Patrick was the nicest, most polite kid you could imagine. He treated the custodian as respectfully as he did the president of the college. If you said show up at eight, he arrived at seven forty-five. It wouldn't be a mistake to call him a sweet person. But when the ball went up for the tip-off, Patrick flipped that switch and didn't back down from anybody. I never saw him initiate any altercations, that's not his nature. He played hard and aggressive, he took a lot of physical abuse because of his size and dominance, and sometimes he retaliated when provoked. Patrick did have a temper, and I had to get on him about losing it, which a few people in our program found amusing coming from me. But like Sister Eunice told me back at Our Little Prison Home, "A man without any temper is not much of a man at all."

Patrick's first season is when media coverage of our team changed. Off the bat, everyone wanted to interview him. Ever since I had been at Georgetown, I never let freshmen do any interviews until January. They had to spend some time here in order to talk intelligently about our program, plus the priority was getting them acclimated to college academics. And I had never let the media into my practices. But a lot of new reporters showed up around our team who were unfamiliar with our program, and our rules made some of them upset or resentful. Not everybody, because I had great relationships with plenty of reporters. George Solomon of the *Washington Post* had covered me at St. Anthony's, and when he became sports editor we remained friendly. I would call the *Post*'s Thomas Boswell at home and spend half the call talking to his mother. I respected the *Post* reporter Mark Asher, even though he was a huge pain and always calling the office acting all curious. Mark claimed that he coined the phrase "Hoya Paranoia." I got in more than a few arguments with Mark. I told him I wasn't going to return his call unless he called twice, because then I would know it was important. He started leaving messages with Fenlon saying, "Tell Coach this is the second time I called," even though it was the first. But Mark was always fair and accurate. If I yelled at him, he didn't act like I was racist because he was white, and he didn't take it personally if we did not do interviews when it was convenient for him. Mark also gave as good as he got, because when he got sick and I went to visit him in the hospital, he started trying to interview me from the bed with tubes stuck in his arm.

Howard Cosell interviewed me around this time and took something I said far out of context. During the interview, Cosell said he didn't see any trace of racism in me. I responded honestly that I wasn't sure I had "no trace" of racism, because I'm a product of my environment. A few years later, Cosell went on ESPN and said I had admitted I was a racist. That was puzzling, because I had defended Cosell when he called a Redskins player a "little monkey." I think Cosell twisted my statement to generate controversy and get ratings, which is what some people in the media do. Cosell always tried to make himself a friend of the Black man, like he did with Muhammad Ali. I didn't dislike him, but he fell into the trap of trying to portray me as a racist based on some of the issues I raised rather than dealing with the issues themselves.

A lot of media people over the years have tried to compare me to Martin Luther King and Malcolm X. I have tremendous admiration for both of those men, and I consider any such comparison the highest honor, but I would rather not be defined by who they were. I want to be me. Besides, a lot of people who tried to compare me to Malcolm X were implying that I hated white people.

I got along with numerous reporters, and I hope they're not disappointed that I can't name all of them. But some writers started to mischaracterize my educational priorities as being militaristic. I admire the American military, so I considered that, too, a compliment. Then they said I had too much control. Of course I was in control. That was my job. Dean Smith controlled everything, down to the temperature of his arena. But my actions were perceived differently because of my color, size, and refusal to be apologetic. A lot of reporters couldn't understand why I wouldn't give them a ten-minute interview with Patrick or Sleepy. Well, there are twenty other reporters who want ten minutes. You do the math. I had a responsibility to protect the kids' time, since a lack of time was the biggest obstacle to their education. I didn't feel any obligation to explain or apologize to anybody, and refused to defend myself against false accusations. We just followed our protocol and let the ball bounce where it may. I understood that reporters had a job to do, but so did I, and I wasn't about to punish the kids for the media's convenience. It's hard for you to write your story? Try taking an exam the day after losing to St. John's. Fenlon was protective of our kids when it came to interviews, and she spoke sharply to a lot of reporters. I think they resented her, or were scared of her, or both.

Steve Hirshey from the *Washington Star* came up to me one day when nobody was around and said that his editor had instructed him to "get Thompson." I respected Steve for telling me that. He didn't like me much, but he had enough integrity not to let somebody put words in his mouth. In a strange coincidence, when I was in high school, my mother had done day's work for the *Star* editor's family. She knew this editor when he was young. Maybe what he said wasn't a coincidence after all. Maybe the editor had a problem with covering the son of a Black woman who cleaned houses.

Very few reporters were Black in the early days. When our team got good, I started seeing more Black faces come around, like Mike Wilbon from the *Post*, Bill Rhoden from the *New York Times*, Ralph Wiley from *Sports Illustrated*, and Bryan Burwell from the *St. Louis Post-Dispatch* and then *USA Today*. I got close to some of those guys, especially Wilbon and Wiley, and let them know me in a different way. Later on, I saw David Aldridge and J. A. Adande coming to our games. I said to myself, "Huh, this racist tag may not be so bad if white newspapers think I'll only talk to Black reporters. I can integrate the media with my reputation." I let it be known that I thought newspapers and TV stations should hire more of us. I don't want to make it seem like I'm the reason these guys got jobs, because they earned it with their own abilities. But I did enjoy the fact that the perception of me as a racist helped create opportunities for Black writers.

We started the 1981–82 season ranked fifth and stayed in the Top 25 almost the whole year. Our games were frequently on television, thanks to Dave Gavitt. A lot more fans and media people saw for the first time what we had been doing the past nine years: pressing and trapping full court, running a fast and disciplined offense, playing hard and physical, coming after people. We didn't start any fights, but we knew how to end them. When the point guard from Western Kentucky sucker-punched Patrick, Fred Brown almost knocked him out cold. I thought Patrick was the one who hit him and cussed him out in the locker room until Fred Brown said, "I'm the one who did it, Coach." The casual basketball fan became aware of the Black coach with the Black team that didn't back down.

People like to think Patrick is the one who made Georgetown basketball what it became. Patrick didn't come to Georgetown to make us good. He came here because we were good. That 1981–82 team was loaded. Sleepy was a senior and could score with anybody in the country; he ended up as Georgetown's all-time leading scorer, a first-round NBA draft pick, and a seventeen-year pro. My other seniors were Eric Smith, Mike Hancock, Ed Spriggs, and Ron Blaylock. They all had important roles, including some who didn't play a lot but contributed greatly to our success. The players with the most ability often aren't the leaders of the team. Blaylock was one of the kids who seeded the clouds and helped the environment of the team with his intelligence. You don't want a team full of idiots. I needed players who reinforced my educational messages and influenced the borderline kids I was trying to change. Ed Spriggs was another smart and unselfish kid. He was a good big man and started every game his junior year. Then Patrick arrived. Ed immediately took Patrick under his wing and helped Patrick take his spot as the starting center. I'll never forget a game we played in Reno, Nevada. An opponent was beating the hell out of Patrick. Eddie stood up on the bench and told the other guy, "Guess what? I'm coming in the game soon. Let's see how tough you are then." Every time they came to our end of the court Eddie yelled out "I'm coming!" He was a protector and teacher of Patrick.

Here's another story about Ed. Fenlon controlled all the meal money on road trips, and if kids were messing up she would sometimes give them less money, or none at all. We did everything as a team, so if one kid messed up, nobody got paid. A kid screwed up and cost them some meal money. When Fenlon left the locker room, Ed stood up, slammed his fist on a locker, and said, "Man, go to class! I need that money!" But the concept of them experiencing everything as a group was important. Once I got mad at how a few guys were behaving, so I made the whole team shave. Some of them were at the age where they worked hard to grow what little mustaches they had. I told them, "If y'all gonna act like fools, you might as well look like gentlemen." I probably mixed in a few profanities for emphasis too.

Eric Smith was one of the best all-around athletes I ever coached. I don't care what kind of game you played, Eric would win. The kids used to play Pac-Man and Eric killed everybody. He reminded me of Sam Jones with the Celtics, because Sam and Eric could learn any new game in five minutes and then beat everybody else. Eric was outstanding defensively and the ultimate team guy. He had some high-scoring games, but he could impact the game without scoring a point. Eric was the definition of a sound player.

Mike Hancock was another senior who wasn't a superstar but had a major influence. Coming out of high school, I thought Mike was an underachiever academically, because he was smart but his transcript was not good. When I offered Mike a scholarship, I told him that for every grade C or below, he would have to pay for that class. For every grade B and above, I would pay for the class. He got excellent grades here, and he was one of the guys who was not heavily recruited and played extra hard because of that.

Sophomore Fred Brown had just been named Big East Rookie of the Year. Fred was a tough kid. When I went to watch him play in high school, he got in a fight at the opening tip. That's when I knew he was special. He was a good point guard, a defensive specialist, and an excellent rebounder for a guy who couldn't jump over a postage stamp.

Gene Smith was one of my best-ever defensive players, particularly guarding the point position. We got a lot of credit for our pressure defense, but that would not have been possible without Gene dictating pressure to the other team's primary ballhandler. Gene's high school was McKinley Tech in Washington. I went there to see a six-foot-ten guy and discovered Gene instead. I went back about five times and told the coach

I was looking at the big kid, when really I was interested in Gene. I didn't want people to know because there was often a herd mentality in recruiting. When I finally told the McKinley coach I wanted Gene, he said he wasn't good enough to play at Georgetown and was headed to Morgan State. See, Gene was not a great shooter, although he could score. He was smart, very tough, and just knew how to play. I knew he was a piece of the puzzle I was trying to put together with pressure defense. With him on the floor, some of the other guys didn't need to be great defenders.

People used to say we had two guys in the backcourt, Gene and Freddie, who couldn't shoot. Well, our team shot 50 percent from the field in 1981–82 and almost broke an NCAA record for shooting percentage, all with two guys who couldn't shoot. We took the ball with our press and got layups.

In addition to Patrick, the other freshmen were Bill Martin and Anthony Jones, who were high school All-Americans, and the big man Ralph Dalton. Billy was a talented forward who made it to the NBA. Anthony was highly recruited out of Dunbar in Washington, people had him rated as better than Michael Jordan. He could play, but he decided to transfer after his sophomore year. Georgetown was not for everybody.

How Ralph Dalton got here is a funny story. I found him on Sherwood Playground in Washington. Like I told Morgan Wootten, I live where you come to recruit. Ralph played for a couple years in prep school, under the radar, and we wanted to keep it that way. Nobody had seen him play in high school. When he played summer league, I told him to list his name as Ralph Brown. The kid went and scored thirty points, and Lefty Driesell happened to be there. He figured out Ralph's name was not Brown. Lefty or one of his people told the *Post* and they did a story, but there was nothing illegal about it. It was summer league. When Dr. J played at Rucker Park, the scorebook didn't say Julius Erving. I didn't want somebody else to capitalize on the work I did finding him. I laughed my ass off when people got on their high horse over Ralph using an assumed name. I was just doing what Red taught me. Bend the rules, don't break them.

During a preseason practice his freshman year, Ralph tore his knee up so badly, doctors thought he might never play again. Our trainer, Lorry Michel, saved Ralph's career.

We had an excellent trainer before Lorry, but he had obligations that sometimes prevented him from staying late or working weekends, and my crazy ways did not accommodate a nine-to-five job. Lorry was one of the assistant trainers for another team, and I noticed she was always at the gym taking care of the kids. Late nights, weekends, Lorry was there. In 1981, I brought her over to the basketball team full time. Ralph was our first major injury she had to deal with. She and Ralph worked as hard as anybody I'd ever seen to rehab his knee. Then Lorry designed a special high-top shoe with Nike that went all the way up to the middle of Ralph's shin, which allowed Ralph to eventually get back on the court.

I'm not sure how many men's teams, if any, had women trainers then. We had a woman as head trainer and another as academic coordinator. Dr. Anita Hughes had a strong influence on my giving opportunities to women. To whatever extent I helped women get ahead, I'm as proud of that as I am of what I may have done for Black people.

IN THE MIDDLE of the 1981–82 season we won thirteen games in a row. There were some scuffles and fights along the way, because people came after Patrick with elbows, fists, words, you name it. His first game at Boston College, the crowd screamed all kinds of racist names at him. One opposing player from some no-name school played so dirty, and the refs were so indifferent, that Patrick grabbed the kid around the throat with both hands and started choking the boy right on the court. The only thing that saved him was I ran out there and hollered at Patrick, "Son! What are you doing!"

In January, we went into Madison Square Garden and destroyed twentieth-ranked St. John's, 72–42. The game was on national television and Patrick absolutely dominated. At one point we were up 41–9. The whole country took notice. And who was running the show but a six-foot-ten, dark-skinned, loud-voiced Black man who refused to be apologetic or grateful for the rights God intended him to have.

Think about how few Black coaches, if any, were in the national spotlight at that time, in any sport. Then think about me being the first Black coach most white people saw. Think about how our team played.

Let's just state the obvious: we scared a lot of people.

They shouldn't have been scared. We were playing basketball, not robbing banks. But American society often assumes, unconsciously or deliberately, that Black people are dangerous, violent, animalistic, or criminal. People think we need to be controlled, kept in our place. I refused to be confined to anyone's idea of my place. I would not tell my team to back off because some people were scared for no good reason. I would not inhibit myself from yelling at refs the same way white coaches did, the same way Red worked refs to get the next call. It didn't take long for a certain word to become attached to our program, our players, and myself.

Intimidating.

When Georgetown pressed full court, we were intimidating. When Patrick blocked a shot, he was intimidating. When I protested a call, I was trying to intimidate the officials. But when Bobby Knight's Indiana team played great physical defense, they were "tough." When UCLA center Bill Walton blocked a shot, he was "talented." When Louie Carnesecca argued with the refs, he was "feisty" because he was a little white man. But big Black John Thompson was trying to intimidate when I simply spoke my mind.

I don't think some people were used to seeing an unapologetic Black man. Maybe they just didn't like it. Listen, when I believe something, I say it. I'm six feet ten inches tall. I have a large mouth, a big head, and a deep voice. I naturally make a big noise. Not only am I Black, but I have dark skin. My feet are big, my body is big. Sometimes I'm loud, but I'm loud because I'm composed of big things. I take up more space. Big people often get judged by their size instead of their mind, which is a disservice. I never went around trying to overpower people.

Hell, when I played, I was a finesse guy. As a kid, everybody thought I was soft.

I don't know if some people were intimidated by my intellect. I hope they were. I think they preferred to say I was a bully rather than say I was intelligent. But because I am large, because I am dark, because I made factual arguments that some people found uncomfortable, it was easier for them to define me as intimidating.

This double standard came from racist ideas about Black men. I knew it as surely as I knew the sun would come up the next day. But my team and I didn't have time to complain about it. We just used it as fuel for the fire and turned it into us against them. That's another thing people criticized me for, that I set up a "Georgetown against the world" mentality for our program. Listen, this is sports. We are trying to beat the other team. It is literally us against them.

We rolled through the 1982 Big East tournament and got a top seed out west for the NCAA tournament. The games were in Logan, Utah, but we stayed an hour away in Salt Lake City. Removing ourselves from the central location is something else I had always done. I thought when we got to the tournament, we would have a better chance of winning if we removed distractions like fans, parents, media, and the other teams. That's why I always liked when we got sent to the West or South region for the NCAAs. Frank Rienzo and I enjoyed finding out-of-the-way hotels in places like Snow Hill, North Carolina, or Goat Island, Rhode Island. Staying far from the action helped us get in the right frame of mind. The NCAA later made a rule, because of us, that required teams to stay within a certain distance of the game arena.

We easily handled Wyoming, Fresno State, and Oregon State. Maybe the games were so lopsided that the reporters needed to stir the pot, because a local Salt Lake City columnist called me "the Idi Amin of college basketball." Amin was a Ugandan dictator who killed hundreds of thousands of innocent people. I'm still trying to figure out who I'm supposed to have killed. Maybe Oregon State, because we beat them 69–45 to reach the Final Four.

As we made our way through the bracket, I saw Dean Smith over in the East winning his games and thought, *Uh-oh.* Both of us knew there was a good chance we would meet in the championship, which is exactly what happened. We didn't have any meaningful conversations during the tournament, but we spoke in passing at the media events at the Final Four. Dean told me, "We don't need to be out there hollering at each other." What he meant was that I would look bad if I yelled at him during the game. He thought I was capable of that, and for good reason, but I don't think I could ever have treated him that way.

The Final Four was in New Orleans, with games played in the Superdome. Our team stayed in Biloxi, Mississippi, ninety miles away. We beat Louisville in a sloppy semifinal game. The day before facing North Carolina in the finals, I mentioned at a press conference that earlier that season, someone had called the Georgetown switchboard and told the operator, "Please tell me Patrick Ewing's room number because I want to kill him."

They can talk about Hoya Paranoia all they want. It ain't paranoia if they're really out to get you.

Dean's team was a powerhouse. Michael Jordan was a freshman, but the star was James Worthy. That's two of the best players in NBA history. Their center was Sam Perkins, who played seventeen years in the NBA. Dean had been to six Final Fours, lost three times in the semifinals and three times in the championship. People said he couldn't win the big game. I always said, "You have to win a whole lot of big games to even get to losing the big game."

The difficulty with playing Dean was that I liked to generate some competitive dislike of my opponents. I searched for something about them to get myself fired up, but I couldn't do that with Dean. I tried to create something about people putting the Atlantic Coast Conference on a pedestal, or we won't let the name on their jersey beat us. My heart wasn't in it, though. Dean deserved to win a championship. But as we prepared to play them, I thought, *It doesn't have to be against me.*

I knew what Dean was going to do with his offense and defense. I didn't know when he was going to do it. One of the best things a coach can do is teach the opponent his offense. The opponent thinks they know what to expect. Then a good coach can put in a wrinkle to surprise the team that thinks they know what he's going to do. When you know that they know your offense, you can do things to fool them. Understand what I'm saying? There wasn't any play Dean could run that I didn't know. But Dean knew that I knew. That made me question what I thought he was going to do. Which left me back at square one.

We started the game in our full court press. Dean's team didn't turn the ball over much in the first half, but getting steals is not the only purpose of a press. We also used it to make them play at a slower pace, or to shorten the game. A lot of people evaluate the press on whether you steal the ball, but that's not the only thing that makes it successful.

Everybody was shocked when Patrick goaltended the ball five times at the beginning of the game. They acted like he was too hyped up or out of control. Not at all. Patrick was following my instructions. I told him, "Anything that comes near the rim, send it back at 'em! Block everything and don't worry about goaltending." My strategy was based on the fact that players want the satisfaction of driving into the lane and making a nice shot, so their ego gets involved when Patrick rejects everything, goaltend or not. Think about it: you have Worthy out there, Perkins, Michael fucking Jordan. That caliber of player won't miss a shot from in close, so if Patrick goaltends, what have we lost? Nothing. And the next time, they're thinking about where Patrick is. The strategy worked. We were right there with Carolina, and they were a truly great team. We were right there until we threw the ball away.

Worthy is who killed us. If you watch that game today, Michael Jordan is not yet Michael Jordan. He's not the player we remember who had the ball all the time and dominated everything about the game. Michael was a role player at that time. In that championship game, he scored 16 points mostly off offensive rebounds and putbacks. He didn't dribble around looking to shoot the ball like in the NBA. That's not how Dean's teams played, or mine either. Our players passed the ball until a good shot presented itself. Everything Worthy threw up that night was a good shot. He was the matchup problem: too big, quick, and strong against man-to-man defense, and when we went zone he made shots from the high post. If Patrick came up from the bottom of the zone to challenge him, Worthy made some great passes down low. He finished with 28 points on 13-of-17 shooting from the field.

As great as Carolina was, we still had them. Patrick played the game of his life: 10 for 15 from the field, made all three of his free throws, and finished with 23 points, 11 rebounds, two blocks, and zero turnovers. We led by a point at halftime and went back and forth the whole second half. Patrick hit a tough jumper with two minutes left, and we were down one. Dean went into his stall game, and since there was no shot clock, we trapped to try to force a turnover. Eric Smith almost stole the ball off Matt Doherty but got called for a foul. Doherty missed the front end of the one-and-one with about a minute left, and we got the rebound. Sleepy made a great move to fake Worthy off his feet and sink a double-pump jumper. We were up one with 53 seconds left.

I put my guys in a 2-3 zone. We couldn't play Worthy man-to-man in that situation. Dean called time-out with 32 seconds left and I was sure he was going to Worthy, probably in the high post. Sure enough, Worthy came up to the elbow. But they skipped a pass to Michael over on the left wing, and he let it go with no hesitation. *Swish.* We were down one with 16 seconds left.

Did Dean know that I thought he would give the ball to Worthy? In all our decades of friendship, we never spoke about the details of that game. Dean knew how painful it was for me, because he had been there so many times himself. But I think Dean knew I was focused on Worthy. Michael shot the ball as if he was expecting to get it.

That was the beginning of Michael's legend. All his NBA late-game heroics and last-second shots, he knew he could make those shots because he did it first against us. Over the years, Michael liked to tease me and say, "I got that shot because y'all were guarding Worthy." I'd tell Michael, "You got that right, motherfucker. Worthy was a number one draft pick, and you were just a skinny freshman."

We still should have won the game. I had one time-out left, but I didn't want to use it and give Dean a chance to set up. They were scrambling on defense. Sixteen seconds was plenty of time. Fred Brown brought the ball to the top of the key and started to pass to Eric Smith. Eric played great that game, he shot six for eight with 14 points. Worthy jumped out to steal the pass, but Fred held on to the ball. Worthy flew past Eric, and all of a sudden it was four-on-five. Sleepy was open, Patrick was open. Worthy had gambled and got stuck five feet beyond the top of the key, out of the play.

Then Freddy threw the ball to Worthy.

What do you think in that moment, with sixty-one thousand spectators in the Superdome and another twenty million watching on television? You don't think. You react, based on everything that you've experienced in your life up to that moment. You react based on heredity, environment, and time.

My mother loved me unconditionally. When I had the most trouble as a young person, she hugged me. After Freddy got confused and gave away the ball, after the buzzer sounded and we lost the national championship to North Carolina, 63–62, the first thing I did was hug Fred Brown. I hugged him tight.

Everybody made a big deal out of that, which I appreciate. But it was not a conscious decision on my part. It was my natural reaction, based on what I was taught by my parents, by Sametta Wallace Jackson, by Dr. Anita Hughes, and by many other people. I thank God that I reacted correctly, because I could have said or done something hurtful due to the emotions of the moment. I give my mother more credit for that hug than I give myself.

What's more amazing is that in the locker room afterward, Freddy's teammates accepted what happened. I'm in catechism books for the hug, but it's never discussed that the team was equally kind to him after the game. That was not easy for the team to do. Fred was somewhat antisocial, and while his teammates didn't dislike him, Fred was not a beloved person. Still, the players supported him in that difficult moment. We win together, we lose together. Fred's teammates worked incredibly hard that season, and they knew we could have beaten North Carolina. We should have beaten them.

When the game ended, before Dean celebrated with his team, he came over and gave me a hug. Then, as he walked away to congratulate his players, he looked back over his shoulder at me. Even in his moment of triumph, Dean was concerned about how I felt.

Later, Dean told me how well my team had played. His did too. It was one of the best championship games in NCAA history. Dean also told me the only reason Fred gave the ball away was that Worthy wasn't where he was supposed to be. I told Dean he taught me how to coach so he could beat me in the championship.

It hurt badly to lose that game, very badly. But not as much as if I had lost to somebody I hated.

11

THE MOUNTAINTOP

After my father died, my mother lived by herself for a while. She had gone back to school and earned her nursing degree, and while I was at Georgetown she worked in hospitals and other medical facilities. I used to pick her up from work, still dressed in her white nurse's uniform, and drive her to the house off Benning Road. She hardly ever came to my games. During the last few years of her life, she lived with me, Gwen, and our children. Toward the end she had dementia, and sometimes she called me Lewis, the name of my poet uncle, her brother. That made me happy and sad at the same time. My mother's bedroom was down the hall from ours, and each morning I peeked inside to see if she was all right. Gwen shouldered all the responsibility for taking care of her, which was a huge task, because I was always gone. I did bathe my mother once, and a few times I carried her in my arms.

As our season got under way in the fall of 1982, my mother got sick, then died in December, at age seventy-five. For the first time in my life, I could not focus on basketball. Sometimes I wondered why I was even coaching. That was the only time I questioned whether winning was important. I stepped away from the team for two games but found that I couldn't stay away any longer. The safest place I ever felt was in my mother's arms, and even though I was now wealthy, famous, and at the top of my profession, my mother's death left me feeling afraid and alone. I felt better when I returned to my team.

Billy Stein left before the start of the 1982–83 season to become the athletic director at St. Peter's University. I was happy for him and couldn't blame him for wanting to get off the recruiting trail and spend more time with his family. I hired three new assistant coaches that season: an experienced local guy named Eddie Meyers, and two of my former players—Craig Esherick, who had just received his law degree from Georgetown, and Mike Riley, who was teaching and coaching at Gonzaga High School in Washington. Craig and Mike stayed with me for the next seventeen years.

There was a lot of talk about Patrick Ewing entering the NBA draft after his freshman year. In those days, for a player to leave college before exhausting his eligibility, he had to make a "hardship" case that his family needed the money. Patrick's father was a manual laborer and his mother worked in the kitchen at a hospital. They absolutely needed the money, and as much as I wanted Patrick to remain at Georgetown, I had to be sensitive to their needs. I had a responsibility to communicate to them the value of their child. Mary Fenlon and I made a trip to Boston to speak to Patrick's parents in person.

We sat down at the same table where they had signed the letter of intent. I explained that if Patrick left—not that he should leave, let's be clear about that, but *if* he left—he could make about a million dollars per year. I explained that if he got injured, the money might never be there. I said he could return to Georgetown in the off-season to earn his degree. That's when Mrs. Ewing had enough. She banged her fist on the table and said, "Patrick will finish his education!"

You know what happened next. "Nice to see y'all," and I was gone.

Even with Patrick back, our team struggled. Sleepy, Eric Smith, Mike Hancock, and Ed Spriggs had graduated. Freshmen Michael Jackson, David Wingate, and Horace Broadnax needed time to develop. Fred Brown was coming back from knee surgery. We had a bull's-eye on our backs from going to the championship game the previous year.

I usually went easier on my players when we lost. I was taught to be careful about what I said immediately after a defeat, because it's easy to say something you will regret. The kids you're beating up are already deflated. I beat my team up when we won. That's when I could point out errors on film and the kids felt good anyway. You can be totally mad at a kid sometimes, but you have to suppress it because you're trying to get him to act. There's a difference between communicating with a person and motivating a person. Communication is when someone understands what you are saying. Motivation is when they act on it.

All of this was part of my teaching. My assistants and I set up chairs on the side of the practice court, and when I blew the whistle and motioned toward the chairs, the kids hustled over and waited for class to begin. I brought in visiting speakers, Black corporate executives who had nothing to do with sports, to give my players the examples of success that I was deprived of as a boy. "Far more money is made sitting down than standing up," I told them. I always hammered home the point that they had to make something more of themselves than as athletes, and the only way to do that was education. "You're not a basketball player," I told them. "You play basketball." During Black History Month, I gave them a two-hour lecture breaking down the legacies of Martin Luther King and Malcolm X. It might have been three hours, I don't know, I was on a roll. I encouraged them to question conventional wisdom. When I blew the whistle at practice, I might curse out Michael Jackson about the defense we were supposed to be running, or I might ask David Wingate, "What happened in Iran today?"

By this time, Georgetown and I had a sponsorship deal with Nike. One day, I saw Anthony Jones wearing another brand of sneakers. The next day at practice I pointed the kids to the chairs. They ran over and waited for me to say they could sit down. Sometimes I didn't let them sit down, but today I did.

Anthony's nickname was Red. "Hey Red," I began, "help me understand why you're wearing those other shoes."

He named some guy from the neighborhood who gave them to him. Anthony was one of the top high school recruits in the nation coming out of Dunbar, and a celebrity in the city before setting foot on Georgetown's campus.

"Do you know why he gave you those shoes?" I asked.

"Umm, not really. He's a nice guy."

"C'mon Red, you're smarter than that," I said, then turned my attention to the whole team. "You guys have to understand that you are extremely marketable. People are going to give you things to wear because you can influence sales of that product."

I yelled up to Fenlon, who was watching practice from the upstairs balcony. "Hey Mary! Go get my contract!"

I had told her I was planning this lesson, so she brought down the paperwork for my Nike deal. At this point I was Nike's highest-paid coach, making more than $100,000 per year from the company, on top of my Georgetown salary. I proceeded to explain to the players that Nike paid me, the coach, to have them, the players, wear the company's sneakers. I wore dress shoes to games, not Nikes, but I got the money. I was getting paid for their labor.

I let the kids marvel at the dollar figures for a minute, then hit them with the real lesson.

"Okay, now help me understand why none of y'all motherfuckers have asked me for any of this money."

And people wondered why I kept reporters out of practice.

WE WERE RANKED second in the country to start the season and won our first six games before facing No. 1 Virginia and their great senior center, Ralph Sampson, at the Capital Centre. Patrick was still the new kid on the block, and his matchup with Sampson got a lot of hype. After the sale of television rights and tickets, Georgetown got a healthy six-figure paycheck from the game. I personally made money on the game too, though not nearly as much as the school, through a clause written into my contract. I didn't do any of those big games without money involved, and I didn't consider that a sin, either. It was not a violation of any NCAA rule, and is a common practice for coaches today.

Virginia beat us, 68–63, and Sampson played well with 23 points. Patrick scored 16 and had one vicious dunk on Ralph that sent a shock wave out to the national TV audience. People thought Patrick's dunk was so intimidating, which aligned with the growing image of our team. Newspaper headlines called us things like THE BAD GUYS OF THE BIG EAST and THE TEAM YOU LOVE TO HATE. Even the TV commentary of our games took on a different tone. The broadcaster Billy Packer was a prime example. I like Billy a lot, he's a good guy who played at Wake Forest when they went to the Final Four. He coached in college before getting into broadcasting, and I remember him coming to gyms in Washington pushing his baby in a carriage, looking for players to recruit. But sometimes on television, Billy described our team as "rough" or "intimidating" and said the refs should call more fouls. Patrick would do something like sky for a rebound and Billy would exclaim, "What an intimidating rebound by Ewing!" When did it become intimidating to grab the ball? Well, a lot of referees watched the broadcast, and Billy was implying we were a bunch of hooligans who fouled all the time. That affected how the refs listening to Billy's commentary officiated our games. During one Big East tournament game, Billy was on TV talking about how the refs should call more fouls and we needed to be careful in the NCAAs. The very next game, the refs whistled us out of the arena.

Opposing teams reacted to this image too. They thought our intention was to punk them, so they played rougher than they normally would. I usually stayed in the locker room while our team warmed up, and I once heard the opposing coach talking to his players in the tunnel, telling them to hit us before we hit them. He didn't know I was listening. This coach hyped his players up to come at us with force, which made us play more physically than normal, but we were always portrayed as the ones who started it.

Other teams played us downright dirty. Especially against Patrick, because he was so dominant. His sophomore year, people absolutely mauled him. Several players blatantly tried to provoke him to fight, and Patrick gave a few of them what they wanted. The worst offender was a kid from St. John's who literally jumped on Patrick's back. Patrick punched him in the mouth and bloodied his lip. Overall, the situation got so bad, I told reporters that if the refs didn't start protecting Patrick, I'd make him leave for the NBA. Every time someone undercut him or slammed into his knees, he risked a career-ending injury. But when he retaliated, as any human being eventually would, people made him out to be the bad guy.

On the one hand, we had referees calling nonexistent fouls on us when we pressed or defended the perimeter. On the other hand, the referees let the other team beat Patrick to death. Okay, so be it. We had to be good enough to beat the cheat. That was the phrase we used, "beat the cheat." If they shoved one of us, we shoved back. If they cheap-shotted us, we retaliated. Yet a whole bunch of people who never played the game saw a Black team defending itself and called us thugs. I'm not saying we never overreacted to situations. We should have kept our cool better at certain times. But I never, ever instructed my team to fight anyone, or to instigate anything physical. I didn't have to tell them anything. They knew how to handle themselves. I didn't recruit kids because they liked to fight, but I knew they weren't going to lose the game on the bus ride to the arena. I'd rather calm down a fool than resurrect a corpse. What a lot of people didn't understand is that if you want to win, you cannot allow people to do certain things to you on a basketball court. If you permit yourself to be shoved, undercut, or cheap-shotted, and the refs are not calling those fouls, you have to defend yourself.

I have a close friend in Las Vegas who used to work for the mobster Meyer Lansky and did a few years in prison for him. My friend had a saying: "Sometimes you just have to let 'em know." Sometimes my team just had to let 'em know.

Some of the physical tactics they used against us was strategy, which is a part of sports. Patrick had special talents and got special attention.

But more often, people came at us overaggressively because of a false perception fueled by racist perceptions of a Black team. And when we refused to back down, or apologize, or play less aggressively to appease the critics, we were demonized. It's as simple as that.

What compounded the problem was racist abuse from fans. At one away game someone held up a sign that said EWING CAN'T READ. At another arena, there was a bedsheet printed with EWING IS AN APE and another sign that said EWING KANT READ DIS. They threw a banana peel on the court. Some of the signs were visible on television. People screamed all kinds of racist language, but the signs were hard evidence of the conditions we played under. I don't want to name the schools where these things happened, but they were supposedly religious institutions in the Big East. What really incensed me was that university administrators and NCAA officials were at those games but did nothing. They sat in the stands and let these racist attacks play out until I pulled my team off the court and made a fuss about it. Then I was the one who looked belligerent. The NCAA was waiting to punish me if I gave a kid a stick of bubble gum while bananas were flying at Patrick on the court.

Ultimately, it added fuel to our fire. Especially for Patrick, who responded by destroying those other teams. The racists thought they were helping their team win, but what they actually did was encourage one of the greatest players in the game to play at an even higher level. The abuse brought the whole team closer together and inspired everybody, including me. We became a family that took care of our own. I also realized that if I didn't become defensive about things, righteous people would defend me. But if I defended myself, it became an argument between pro and con. So when we were kicking ass and taking names, we didn't apologize for anything. The players started to embrace their image, like the Oakland Raiders. Some of them liked playing in hostile arenas more than at home, because they loved shutting up those crowds. Patrick's sophomore year, it truly became us against the world.

The world won that year. Fred Brown played only about half the season. We needed more experience. We lost to Syracuse 79–72 early in the Big East tournament, and then Memphis State beat us 66–57 in the second round of the 1983 NCAA tournament. But I didn't get too down. I knew what we had coming.

Some of the biggest contributors to my success were Black high school coaches who trusted me enough to let their players come to Georgetown. A lot of Black people at that time were conditioned to think that everything white was better, and to seek approval from whites in order to get ahead. The result was that some Black people discriminated against us too. We were conditioned to question the validity of our own people and institutions. We still are, to some extent. Why don't more of us put our money in a Black bank? Why don't we go to a Black hospital? Why don't today's top players attend historically Black colleges? When I got rolling at Georgetown, the most successful college basketball teams in the country were white schools coached by white men, and they still are. We missed a lot of prospects because their high school coaches told them that they should attend a "big-time school." I give Mike Jarvis, and Patrick's parents, a lot of credit for believing that I was the right coach. Jarvis, Joe Dean Davidson at Dunbar in Washington, Bob Wade at Dunbar High School in Baltimore—those guys sent a lot of great players my way.

Going into the 1983–84 season, Patrick's junior year, Bob Wade helped me sign one of the best players in the country, the high-scoring forward Reggie Williams. My other recruit was Michael Graham, a six-foot-nine big man who became one of the most memorable players at Georgetown. Reggie was smooth and skinny; Michael was rough and tough. Reggie had by far the better basketball career, but more people remember Michael, even though he played barely one full season.

Michael went to Spingarn, the Rabbit's school, around the corner from my old house on 19th Street. He tore up high school competition, and a lot of colleges recruited him, but he had a reputation as a problem child. His grades were terrible, he didn't go to class consistently, and he had a problematic family situation. His neighborhood was full of drugs and violence. When I went to his house on a recruiting visit, there was blood on the ground near his front porch. The electricity was off, and the family left the front door open to let the light in. Michael acted like a tough guy because that's what he needed to survive in his neighborhood. He was a big, strong kid, and he shaved his head a long time before it became fashionable. He needed that image around his way. You had to have a certain walk in those streets, wear your hat or clothes a certain way, have an attitude, in order not to be a target. If Michael had walked around with eyeglasses and a coat and tie, he would have got beat up every time he left the house.

Michael's character was spoken of poorly in Washington, but my nephew Eddie went to Spingarn with him and they were best friends. I asked Eddie what kind of kid Michael was, and if he would cause trouble if he came to Georgetown. Eddie said, "Uncle John, Michael is not like people think he is." When I finally got to speak with Michael, he was as nice and respectful as anybody you'd want to meet. He was intelligent and spoke well. After speaking with people from Spingarn, I believed he could do the work at Georgetown. I decided to try to get him admitted. Charlie Deacon was not enthusiastic, and I needed President Healy, the Big Irishman, to sign off. Michael took several summer courses and was tutored by a great educator and family friend named Jackie Waddy-Lewis. At the last minute, we got him into school and academically qualified to play.

The season began on a difficult note when Patrick's mother died of a heart attack, in September 1983. She was only fifty-five years old. Dorothy Ewing was the rock of that family. If it hadn't been for her bravery and sacrifices to bring her family over from Jamaica, we never would have known the name Patrick Ewing. We mostly kept her death secret from the media, because it would have been even more painful for Patrick to be asked questions about it all season long. Ralph Dalton's mother died around that time as well, and so did Craig Esherick's brother and David Wingate's mother. All of these personal tragedies brought our team closer together.

Anthony Jones had transferred to the University of Nevada, Las Vegas, but we had everybody else back. You should have seen our practices that fall. We had big fellas battling each other—Patrick, Michael

Graham, and Ralph Dalton. David Wingate, Reggie Williams, and Bill Martin were long and fast and could shoot and handle the ball. Michael Jackson was right up there with John Duren as the best point guard I ever had. Michael gave up a lot of his game to fit in with the team; he could have been a big-time scorer someplace else. Fred Brown was back from his injury, and he and Gene Smith were still two of the toughest defenders anywhere. Horace Broadnax was a tough, smart little point guard with a nice jump shot. You had six NBA draft picks on that team, and nobody gave an inch to anybody else in practice.

That team might have had the hardest time following my longstanding rule not to swing on the rim after dunks. I thought it was a stupid thing to do. Instead of getting focused and organized after scoring the basket, you're showing off and going against my concept of what a team is. Just continue to play. It's more acceptable today and doesn't bother me anymore, but back then I didn't tolerate it. Someone swung on the rim one day and I stopped practice. "That's nice, son," I said. "I saw a monkey in the zoo do the same thing too."

That was the year people started saying that the best team in the country was Georgetown, and the second-best team was Georgetown's bench. Sometimes we had to cut practice short because the bench was killing the starters. The bench guys didn't see themselves as being second-best, but they were unselfish enough to understand the value of winning.

Also, for the first time, my team was all Black. Our only white player, David Dunn, wanted to play closer to home and transferred to the University of Georgia, where he had a productive career. We had a whole lot of Black fans already, based on our success and me being the coach, but during this period we became Black America's favorite team. Black folks liked how we stood up for ourselves and refused to be apologetic about how we were perceived. Also, our community tends to rally around Black people who are subjected to racist attacks, so all those signs and biased newspaper articles garnered us more support. People from coast to coast wore Georgetown jackets, caps, and T-shirts. These items became a status symbol in Black neighborhoods, to the point where a kid was stabbed to death while being robbed for his Georgetown jacket inside a Baltimore junior high school. The jacket made it a national story because people wanted to tie my team to something violent, but I rejected that notion. Poor people committed robberies out of desperation and lack of opportunity, and when they did, they stole things of value. It didn't matter whether thieves saw value in a watch or a jacket. The real issue was, what made them want to steal in the first place? Not Georgetown's basketball team.

Black folks knew better than to fall for that line of thinking. I can't count how many Black people came up to me in airports and other public places to say, "Thank you for what you are doing." They weren't just talking about winning games. They were talking about how we represented ourselves as a group of proud, intelligent Black men who showed up wearing coats and ties, who graduated, who were faced with racism and overcame it. And yes, who also won a lot of games. More than a few people thought Georgetown was a historically Black college, based on our team. That always gave me a good feeling.

My relationship with Nike became important about this time. I had signed my first endorsement deal with the company in 1977, after having been told that they were paying college coaches to outfit their teams in Nike gear. I was an economics major, so you didn't have to tell me twice. I went out to the company's headquarters in Oregon and met with Nike founder Phil Knight and marketing chief Rob Strasser. To say they were small-time then would be generous. We met in a hotel room where they had clothing hanging up on racks, the kind with wheels that you can push down the street. I decided to work with them, mostly because I liked Phil. He had a lot of rebellious ideas, which appealed to that part of my nature. Plus, compared with companies like Adidas and Converse, who had all the big colleges, Nike was an underdog. That's how I felt too.

In the 1983–84 season, we wore custom gray and navy blue Nikes with HOYAS printed around the heel. This was before Michael's first

Air Jordan. Black kids were starting to make sneakers popular for fashion at that time. They loved Georgetown, and when they wore our shoes, it helped Nike establish the rebellious image it wanted to project.

It also helped that we played in the Big East, which had become one of the best conferences in the country. Aside from talent, we had characters and story lines. We had a mystique. It was Big John vs. Little Louie. Syracuse vs. Georgetown. Tough, physical, gritty games, similar to the cities we came from. Star players like Chris Mullin, Pearl Washington, Mark Jackson, and Michael Adams. Syracuse's Carrier Dome was the biggest college basketball arena in the country with more than thirty thousand seats. Television loved us. Dave Gavitt's brilliance was now obvious to everyone.

I used various starting lineups that season, depending on who was playing well, the opponent, and other factors. Our players were extremely unselfish and sacrificed points or playing time for the sake of the team. Not everybody was happy about it, but they were mature enough to handle it. It helped that Patrick didn't care about scoring all the points and always shared credit with his teammates.

I deliberately scheduled easy nonconference games at the start of the season. The Big East was tough enough, we didn't need to beat ourselves up before those games. We won some early games by 40, 50, and 60 points before losing by two at DePaul. We won the next eight games before Rollie Massimino and Villanova used a sagging zone that clogged the middle to beat us at our place in double overtime. Then came another ten-game winning streak. Teams tried everything against us. Boston College tried to run with us; we beat them 92–83. Providence slowed it down; they lost 59–38. We won the rematch against Villanova at the Spectrum in Philly, but we lost to St. John's, 75–71, when Chris Mullin had 33 points.

Mullin is the only player I ever told my guys to touch. We couldn't get him to stop shooting, and when Chris let it fly, you could take it to the bank. I told my guys, "When Mullin comes through the lane without the ball, make sure to show him some affection." But it didn't work that game, and Louie beat me at the Capital Centre.

Meanwhile, Michael Graham was in and out of the lineup because of academic problems. I suspended him outright for two games, because the boy didn't want to go to class. When he attended, he had no problem doing the work. He acted respectfully, didn't give us any back talk, he just did not like school. Graham's problem was he could not tune out what I described as the "Call of the Wild." He listened to his neighborhood calling him back: "Miiichaaael, Miiichaaael . . ." He couldn't stop hanging out with people who were detrimental to his future. I told him, "You are not like those kids in your neighborhood. You have an opportunity to change your life." But when he didn't listen and missed classes or assignments, he was not allowed to play.

Graham was portrayed in the press as a bad guy because he played for Georgetown, and because he played with an edge. He looked fierce with his shaved head. Off the court he was articulate and gave great interviews, but he played with a scowl and an attitude. He was the first person I heard use the term "game face." I would never call him dirty, just extremely aggressive and tough. If you pump-faked him into the air, he'd clobber you on the way down to prevent the and-one. If you shoved or swung at him, he swung back. He was not a bad person who tried to hurt people. He was the kind of player the other team hated to face. He played to win, not to look good. Reporters painted him as some sort of hardened criminal, but we laughed because he was scared to death of Mary Fenlon. If he saw her coming, he'd take off the other way. That's not what a thug would do. But that's what they called Graham, and the rest of us too.

As the Big East tournament approached, *Sports Illustrated* sent Curry Kirkpatrick to campus to write a Georgetown story. Curry already disliked us because the year before, he didn't get an interview with Patrick, and he felt entitled to everyone giving him what he wanted. Curry wrote thinly veiled racist stuff that white people at the time would deny was racist. As Curry came to campus, another *Sports*

Illustrated person went around asking students and administrators if I was a racist who didn't want white players on my all-Black team, and if alumni wanted me fired.

Here's the thing about the complexion of my teams: I recruited who I could get. I was born, raised, and coached in a majority Black city. I worked in a sport with mostly Black athletes. It was logical that my teams would be mostly Black. If I had been a hockey coach, my teams would have been white. When I came to Georgetown, I had no problem recruiting white players until people started telling white kids I was racist and wouldn't give them playing time. After a while, I knew that if I were a white player, I wouldn't come to Georgetown either. Think about it. Would I, as a Black parent, have sent my son to play down in Mississippi during Jim Crow? I wouldn't risk my son's future like that.

Based on the way I was falsely portrayed, to a white parent, I was Mississippi.

Something I always thought about was that I had more close white friends than most of the people who called me racist. People saw the public part of my life with an all-Black team, and they heard me tell the truth about the world as I saw it. But if I ever got in trouble, I could have more white people instantly come to my defense than the people who called me racist could get in a month.

Frank Rienzo found out what kind of questions *Sports Illustrated* was asking. We met with Curry in my office, and Rienzo got on the phone with the guys who ran the magazine. None of these discussions went well, to say the least. They acted like I had something to hide. That completely missed the point, which I did not feel obligated to explain to them. Curry went home without his story, and we went to New York for the Big East tournament.

We beat Providence and my old coach Joe Mullaney in the first round. I have to admit, it gave me some satisfaction to consistently beat him. Not because I had felt neglected when I played for him, but I enjoyed beating short guys. The stereotype is that guards are the thinkers on the team, and that leads to the perception that big men are not smart. I've played with some pretty dumb guards. Every time I beat a short guy, I considered it a step forward for the rights of big people who are stereotyped as stupid.

In the semifinals against St. John's, Mullin gave us 29 points despite all our affection, but we kept the rest of his team in check and won 79–68. That put us against Syracuse for the championship, in a sold-out Madison Square Garden.

Syracuse's star guard, Pearl Washington, had been phenomenal all season, and we couldn't stop him. He dribbled through our press and nobody could contain him one-on-one, not even Gene Smith, who was one of the best defenders in the country. Before the championship game, I told our team to back off Pearl and let him take jumpers, because he had the reputation of not being able to shoot. I'll be damned if he didn't make jump shots *and* slice up our defense on his way to 27 points and six assists.

Pearl had Syracuse ahead 57–54 with under four minutes left when Michael Graham grabbed an offensive rebound and missed the putback. Syracuse center Andre Hawkins came down with the ball, but Graham had his hands on it too. Hawkins had been taking shots at Graham all game, he was one of those guys who tried to prove to Georgetown how tough he was. Hawkins tried to rip the ball away and swung an elbow that glanced Graham on the chin. In the process, Hawkins lost his balance and stumbled backward, and at the same time Graham swung at Hawkins and missed. Hawkins fell down. The ref, Dick Bavaro, tossed Graham out of the game, but then the officials got together and Bavaro reversed his ejection. Instead of Syracuse having four free throws plus the ball, Hawkins hit two and we got the ball back, down five points.

As great as Pearl was, he didn't play defense, so we gave Michael Jackson the green light to go at him, which helped us cut into their lead. Michael tied the game with a jumper from the top of the key with 36 seconds left. Boeheim called time-out and tried to get the ball to Pearl, but Gene face-guarded Pearl and didn't let him catch it. The game went to overtime, and we won easily, 82–71. In the postgame press conference, Boeheim flipped out over the reversal of the call on Graham, then threw a chair as he left the podium. If I had thrown a chair, I would have left the Garden in handcuffs.

The next week, *Sports Illustrated* published a story about the Big East tournament that shows what we consistently had to deal with in a significant portion of the media. Fresh off his rejection on our campus, Curry Kirkpatrick pulled out all his racist tricks. His first sentence basically called our players stupid, apropos of nothing. In the second paragraph, he said our strategy was to "hit 'em while they're down." He criticized us for staying at a hotel in Harlem. He brought up the old intimidation business. After briefly praising me as a "surpassingly bright, deep, discerning and articulate fellow who genuinely cares about his players' academic attainments," he quoted Lou Carnesecca comparing my team to Nazis and another writer calling me "sick, paranoid, petty, pompous and arrogant." When I responded that Black people were tired of defending themselves against biased people, Curry accused me of wielding race "like a baseball bat." Even when I was just talking, he colored me violent.

Sports Illustrated had millions of readers and was the biggest sports outlet in the country. A lot of writers followed Curry around like he was royalty, and a lot of them echoed his biases in their own stories. Weak writers tried to mask their deficiencies by aligning themselves with a group. They said "John doesn't like the media." No, I talk to plenty of reporters, I just don't like *you*. I did appreciate what some people wrote about us, like John Schulz at the *Washington Star*. After Curry's hit piece, Schulz wrote a column that said, "Some people simply aren't ready to accept the fact that a Black man is smart enough and works long enough and sacrifices enough to reach the pinnacle of his profession." But that was one local story. Curry's narrative was already established as we entered the NCAA tournament as the top seed in the West region.

In the first round we played Southern Methodist in Pullman, Washington. Our hotel was right near the Seattle airport, but everybody thought we were staying in Canada. Our season almost ended in Pullman. SMU followed Villanova's playbook and used a sagging 2-3 zone to clog the middle, with big Jon Koncak at center. Our jump shots weren't falling and we trailed 24–16 at halftime. Then we clamped down on defense in the second half, took the lead with thirteen minutes left, and went into our stall game. I wanted to pull them out of their zone, but instead we made some mistakes and let SMU tie the game 34–34 with 51 seconds left. Gene Smith got fouled and went to the line for a one-and-one. I instructed the team to set up our press and told Patrick to go back and protect our basket.

Patrick ran over to me on the sideline and said, "Coach, Gene's gonna miss."

Gene was not a good free throw shooter. Patrick said, "Let me line up for the free throw, I'll get the rebound."

Thank God I listened to him. Gene missed the free throw, but Patrick somehow evaded the box-out and tapped in the rebound. We ended up winning 37–36. That play isn't talked about, but it saved our season. Michael Graham also played well that game, with eight rebounds, six points, and two assists. Michael didn't do much early in the season, he averaged less than five points and four rebounds. But he had a great tournament, which is why so many people remember him.

We won our next two games easily, against UNLV and Dayton, and advanced to the Final Four in Seattle. Before the semifinal against Kentucky, I called Michael Graham all kinds of bitches to get him ready for their front line of Sam Bowie and Mel Turpin. I told him things like "People think you're tough with those scars on your face. You must have been the one who got beat up!" That was some more of Red Auerbach's strategy. Patrick had foul trouble and spent most of the first half on the bench. Ralph Dalton played well in Patrick's place, and Graham wrecked Kentucky with six rebounds, three blocks, eight points, and great defense on Bowie and Turpin. We were down twelve points early in the second half, but I felt good about our chances. During a break in the action I spotted Curry Kirkpatrick sitting in the courtside media section and said hello just to mess with him. He looked over his shoulder because he thought I was talking to somebody else.

Once we made our move, we held Kentucky to 3-for-33 shooting the rest of the way and won 53–40. David Wingate killed the kid who was guarding him, blew past him over and over. But Graham is who really imposed his will on the game, in ways the stat sheet doesn't measure. Years later, I ran into one of the Kentucky players and he told me, "That bald-headed boy won y'all that game."

We would now face Houston and the great center Hakeem Olajuwon in the championship. This was the year after their Phi Slama Jama team with Clyde Drexler and Larry Micheaux, which lost to North Carolina State in the 1983 NCAA championship game. But they still had Alvin Franklin, Michael Young, and Rickie Winslow, with Benny Anders as their sixth man. I was concerned about their athleticism, which was equal to ours. I felt our depth was superior, even though Gene Smith had injured his foot against Kentucky and could not play. Our biggest challenge was how to contain Olajuwon's offense and deal with his shot-blocking ability. I told our guys to pump-fake him and try to draw fouls.

The Final Four is a national convention for the coaching profession, everybody is there. Before our game, while the players were warming up, a Black coach named Fred Snowden came down from the stands and stood near the tunnel that led to the referees' dressing room. Freddie the Fox was hired at Arizona in 1972, the year I got to Georgetown. I was told by a friend that Freddie stood near the tunnel and waited for the referees to come onto the floor. One of the refs in the championship game was a Black guy and a terrific official, Booker Turner. Freddie stood there and stared at Booker. Didn't say a word, just stared at Booker until the ref had no choice but to make eye contact. The unspoken message was: "Don't screw Thompson over tonight." Booker didn't give us any calls that night, but we didn't have to beat the cheat, either.

Before the game I paced back and forth in the locker room, the way I usually did. Patrick came over and said, "Don't worry about it, Coach, we're going to win you a national championship tonight." That's the kind of kid Patrick was. He said they would win it for me. I left the locker room before the players. While I was gone, Fenlon told them, "Look around this room." What she meant was, this is more than just a game for a Black team. You have a chance to do something unprecedented.

I put Ralph Dalton in the starting lineup, which was unusual, just to shake things up and counter Houston's physicality. The other starters were Patrick, Michael Jackson, Fred Brown, and David Wingate. My first subs were Michael Graham and Bill Martin, who would be starters on most other teams, and then we came with Reggie Williams and Horace Broadnax. I had some players that year, man. We rolled deep.

We didn't press Houston much, or go out of our way to run with them. People liked to make a big deal about how fast we played, but that depended on the situation. Houston played a 2-3 zone, so we moved the ball and took open shots. We played a controlled, patient, organized game. We played Georgetown basketball. Everyone played unselfishly for the good of the team. Watching the Houston game today, you might think it was boring. Not to me, though. To me, it was an expression of our excellence.

With a few minutes left in the first half, David Wingate pump-faked Olajuwon, drew the foul, and scored the basket. That was Olajuwon's third foul, and he had to come out of the game. At halftime we were up ten, and although they scared us at times in the second half, we led the rest of the way. Patrick, Ralph, and Graham controlled the lane and held Olajuwon to 15 points. With Houston focusing so much attention on Patrick, Graham scored 14 off the bench. Patrick even threw him an alley-oop at one point. Reggie led us with 19 points and won the MVP. Fred Brown grabbed several crucial rebounds. All ten of our players contributed something to the win, even Gene, who stood the entire game on his injured foot and cheered on his teammates.

In the last few minutes of the game, when I could see the light at the end of the tunnel, I saw Dave Gavitt behind the scorer's table. I slid over and said, "How about the Big East now?"

When the buzzer sounded, I made a beeline for Fred Brown. It was the last game of his college career. This time, our hug was joyful. Dean Smith came onto the court and we slapped hands. I waved at Gwen, who was sitting with John and Ronny a few rows behind our bench.

When it was time to walk off the floor, I caught my sons' attention and did a little Michael Jackson moonwalk.

Just because we won didn't mean some of the media treated us any better. When they interviewed Reggie Williams on live television in the moments after the game, he got tongue-tied. He was trying to say that it had been a difficult year because of all his teammates' mothers who died, as well as Craig Esherick's brother. Commentators tried to say Reggie was stupid and went back to that whole thing about our players not deserving to attend Georgetown. They ignored that Georgetown is an educational institution, where kids are supposed to learn how to handle different situations, including interviews. Kids come to college to make mistakes and learn from them. Don't throw that judgment on a shy freshman who's thrust onto live television and gets nervous. I've seen a lot of inarticulate writers, too. Ask a college professor or a business executive to do a live, off-the-cuff TV interview, and a lot of them would stammer. But what happened to Reggie is part of the value and beauty of sports. It exposes you to things that will happen in the rest of your life.

My main emotion upon winning was relief. The monkey was off my back. Now that I had won a championship, I could admit I had been obsessed with it. I had won championships in high school, at Providence College, with the Celtics, and in the Olympics, so I burned to win one at Georgetown. I wanted it selfishly, probably to the detriment of other parts of my life. At the same time, I knew I only had to win one. I didn't have to be John Wooden. All it took was one championship to destroy the notion that we were not intelligent enough to do it.

At the postgame press conference, I was predictably asked what it felt like to be the first Black coach to win it all. I responded that the question was insulting, because it implied that Black coaches before me had not been good enough to win a championship. The only reason I was the first Black coach to win one is because I was the first Black coach afforded the opportunity to do so. The great coaches who came before me at the historically Black colleges, guys like Clarence "Big House" Gaines, John McLendon, and Cal Irvin, they all had more than enough ability to win a championship. They invented and innovated a lot of modern basketball, but they were not permitted to compete on an equal level. So don't expect me to be grateful for being the first Black championship coach. I'm still thinking about all of us who were not permitted to win.

One day I was someplace fussing or arguing about something, and Cal Irvin from North Carolina A&T was there. When I was growing up, he was a legend in my neighborhood because A&T was a Black college with great teams and the white schools didn't usually recruit us.

Coach Irvin came up to me and said, "Boy, where'd you go to college?"

I said, "Providence. Why?"

"Really?" Coach Irvin said. "You sound like you came from one of our schools."

That meant a lot to me, that he thought I went to a Black school. And I did.

That school was called life.

12

BET THE JOCKEY, NOT THE HORSE

After we won the NCAA championship, Michael Graham still wouldn't go to class, so I had to put him out of school. We worked with him all spring and summer, and I warned him again and again: "If you don't handle your schoolwork, you'll be gone." He didn't, so he had to go. Even the president of the school, Father Healy, urged me to keep him, but I felt it would be wrong to compromise just because Michael had helped us win a title. I didn't want to become what I professed I was not. I blamed myself for a lot of Michael's failure, because I wasn't able to work with him in a way he responded to. My biggest frustration was that he had more than enough intelligence to graduate, but I couldn't blow that spark so it became a flame. I was glad when some players were gone, but not him. Michael was not unpleasant to be around. He was his own worst enemy. Our relationship became closer years later, although I find it interesting that he acts like an alumnus. In 2013, he hit the lottery for a million dollars and brought the ticket to me here at school. I kept it in my office safe for a few weeks.

Patrick won a gold medal that summer with the 1984 Olympic basketball team, coached by Bobby Knight. I respected Bobby, and by this point we were friends. We also had to make a decision about whether

Patrick would return for his senior year or turn professional. In that era, it was rare for players to leave college early. Even Michael Jordan stayed in college for three years. Patrick wanted to come back, and he told me one day, "Coach, you know I can't leave you without a center." But I felt a responsibility to make sure he was doing the right thing, and I was concerned about protecting Patrick from my own selfish desire for him to play one more season.

I picked up the telephone and called my lawyer, David Falk, who was another diamond I found in the rough. In the early 1970s, Falk was working for a firm in Washington called ProServ that was owned by Donald Dell and Lee Fentress. ProServ represented players from big-time schools like Kentucky, UCLA, Maryland, and North Carolina. Dean Smith was tight with ProServ, because Dean had the best of everything. Falk was a junior associate and basically a nobody, but my old friend from Boston Harold Furash was friends with Falk's father-in-law. Furash told me I should connect with this young guy Falk who was scuffling around like me. When Bay Bay and Craig Shelton were about to get drafted, Dean urged me to go with ProServ. But I perceived Dell and Fentress as being part of the white establishment, which I subconsciously considered to be racist. If it hadn't been for Dean, Donald Dell probably wouldn't have even wanted to speak to me, or so I thought. Falk was a thirty-one-year-old Jewish guy, and he represented the Black tennis champion Arthur Ashe, so I decided to go with the underdog. Falk did a good job with Bay Bay, Craig, and then Sleepy. When Nike started offering coaches stock options in our contracts, I invited Falk to lunch and asked his opinion. He said, "I'd love to help you with all this, but ProServ has a policy against representing coaches." They thought it would prevent them from signing players out of other schools. As soon as I heard there was a policy against it, I wanted it. "I don't give a damn about your policy," I said. "Do you want to help me or not?" He was tongue-tied for probably the first and last time in his life. That's how David Falk became my lawyer. He still is, and we have become close personal friends.

I asked Falk what he thought about Patrick going pro. He said that it would be a bad idea. Normally an agent wants the kid to go pro as soon as possible, so he can start making money. Falk didn't think selfishly, which was one reason I liked him. Falk said Patrick's mother had wanted him to graduate. He said the Houston Rockets had the first pick and were a lock to draft the hometown hero Hakeem Olajuwon. The highest Patrick could go was second, to Portland.

I said, "If Patrick makes a million dollars per year, he can pay for as much education as he wants. What does it matter if he's drafted second?" Ralph Sampson made about a million when he was drafted No. 1 the year before, and everybody knew Patrick was as good as Ralph, if not better.

We argued back and forth for a while, and I started to get frustrated.

"I thought you were my friend, David, but you're telling me what you think I want to hear, and you're wrong," I said. "I don't want Patrick to come back."

The reality was that I felt an enormous amount of pressure to tell Patrick to leave for the NBA. I knew lots of things could go wrong over the next year that could cost Patrick a lot of money, and I felt he should capitalize on the opportunity he had at that moment. If Patrick came back and something derailed his pro career, it would be my fault. It was stressful because I had a lot of influence over the decision, and I worried that my own self-interest would cloud my judgment.

The conversation with Falk got heated, but it was backwards. The coach was arguing for a great player to leave for the NBA, and the agent was arguing for him to stay in school.

In the end, I decided that Patrick could come back and graduate. That's what he wanted to do, and his mother had made it clear that she wanted him to receive his diploma. I didn't have the right to override her wishes.

When the season started in November 1984, *Sports Illustrated* put us on the cover. The magazine replaced Curry Kirkpatrick with an outside writer, the Black author John Edgar Wideman, who had played college basketball and was well known for his stories about Black life. I got along well with Wideman and liked his story, but the cover photo was my favorite part of that experience. They arranged to photograph Patrick and me with President Ronald Reagan, each of us holding a basketball. Falk had negotiated me a nice five-figure sponsorship deal with the Wilson basketball brand. I told Falk to ask Wilson how much it would be worth for its brand name to appear on the cover of *Sports Illustrated*. While they were setting up the photo, I kept subtly turning the basketball so the name Wilson would be in the picture. Reagan realized what was going on and kept moving his ball to hide the name. I laughed about that and kept on doing what I was doing. The photographer tried to get me to turn my ball around, but in the end mine was the only ball with the logo front and center.

As we began our title defense, Fred Brown and Gene Smith had graduated, but we added the freshmen Perry McDonald, Ronnie Highsmith, and Grady Mateen. Alongside Patrick in the starting lineup I had Reggie Williams, David Wingate, Bill Martin, and Michael Jackson, with Ralph Dalton and Horace Broadnax off the bench. Our team was still all Black.

We went to Puerto Rico for a tournament before the Big East season began, and I used my leverage to include Tennessee State and North Carolina A&T. That might have been the first time historically Black colleges played basketball on national television. I always scheduled Black colleges, as a way of giving back to schools that did not have equal opportunities. I did have winning in mind, of course, but I could have beaten a lot of white schools easily, too. When I put Black schools on our schedule, it gave them more money and exposure.

Before integration, Black athletes were discriminated against and Black schools were powerhouses because of it. White schools didn't want to play John McLendon's team at Tennessee State back then. Growing up, I wanted to play for Coach Mac, because that's who I heard about under the tree at the playground. But people encouraged me to go to a white school because I could get more exposure and recognition there. A white school was perceived as the best way to get ahead and make more money, both in basketball and in society. It will be interesting to see what happens now that some of the best high school players are skipping college. They're choosing money over the white schools, the same way we chose white schools over Black. It's the same principle.

After they let us into the white schools and took our best players, they said those same Black schools were inferior and made it hard for them to get into tournaments or receive a high NCAA bid. The only reason those schools struggled athletically was because of integration. They paved the way for Black athletes, and I put them on my schedule to give them the respect and recognition they deserved. Maybe a little too much recognition, because after we beat Tennessee State in Puerto Rico, North Carolina A&T gave us a tough game before we pulled it out, 61–56.

We had a new sports information director, and he underwent a trial by fire because the animosity directed at us would reach an all-time high that year. I found Bill Shapland working in the equipment room at McDonough. He was the guy who gave out towels, socks, and whatever else to players from all the Georgetown teams. I got to know him a little bit when he asked me for a letter of recommendation for a job at Amtrak. Shapland had graduated from Georgetown and was studying toward a master's degree in English literature. I liked his humility, but he wasn't a weak person. When I hassled him about equipment, he stood up for himself, so I knew he could stand up to reporters. He didn't have a lick of experience or even the desire to be sports information director, but he was smart, and he could write. When the sports information job came open, you should have seen Frank Rienzo's face when I told him I wanted to hire the kid out of the equipment room.

Shapland turned out to be one of the most valuable members of the athletic department, and he stayed there longer than I did. I called him Big Willie. He protected me from a lot of media nonsense that would otherwise have distracted or angered me. He took a lot of heat for the decisions that I made, and he did it selflessly. He also wrote books and worked in the theater, but I thought some of the best things he ever wrote had my name on them, not his. People paid me for columns that Big Willie wrote.

I always said, "It's not what you know, it's who you find that does know." People like to say John Thompson did this or that because I selected the players. But far more significant was selecting the staff. Buildings and equipment don't win ball games, people do. I was extremely lucky to have people like Shapland, Bill Stein, our first sports information director Fran Connors, Frank Rienzo, Mary Fenlon, Lorry Michel, Craig Esherick, Mike Riley, Brian McGuire—they rolled up their sleeves and fought alongside me.

As we proceeded to run our record to 18–0, we became Goliath, and everybody we played wanted to be David. I had dealt with plenty of vicious boos in my career; you should have heard the Philadelphia crowd when Red's Celtics came to town. But the type of booing our team received that year had a different edge, and it was directed at college students. People booed us off the court after we won. Bands in opposing arenas played the Darth Vader theme music when I walked by. Newspaper stories about me used words like "monster," "ogre," "executioner," and "Hoyatollah."

This was the peak of what had been building up for a long time with our team. At first we were intimidating, then scary, then dirty. When we became champions, they couldn't minimize our ability anymore, so we had to become evil. I think they called us those names to avoid saying we were smart.

People told me all the time, "You don't scare me." What was that really about? I didn't have a Halloween mask on. I never physically attacked another person. I was a mama's boy. I was scared to play football back in the projects because when the helmets clashed, I thought bones were breaking. I never tried to scare anyone, but I brought me with me wherever I went, and I'm a large Black man with strong beliefs that I am not reluctant to express. As God is my witness, I never intended to frighten, intimidate, or physically overpower anyone when I got angry or loud. I was simply exercising my right to behave the same way other coaches behaved, in pursuit of an edge or motivational tactic. If I argued with someone and towered over them, that didn't have anything to do with trying to scare them. It had to do with me being six foot ten. Was I supposed to get down on my knees? Sure, sometimes I lost my temper, but I didn't threaten anybody with violence. I was passionate about my profession and trying to win the argument. The only reason to believe or imply I wanted to intimidate somebody was because of my size and color.

To this day, big Black people don't get jobs because of those kinds of stereotypes, because of people's fear of our physical appearance. It's amazing how few centers from the NBA have ever gotten an opportunity to coach.

Every Big East game in those days was a war. I hated playing at Providence, because I went to school there and wanted them to do well when I wasn't playing them, so I was caught in a psychological trap. I also hated playing at Seton Hall, because they were very good under their coach, P. J. Carlesimo, but people expected us to kill them. That kind of situation makes a coach apprehensive. It was easy to get motivated for Syracuse, and even though they had the huge crowd that threw oranges and said nasty things, I loved that atmosphere. I loved playing at Syracuse the same way I loved going to New York. It didn't get any more big-time than Madison Square Garden. I could fuss with the fans, people there knew the game, the tabloids went wild, and the competition was outstanding. A lot of Big East games matched or exceeded the intensity of a playoff game seven with the Celtics. And when we played at the Garden, it felt like the whole city came to a halt. My teams usually played well in New York.

As much as I feuded with the other Big East coaches, especially Jim Boeheim, I secretly thought of them as family. We were establishing our league against the big-time conferences, and we had fantastic coaches with distinctive personalities, but I could not publicly acknowledge my respect in any way. When Nike started having a retreat for all their coaches in the summer, flying guys and their families out to luxurious resorts, I was the only coach who didn't attend. I didn't want that kind of relationship with my rivals. Phil Knight asked me why I wouldn't go, and I told him, "When you go to a picnic with Adidas and Converse, I'll hang out with Boeheim and Massimino." That's how I was taught.

Bill Russell loved Elgin Baylor, but when Elgin tried to shake Russ's hand before the tip-off, Russ acted like Rabbit wasn't even there. But despite all the competitive anger between us, there also was camaraderie. We wanted to prove that the Northeast could compete. I always resented the fact that when they said I was the first African American to win a national championship, they never mentioned I was the first anybody from the Northeast to win a championship in thirty years.

Although we won eighteen straight to begin the 1984–85 season, we had some close calls. Boston College took us to overtime before we won 82–80. In both of our regular season games against Villanova we were losing at halftime, and we needed overtime to beat them 52–50 at the Spectrum. In January, after winning twenty-nine games in a row going back to the previous season, we lost two straight, to St. John's and Syracuse. That set up a rematch with St. John's late in the regular season, in New York City, at the Garden.

We were ranked second in the country. St. John's was No. 1 and had won nineteen games in a row, including their victory against us. They had Chris Mullin, a senior and one of the best players in America; Mark Jackson, who would become an outstanding NBA point guard; center Bill Wennington, who would have a productive NBA career; and six-foot-eight freshman Walter Berry, who was ahead of his time in terms of being a tall guy who could dribble and shoot like a guard.

Lou Carnesecca had worn this ugly sweater during his winning streak, and the media made it into a big thing. It was brown, with a big red, blue, and green V on the front. Everybody loved Louie's "lucky sweater," and he milked it for all it was worth. I grumbled publicly about it but thought to myself that it was great marketing. Louie was one of the coaches who had recruited me out of high school, and I liked him.

Mary Fenlon and I were talking about Louie's sweater, and we came up with an idea. When I came onto the Garden floor before the game, I kept my jacket buttoned up high. Louie came out and sat on his bench. I walked over and opened my jacket real wide. I was wearing the exact same ugly sweater as Louie.

I told him, "That lucky sweater is bullshit. I got one, too."

Man, the fans went crazy when they saw the sweater. I hadn't anticipated that reaction, because I was just messing with Louie. Then the camera people chased after me and asked me to open my jacket again for TV. When I did, the entire Garden caught on. The fans were there to see us get our ass kicked, but New York loves somebody who can dish it out, and the crowd went absolutely wild. The whole thing deflated the anger that was in the building, not street anger but competitive anger. That's what the Big East was in those days. We fought one another, and we loved one another, too.

What made the whole thing even better is we whipped their ass, 85–69, in what is now remembered as "the sweater game." It's one of my favorite moments. If you can make it in New York, you can make it anywhere. That game, we made it in New York.

The next week, we crushed Syracuse at home, 90–63, and reclaimed the top spot in the national rankings. But then we had to play St. John's and Syracuse again in the Big East tournament. Louie came out for our game with a ridiculously long towel draped over his shoulder, but it was too late. I got him first. We won both of those games, but they were close. The Big East was a monster, with all-time great players from top to bottom.

Although we entered the NCAA tournament as the top overall seed, people didn't realize how close some of our victories had been. People still treated us like Goliath. We ran over Lehigh in the first round of the tournament, which set up a game against Temple, coached by my good friend John Chaney. He was the only Black coach crazier than me in terms of going after white people. We beat Temple 68–46, then had two closer victories, over Loyola and Georgia Tech. Loyola almost beat us, but Ralph Dalton made two free throws with 14 seconds left that sent us back to the Final Four.

The Final Four that year was at Lexington, Kentucky, in the arena named after Adolph Rupp, the coaching legend who did not sign Black players until he lost the 1966 national championship to the all-Black starting five of Texas Western. Our team stayed in Louisville, eighty miles away. Three of the Final Four teams were from the Big East: Georgetown, St. John's, and Villanova.

I didn't like three Big East teams making the Final Four, because the Georgetown reputation didn't faze them. When we played some school from across the country that was supposed to be Top 20, we could throw our jerseys out there and scare them to death. Schools in the Big East would throw it back and say, "Fuck that. You got to beat us."

In the semifinals, we played St. John's for the fourth time that season. We ran a box-and-one on Mullin, held him to 8 points, and blew them out, 77–59. We would have to beat Villanova for a third time that season to win the championship.

Villanova had lost ten games and barely squeaked into the tournament, probably because the field had expanded to sixty-four teams. People thought they wouldn't get far, but I knew how smart a coach Rollie Massimino was. Before the tournament, when people asked me about Villanova, I said, "Bet the jockey, not the horse."

The Big East used a shot clock for the first time that season. I hated it. It reduced the strategy and intelligence of coaching to cater to the entertainment of people who did not know the game. Without a shot clock, I could exploit your weaknesses. I could make you come out and play me. You're not going to hide against my talent. If my best players were in foul trouble, I could stall and shorten the game. If I saw your stars at the table waiting to check back into the game, I could hold the ball. Playing patient basketball may have been boring to the average fan, but it made the cerebral aspect of coaching much more interesting.

In the 1985 NCAA tournament, though, there was no shot clock, because some conferences had not yet adopted it. Rollie was great without a shot clock. In the Southeast regional final, against Dean Smith and his North Carolina team featuring Brad Daugherty and Kenny Smith, Rollie's team got a lead midway through the second half and ran out the clock on them. Rollie was a helluva jockey. I don't understand why he's not in the Hall of Fame.

Of course the media went to town with the David vs. Goliath angle. IT WILL TAKE A DIVINE INTERVENTION TO STOP GEORGETOWN, said one headline. It was Big John Thompson vs. five-foot-eight Rollie. The giant Patrick Ewing against Ed Pinckney. The Hoya Destroyas bullying a bunch of nice boys from Philadelphia's Main Line.

One of their nice fans threw a banana onto the court when Patrick was introduced, but we were long past letting that bother us. Our team was focused and ready. Villanova played us the same way they did during the regular season, with a tight zone and the guards sagging back on Patrick in the lane. From the start, everything Villanova threw up seemed to go in. They made nine of their first ten shots, but we stayed close because our pressure forced some turnovers. Then Villanova settled down. Pinckney was a tough senior from the Bronx who had played on the same high school team as Fred Brown and had gone toe to toe with Patrick for four years. Harold Pressley and Dwayne McClain were talented. Their senior point guard, Gary McLain, handled our pressure better as the game went on.

Not long after that game, I read in *Sports Illustrated* that Gary McLain said he had been high on cocaine while playing in the Final Four. McLain also said he had used and sold drugs while at Villanova, that some of his teammates also used drugs, and that Rollie was told about his illegal activities but did not take action. I kept quiet about it for the past thirty-five years, because I respect Rollie and I don't want to diminish his team's accomplishments, which were well deserved. But I can say now that I am disturbed by how the drug use seemed to be swept aside and basically ignored. If this was the NBA, Major League Baseball, or the Olympics, one or more of their starters could have been disqualified. The NCAA is supposed to enforce these rules, but it never announced any investigation. The fact that it didn't even investigate what McLain admitted to doing feels like a tremendous disservice to my kids who played their hearts out. I had to wonder if drugs made it easier for McLain and whoever else might have been using to perform. McLain said that he generally played better while high. Drugs are outlawed in sports for a reason, because they can provide a competitive edge, and those rules should be enforced. Rollie did not deny being told that McLain was involved with drugs. That said, I'm not sure what I would have done in Rollie's shoes, beyond getting McLain some counseling. I've kicked some kids off my team for using marijuana, and other kids I gave another chance. It all depends on the situation.

With two minutes left in the first half against Villanova, Pinckney sat on the bench with two fouls. Villanova had the ball down one, and Rollie went into his stall. We were winning, so I kept us back in our zone and let Rollie run the clock down. Pressley missed a shot with five seconds left but rebounded his own miss and put them up one at halftime. No big deal, we had been down at the half in both games that season and come back to win each time.

But Patrick got whistled for three fouls in the first few minutes of the second half, and I had to sub him out. Patrick didn't shoot a single foul shot that game, by the way. We took eight foul shots as a team and made six. They took twenty-seven free throws and made twenty-two.

Villanova went up five, then our press turned them over a few times and we took a one-point lead with 4:35 to play. I went into our delay, but an unforced error gave them the ball. Villanova made yet another jumper—they shot 90 percent from the field in the second half, and 79 percent for the game—to take a 55–54 lead with two and a half minutes left.

That was it. We never got the lead back. Villanova won the national championship, 66–64.

As Villanova celebrated on the court, and what seemed like the entire stadium cheered for them, I didn't plan or think about my actions. Like in my other two championship games, I reacted instinctively, based on heredity, environment, and time. I told my team that we would remain on the court for the trophy ceremony. We did not retreat to the locker room with our tails between our legs. We had nothing to be ashamed of. We shot 55 percent from the field and 75 percent from the free throw line. We had more rebounds and fewer turnovers than Villanova. Villanova missed only six shots all night, against one of the best defensive teams I ever coached. Whether you want to call it luck, divine intervention, or the ghost of Adolph Rupp, Villanova beat us.

I always planned to be a teacher, not a basketball coach. I used basketball as an instrument to teach. My classroom was the court. This time, instead of the tiny gym at St. Anthony's or the McDonough practice floor at Georgetown, my classroom was Rupp Arena, with twenty-three thousand fans rooting against us and thirty million more watching on television. Losing is part of sports, an opportunity for the type of informal education that college athletics is supposed to be about. We stood in front of our bench and applauded Villanova as they accepted the championship trophy that should have been ours.

My biggest regret is that it was the last game of Patrick's college career. It hurts that I couldn't give him another championship, because nobody deserved it more. I mean that literally. Think about all the abuse he endured, from the moment he announced he would attend Georgetown to the banana that greeted him in our final game. People called him stupid, ugly, a brute, an ape. Patrick still played his heart out, and when the games ended, he was the most considerate, thoughtful person you could find. You never would have guessed he was a superstar by the way he acted. This boy had the most leverage over me of any player I ever coached, and he used it the least.

There's something else that a lot of people overlook: before Patrick, no athlete of his stature had chosen to play for a Black coach. That's one of the reasons I love his mother and father, because they could have stopped him. Patrick made it safe for generations of Black athletes to play for Black coaches. We should never forget that.

If anybody asks me who's the greatest player in Georgetown history, I'm going to say Patrick Ewing. That is my sincere belief, based on how he played, the character he displayed, and what he did for the program. But if another player came to Georgetown who I thought was better than Patrick, I would lie and still say Patrick is the greatest. I love him that much.

The pain of losing a game like the 1985 championship never leaves you, although it does fade over time. I wouldn't do anything differently, though. If somebody has to shoot 79 percent from the field to beat us by two points, I've done all I can do.

13

SOMETIMES THE LION KILLS YOU

None of my worries came true about Patrick staying for his senior year. He was picked first by the New York Knicks in the 1985 NBA draft. Back then there was no set salary for draft picks, and David Falk negotiated a contract for Patrick worth about $3 million a year over ten years. That was triple what Olajuwon got the year before, the most ever for a rookie, and the highest salary in the NBA. Best of all, Patrick graduated with a degree in fine art. We made his mother proud.

Even without Patrick, we were still among the top-ranked teams in the nation in 1985–86. Reggie Williams was a junior and took over as our go-to scorer. Our seniors were David Wingate, Michael Jackson, Ralph Dalton, and Horace Broadnax. The sophomores were Perry McDonald, a former Golden Gloves boxer from New Orleans, and Ronnie Highsmith, another kid from off the beaten track I found on a military base in Virginia. My New Orleans connection was going strong and I had two freshmen from there: Johnathan Edwards, whose career was held back by an injury, and Jaren Jackson.

Jaren really made himself into something, more than any of my other players. He was a six-foot-four guard who barely played his first two seasons, became a starter as a senior, then didn't get drafted. He played in the minor leagues and overseas before getting a shot in the NBA, where he had a great career, including a championship with the San Antonio Spurs in 1999. Jaren never asked me or Falk for help getting into the NBA, he did it all himself. I have a lot of respect for what Jaren did.

My final freshman that year was an afterthought named Charles Smith. He played for All Saints High School in Washington, which was the new name for St. Anthony's, my old school. Charles was coached by my first Georgetown recruit, Aaron Long, who told me Charles was better than people thought he was. Seton Hall had backed out of a scholarship offer and nobody else wanted him. I went to watch Charles play, and saw a kid just six feet tall and maybe 160 pounds after Thanksgiving dinner. I thought he was way too small for the Big East. But people kept bothering me about Charles, and since I had an extra spot in 1985, I decided to give it to him. I told his mother not to complain when Charles didn't play.

For some reason, Mary Fenlon took a liking to Charles, who everybody called Smitty. As expected, he hardly ever played, but Fenlon always asked me, "What about Charles?" I would tell her to shut the hell up and stop acting like she knew something about basketball.

At the end of the season, we lost to Michigan State in the second round of the NCAAs. The next year, with Reggie Williams as a senior, we kept coming back from double-digit deficits to win games, and people started calling us Reggie and the Miracles. We won the 1987 Big East tournament and got a top seed in the NCAAs, beat Bucknell in the first round, then got ourselves in a bind against Ohio State. We were losing by 15 points in the second half when one of my starting guards, Dwayne Bryant, picked up his fourth foul. I had nobody left to replace him, so I threw Charles in as a last resort. Smitty went completely off, scoring from everywhere on the court, hitting shots he had no business taking, let alone making. At the end of the game I specifically told him not to shoot the ball. Smitty shot it anyway, made the basket that won the game, and finished with 22 points.

Fenlon hustled back to the locker room and waited for me in the doorway. When I walked past she said, "What about Charles now?"

We beat Kansas to make it to the Elite Eight, then lost to Providence, where Rick Pitino was in his second year as coach. Our "Reggie and the Miracles" season came to an end. Reggie graduated and was the fourth pick in the 1987 NBA draft.

Little Smitty then became our go-to guy, averaging 16 points per game his junior year. He made more game-winning shots than anybody who ever played at Georgetown, including Patrick Ewing and Allen Iverson. Up at Syracuse, he took the ball the length of the court with seven seconds left and made an underhanded flip shot at the buzzer for a one-point win. Charles took game-winning shots when everybody in the gym knew he was going to shoot, and he made them anyway.

We had a couple of brawls that season against Pittsburgh. The bad blood went back a few years, to when one of the Pitt guys used an Ace bandage clip like a razor blade to cut one of my players. The fights were not instigated by us, but we didn't back down, and we knew how to handle ourselves. Our former boxer, Perry McDonald, hit one Pitt kid three times before he felt the first punch. Another time Perry just raised his hands into a boxing stance and the Pitt kid took off running. But in all seriousness, the whole Big East was extremely physical then, and the fights were a problem. They led to the NCAA passing a rule that suspended any player who left the bench or threw a punch on the court. People called it the Georgetown Rule, which didn't faze me. The rule showed that you couldn't mess with us, and as much as people tried to stereotype and racialize our team, we still did what we had to do. We didn't break the rules, we went around them. We stretched the rules to the point where they felt compelled to change them. Think about this for a second: after they passed the "Georgetown Rule," did you ever hear about any of my players getting suspended for fighting? No, you didn't. We knew what we were doing.

Our 1987–88 team was not as dominant as we had been in the past. We lost to Seton Hall in our first game of the Big East tournament, then were an eighth seed in the NCAAs. In the first round, Smitty banked in a thirty-footer with no time left and we beat LSU 66–63. After that, my man John Chaney's Temple team killed us in the second round, 74–53.

Chaney won all the Coach of the Year awards in 1988, deservedly so, because he was a terrific coach. Chaney got his start at the historically Black university Cheyney State in Pennsylvania, where he won a Division II national championship. I got to know him when he took over at Temple in 1982. There were still very few Black coaches in college basketball. Chaney and I became close because we were philosophically and temperamentally aligned, and we faced the same obstacles.

I had to laugh when Chaney had that fuss with John Calipari in 1994. Temple and Calipari's Massachusetts team were two of the best teams in the country, battling it out in the Atlantic 10 conference. After UMass beat Temple by one point, Calipari said some things to the officials that Chaney felt were inappropriate. At the postgame press conference, which was televised, Calipari was talking at the podium when Chaney interrupted from the back of the room. Chaney said some things to Calipari, they went back and forth, and all of a sudden Chaney rushed the podium. Thank God people intervened before Chaney got there. He was out of control, said he would kill Calipari, or at least kick his ass. That was unfortunate, but as serious as the situation was, I found it hilarious. I loved the fact that Chaney had the gumption to be on national television chasing a white man like that, threatening to kill him. The thing is, Chaney is a classy and intelligent guy. But I knew if I needed him, he would never back down.

Some time later we were at an event, and when they took me to my seat, I saw Chaney there. I said, "Hell, no, I'm not sitting next him." Everybody looked at me all worried. I smiled and said, "Any time a Black man would chase a white man on national TV and promise to kill him, I don't know what he's gonna do to me!" I never let Chaney forget what he did to Calipari. But he knew how much respect I had for him, on and off the court. So if we had to lose to anybody in the 1988 NCAA tournament, I preferred that it was him.

MANY ASPECTS OF my life were not visible to the public, and it gave me internal satisfaction to do things that people thought were outside of my interests or capabilities. One example was my relationship with Dan Rather, the CBS News anchor. Dan lived near school for a while, his son attended Georgetown Law, and we became friends after meeting on campus. I was surprised when I met him, because he did not act like his television persona, all serious and buttoned up. I expected him to be this stiff-necked type of guy, but he was much more informal and I enjoyed his company. Once I took Dan to Spingarn with me when I was recruiting a player who was interested in studying communications. Spingarn was a very Black environment, in my old neighborhood off Benning Road, and Dan was quite comfortable there.

I also had a friendship with Petey Greene, the Washington radio and television host who turned his life around after a prison sentence. One night we were riding together to a white charity event where we both were supposed to speak. I told him, "When they give the award for outstanding citizen, I'll bet you anything it goes to a Black person." Petey was puzzled. I explained, "You don't get paid well for being nice. You get paid well for being smart, and they don't want to attach that to us." We got to the event and sat at separate tables. When they gave the citizenship award, sure enough, a Black guy got it. Petey leaned back in his chair and caught my eye, and we shared the kind of look that a lot of us exchange when we are in a room full of white folks.

Another good friend was Fred Mathis, an athletic trainer who worked with a lot of young Black kids in Washington taping ankles and caring for injuries at games. Everybody called him Doc. He came to Washington from Georgia about 1960, then worked as a teacher at Ballou High School and as a trainer across the city. High school games, summer leagues, Boys Club No. 2, you name it. This was before they had rules requiring schools to hire trainers, so Fred volunteered his time, unpaid, and provided a valuable service. Fred also was gay, and it was apparent. He didn't feel the need to hide his mannerisms.

Fred and I always had a great relationship. He was highly educated, with degrees from Morehouse and D.C. Teachers College, and he did graduate work at Howard and George Washington. His sports medicine training was from the University of Virginia. I admired how he served the community. He gave a lot of kids food, clothes, bus fare, and other things they needed. I asked him to call me if he saw a good ballplayer somewhere. Or, if I was thinking about recruiting a kid, I asked Fred what he knew about the kid's character, how he acted in school and around his coaches, those kinds of things.

Fred faced a lot of discrimination because he was gay. He came to a game at Georgetown when he was writing for one of the small local newspapers, and one of our staffers called me up questioning whether to let him in. I said, "Of course let him in, you think he can't cover the game because he's openly gay?" Another time, some people at a high school where Fred was teaching started a movement to get rid of him. Some people think that gay people are more inclined to molest kids, which is false. Fred wasn't messing with any kids, but the people at this school tried to insinuate that might be the case. When Fred called me to ask for help, he was scared to ask me to come to the school and talk to the administrators, but that's exactly what I did. See, I accepted him for who he was. Being gay had nothing to do with anything. Maybe my admiration for my uncle Lewis helped me understand that. When I went to Fred's school, I saw some of the cruelest things, in terms of the questions they asked about him and the photographs they tried to use. It was terrible.

It bothered me that Fred thought I would be reluctant to openly defend him. But what bothered me even more was the way those people at his school tried to humiliate him, and said he was a threat to their children. That's like saying all Black people steal, you know? Most people thought I wouldn't want to defend a gay man, because of their own stereotypes. I didn't look at it that way. I defended a good man, and a friend.

My son John turned into a pretty good player at Gonzaga High School in Washington. He was six foot four, tough and smart at the guard position, and was named first-team All-Metropolitan as a senior. I saw him play only a few games, because I was conscious of giving his coach space. I didn't want John's coach to feel I was second-guessing or influencing him. When Ronny was a freshman in high school, he was on varsity but not playing at all. I thought the coach might have put Ronny on varsity because he was my son, when he should have been on JV based on his development at that point. I tried to keep my distance from Ronny's and John's teams for those reasons. Also, although my father saw me play only once in high school, I knew for an absolute certainty that he loved me. That gave me permission without even thinking to keep a distance from John's games, because I didn't feel I had to attend to show that I loved him.

One of the few times I saw John play was against DeMatha. Dean Smith came to the game with me, and John had a triple double. I knew he could be a good college player. Dean offered him a scholarship to play at North Carolina, and he also got offers from Kansas, Notre Dame, Villanova, and Princeton. John wanted to play for me at Georgetown, but I had a problem with that. It would place him under extra pressure from the moment he walked on campus. It would be awkward for me to coach my son under the spotlight. I had always tried to protect my family from the public glare. Mary Fenlon agreed with me that it would be a bad idea for John to play for me. I tried to peek into John's future, considering his personality and his intelligence, and based on those things I thought Princeton was the best fit. Pete Carril was known to be a good coach, and the academic reputation certainly got my attention. You have to yell the name of some colleges, but you can whisper "Princeton" and get people's attention. When John chose to attend, I supported his decision.

The sad thing is, our ancestors fought for opportunities to attend these great universities, and then some of us turn around and resent Black people who go there, call them uppity or Uncle Toms. We experienced some of that with John, but he had a good experience and graduated in 1988. I saw him play one game in college, on senior night. I had my hands full preparing for the Olympics.

SOME PEOPLE MIGHT have called it a setup when I was asked to be head coach of the 1988 Olympic team, but I considered it a great honor.

I knew up front that the rest of the basketball world was catching up to the United States. Dean Smith and Dave Gavitt, who were on the selection committee, told me that this would be our last Olympics with college players. Other countries already used professionals, and kept them together on their national teams year after year. At the 1972 Olympics, the Soviet Union beat us by one point in the gold medal game. People say the Soviets cheated, but they had to be close enough to be able to cheat, you know what I mean? In the 1987 Pan Am Games, Brazil beat us on American soil, at Market Square Arena in Indianapolis, to win the gold. That U.S. team had guys like David Robinson from Navy, Pervis Ellison from Louisville, and Rex Chapman from Kentucky. Brazil's best player was twenty-nine-year-old Oscar Schmidt, a six-foot-eight future Hall of Famer who was deadly from the three-point line. Schmidt scored 35 points in the second half, finished with 46, and lay on the court screaming when Brazil won. That scream woke America up to the fact that we were no longer invincible with the system that was in place.

There's a thing Black folks say among ourselves: when things can't get any worse, that's when they give us a chance. The 1984 Olympics were in Los Angeles, we had Michael Jordan and Patrick Ewing, and the Soviet Union boycotted. Bobby Knight coached that team, deservedly so. When they asked me to coach in 1988, the Olympics were in Seoul, South Korea, the Russians were back, and we needed to bring our pros but didn't.

Still, I had to accept the challenge. First of all, I thought we would win. And I'm a patriotic person, so representing America was something I could not turn down. My Olympic experience in 1976 under Dean Smith had been fantastic. Walking into Montreal's Olympic stadium behind the American flag, especially as a coach selected for my intellectual and not physical abilities, was one of my most emotional sports experiences. I also felt that my response to this offer would influence opportunities for other Black coaches. Yes, it was risky. So was coming to Georgetown in the first place.

I always loved the Gandhi quote about real freedom being the freedom to make mistakes. At that point in my life, I felt free enough to take the chance that I might not be successful.

For my assistant coaches, I selected Fenlon and George Raveling, who was then head coach at the University of Southern California. My manager was Billy Stein. Even though Stein had left for St. Peter's before we won the 1984 title, I gave him the championship ring he deserved, because he recruited and developed that team, and we remained close friends.

We had a good crop of college players to choose from, even after guys like Pervis Ellison, Gary Grant, Mookie Blaylock, and Tim Perry declined our invitations. I didn't blame anyone for protecting their NBA opportunities. I also did something unusual heading into the tryouts and invited a high school senior.

Alonzo Mourning was the No. 1 schoolboy in the nation, and I had already signed him to come to Georgetown. He was a six-foot-ten center from Chesapeake, Virginia, who had dominated in high school, but plenty of guys were his size in college. I thought trying out for the Olympics would give him great preparation for Georgetown. What I didn't think was that he would play so well at the trials. David Robinson was the most physically talented big man at the training camp. Robinson had graduated from the Naval Academy in 1987 and was the first pick in the NBA draft, but he had not yet gone to the league because he was doing his two years on a submarine or wherever the navy put him. Alonzo went toe to toe with David and got the better of pretty much everybody else. We played exhibitions against NBA teams and did a quick tour through Europe, and Alonzo played extremely well. When it was time to make the final cuts, everyone involved in the selection process said Alonzo should make the team. I was the only person who disagreed, and unfortunately for Alonzo, I was in charge. My reasoning was that the Olympics were held in September that year, and if Alonzo played, he would miss the first month of school. That would have put him at a tremendous disadvantage academically. Alonzo is extremely intelligent and ended up doing well, but at that time he was coming out of a foster home and a weak high school academic environment. His letter of intent was signed by his foster mother, Mrs. Threet. He was about to be tossed into the deep end of the pool, academically speaking. I could not risk having him drown just to satisfy my competitive desire to win a gold medal. Alonzo was the last cut, and he felt crushed by the decision, though he understood later it was the right thing to do.

I wanted the first tryouts to be in Las Vegas. I had a lot of friends in Vegas, I liked to relax in the casinos, and the logistics of bringing in more than eighty players was simpler there. Plus, the location would encourage more players to try out. USA Basketball wanted tryouts at its headquarters in Colorado Springs, which was inconvenient and a place nobody wanted to go. The organization had a holier-than-thou attitude about Vegas being "Sin City" and exposing so-called amateur athletes to gambling. It amuses me now, because every summer the entire basketball world goes to Vegas, from youth tournaments up to the NBA summer league and USA Basketball itself. You can bet on college games from your phone. They now have a sports book in the arena where Georgetown plays its home games. But they put the trials in Colorado Springs, where I closed practices to the media like I had done the past sixteen years. Some reporters got predictably riled up. A few news organizations threatened to take me to court, which was hilarious. One of the protesters was the columnist Jim Murray from the *Los Angeles Times*. Murray didn't know I was a huge fan of his. I looked for his newspaper just to read what he had to say, especially about baseball. Murray was among those harassing me about closed practices. I thought to myself, "If you had just asked me for an interview, I would have sat down with you for hours. I would have considered it an honor."

Our roster selections were criticized, of course. This was nothing new. Our big names were Robinson, a future Hall of Famer, and Danny Manning, who had just led Kansas to the national championship and was the top pick in the 1988 NBA draft. After them came Pittsburgh power forward Charles Smith (drafted third in 1988); scoring guard Mitch Richmond (drafted fifth, future Hall of Famer); shooter Hersey Hawkins (drafted sixth, the leading scorer in college basketball at 36 points per game); forward Willie Anderson (drafted tenth); and the big guards Jeff Grayer and Dan Majerle (drafted thirteenth and fourteenth, respectively). The rest of the team were the six-foot-nine J. R. Reid, the versatile wing Stacey Augmon, the point guard Bimbo Coles, and last but absolutely not least, my man Smitty. People could accuse me of favoritism all they wanted, but Charles earned his stripes with me. I trusted him in the heat of battle. We had outstanding three-point shooters in Hawkins, Richmond, and Majerle. Manning was the best all-around player in college basketball. David Robinson was David Robinson. There were good reasons we didn't pick some guys with big names, and I think their pro careers validated our decisions. Also, once you chose the stars of the team, the other guys needed to fill complementary roles. I was coaching human beings, not chalk. Our team had seven of the top fourteen picks in the 1988 NBA draft, plus Robinson. The other four players had to fit in with them and be able to play the pressing, fast-paced style that I planned to use.

What bothered me more than griping about our roster was the fact that Arvydas Sabonis, the seven-foot-three Soviet center, spent the months leading up to the Olympics working out with the Portland Trail Blazers. I knew that Portland had drafted Sabonis, but the guy didn't come play in the NBA for another eight years. Also, several NBA teams played exhibitions against the Soviets ahead of the Olympics. Like Lenin said, we sold the Russians the rope they used to hang us.

When our games started, we got an early scare from Canada in the second round and beat them by six. Our next opponent was Brazil. I showed our team a tape of that Pan Am loss. Oscar Schmidt scored 31 on us, but we beat them 102–87. In the next game, a blowout of China,

Hawkins hurt his knee. He volunteered to play through it, but I didn't want to ruin his NBA future, so I shut him down for the rest of the Olympics. We won the next two games easily to advance to the semifinals against the Soviet Union. The Soviets had lost a game to Yugoslavia but were formidable with Sabonis in the middle and the professional guards Sarunas Marciulionis, who brought the Eurostep to America during his eight-year NBA career, and a deadeye shooter named Rimas Kurtinaitis.

The Soviets beat us, 82–76. Manning picked up two fouls in the first two minutes and did not score the whole game. We missed Hawkins's shooting. Kurtinaitis hit a bunch of threes. Sabonis was one of the best centers in the world at that point, and had 13 points and 13 rebounds. Unlike my NCAA championship losses, where my teams played great, we were not at our best that game. It happens. Sometimes you have an off night. In the locker room afterward, I didn't blame them for losing, and I told them we had nothing to be ashamed of.

The Soviets beat Yugoslavia to win the gold medal, finishing the tournament 7–1. We finished 7–1, too, after we beat Australia for the bronze. I lost the wrong game.

I don't wish for one second that I had turned down the Olympic job. That's like wishing we hadn't come out on the floor to play Villanova. I earned the right to coach those games, and whatever comes with that, I have to accept. As great as Muhammad Ali and Joe Louis were, they lost fights. But first they had the courage to get in the ring.

Sometimes you kill the lion, and sometimes the lion kills you. Either way, you hunt.

14

RAYFUL

The Olympics were just the beginning of the most challenging twelve months of my career.

I returned to Georgetown in October, well after school had started, which was a bit disconcerting. I expected us to have an outstanding team that season. I already knew what Alonzo Mourning could do based on the Olympic trials. Smitty and Jaren Jackson were seniors. And my son Ronny was a freshman on that team. Ronny was a different type of kid than John, with more of my characteristics in him. I needed to keep Ronny under my thumb—actually, more like under my fist—so it worked out for him to play at Georgetown.

We also had a new kid from Central Africa by the name of Dikembe Mutombo.

I first heard about Dikembe in early 1987 when a guy named Herman Henning showed up at the basketball office and said there was a player in the Congo we needed to check out. Henning was not a coach or scout. He said he worked for the U.S. Agency for International Development, but I always thought he was CIA.

"This African kid can really play," Henning said.

"How tall is he?" I asked. That was always my first question.

"Dikembe is seven feet tall," Henning said.

I walked him to the balcony overlooking the practice court and pointed to our seven-foot center, Ben Gillery.

"Is your kid as tall as Ben?" I asked.

"He's taller."

At that point it seemed wise to take down Henning's information, and he sent us a videotape of Dikembe. The boy had a rag tied around his head, was playing on what looked like grass, and was blocking all kinds of shots. I was intrigued by his combination of size, agility, and athleticism, although part of me wondered if he was really as tall as they said he was. Eventually I decided to put him on my team and sit him out for a year as an adjustment period, when I could also evaluate his ability. If it worked out, great. If not, Henning could ship him back on one of his CIA planes.

I sent Mike Riley, Craig Esherick, and Michael Jackson to pick up Dikembe at the airport. Michael brought an African girl he was seeing who spoke several languages. I told them, "When the kid gets off the plane, if he doesn't have to duck his head way down to walk through the door, turn around and leave his ass at the airport." Michael Jackson and his girl greeted Dikembe at the gate, and when he revealed himself to be seven feet two, Riley and Esherick came out from hiding behind a couple of plants.

Dikembe sat out for a year as planned, then began his first season in the fall of 1988. Mike Riley and Craig Esherick supervised the team as I eased back into the flow of things that October. All my easing came to an abrupt end when my people around Washington told me that Alonzo Mourning and another kid on my team, John Turner, were hanging out with a drug dealer named Rayful Edmond III.

I knew that Rayful was the biggest dealer in Washington at that time, and I was extremely concerned. First of all, Alonzo's and Turner's futures as young men were at risk, let alone as basketball players. Len Bias had died of a cocaine overdose just two years earlier, right after the Celtics drafted him out of Maryland. Lefty Driesell lost his job over that. If Alonzo and Turner weren't using cocaine, were they selling it? Even if neither was true, just associating with a drug dealer could ruin their lives. There also was a great danger that Georgetown could have its name dragged through the mud. I had a responsibility to protect the school. The press was already painting us as bad guys, and I knew some reporters would love to put us in a story with a real criminal. I had no idea about the extent of Alonzo and Turner's involvement, so the first thing I had to do was question them about what was going on.

Here's the philosophy of how I approached it. I had a friend from Baltimore we called Pitty Pat. My man Pitty Pat told me that one day he was walking down the street in a dangerous neighborhood and saw four rough guys coming his way. Pat got scared as hell. We get mad when white people are scared of us on the street, but we can get scared, too. Pat told me he knew he was about to get jumped, so he started yelling, acting crazy, and cursing into the air. Those four thugs crossed to the other side of the street and left him alone. Pitty Pat told me, "When you mess with a crazy man, you got to be more crazy than him." I always kept that in mind with my players. I wanted them to think I was capable of anything.

I brought our athletic director, Frank Rienzo, up to speed on the situation. I asked Frank to bust through the gym door during practice, storm over to Alonzo and Turner, and tell them to get upstairs to my office right away. Frank was a low-key guy, so when he came in angry, Alonzo was petrified. Turner was older—he had come to us from community college—and he reacted more nonchalantly. I thought scaring Alonzo would make him tell me the truth about what was going on. The Alonzo Mourning now known to the public is a big, tough, sophisticated man, but when he arrived here he was an eighteen-year-old country bumpkin. We took Zo and Turner upstairs and I went completely off. More than a few profanities were used. The nice version of what I said was that they had exercised exceedingly poor judgment and were in immediate danger of losing their scholarships. Alonzo and I like to laugh about it now, but that day in my office Frank and I worked him over so thoroughly, he was almost in tears.

I figured out that while I had been away at the Olympics, Alonzo and Turner got tight. Turner, who everybody on the team called JT, was from suburban Maryland but had an uncle who lived in the city, up the block from Rayful. Turner and Rayful had become friends at an early age. By the time Turner got to Georgetown, he was enamored of the street image of the drug dealer lifestyle and liked to hang around with those guys. Now he was bringing Alonzo with him.

Rayful was crazy about basketball. He had gone to Dunbar, my mother's school, and was a good playground player. He kept a crew of talented local stars around him, and they played together all over the city. Alonzo and Turner told me they played ball with Rayful and his friends, hung out with them at their homes and at different nightclubs, and went out to eat sometimes. They didn't mention it, but obviously they enjoyed that Rayful always picked up the check and sprinkled his money around in different ways. They insisted that they never saw or even talked about any drugs and that they weren't involved in anything illegal. I didn't find out until much later that Alonzo had played on Rayful's teams against other squads run by drug dealers, and there was big money bet on those games. Alonzo was a naïve teenager who got caught up in the celebrity of being a Georgetown player in the big city. Turner probably knew more about what was going on. I liked JT—he was a nice kid to be around and a very good player. But he had spent enough time around the neighborhood to know who and what Rayful was.

I told Alonzo and Turner to stay away from Rayful, and repeated the message to the entire team. There was one popular nightclub, Chapter III, which I declared completely off-limits. Everybody promised to do the right thing.

But that only addressed half of the problem. I had to talk to Rayful.

Over the years, people made a big deal out of my decision to meet with a person like him. A judge once asked me, "Are you the coach who met with Rayful Edmond? You had more nerve than Jesse James!"

Well, Rayful was not the first person I'd encountered who had difficulty with the law. I delivered the *Washington Daily News* to numbers houses when I lived on W Street. The first sports uniform I ever wore was bought by a numbers runner. I played one-on-one against my drug dealer friend Big Roy. I did my master's degree practicum at the city jail, where one of my kids was later identified as a contract killer. I have a friend right now with the key to my house who spent years locked up. One of my best friends in Vegas worked for Meyer Lansky. Rayful's type was not alien to me. Of course we should talk. I'm not saying I didn't recognize the danger, but I was not as terrified about it as some other people were.

When I was a boy, if my mother heard about some trouble I got into in the street, she would take off her apron and come outside to see what was going on. That's all I did with Rayful.

He wasn't too hard to find. We knew someone in common. Clarence "Bootney" Green had played basketball at Spingarn, grew up in Boys Club No. 2, was Division II player of the year at Cheyney State, and was a young basketball legend in the city. A lot of the Washington kids on my team admired Bootney. He was not involved with drugs, but he played on the team that Rayful took with him around the city. Rayful would leave his drug crew, go pick up Bootney and a couple other guys, and play basketball all day. From what I've been told, Rayful was a solid player with an accurate jump shot, and he liked to shoot the ball a lot.

I questioned various people and figured out that after Bootney and Rayful finished playing ball with Alonzo and JT, they usually drove them back to campus. Sometimes Bootney and Rayful hung out in the dorms where all the players lived, buying them pizzas and whatnot. For a broke college student, pizza with all the toppings is like steak and lobster. Hanging with Rayful also gave them status, and Rayful got status from associating with my team. That coin had two sides.

I put the word out that I wanted to talk to Bootney. When I got him on the phone, I said I needed him to bring Rayful by my office at McDonough. Bootney said he'd ask, then called me back and said Rayful would come at a certain time, but it didn't happen.

Soon I got Bootney on the phone again. He was on campus, in one of our dorms. "Rayful didn't show up," I said. "Can you get him over here to meet with me? I need to talk to him."

I heard Bootney talking to somebody and realized he was with Rayful at that very moment. I heard them going back and forth. Bootney said, "Aww, Coach, Ray is scared. But he said he'll come see you. What time?"

"How about tomorrow between noon and one o'clock."

"Okay," Bootney said. "We'll be there."

Now, why would a guy like Rayful Edmond be scared to talk to me? Clearly it was not based on any physical threat that I posed to him. Violence is not part of my profession. He also was not afraid I would run to the police. I didn't have anything to run to the police about. Yet here I was being perceived as fearsome again. People said it showed my power in the city that Rayful came when called. But it wasn't about power. Rayful respected me based on what I represented to Black people in the city of Washington. What scared Rayful was the idea that he was causing me a problem. He had a conscience. His thought process was similar to that of a young man who got in trouble with his father.

The next day, as I was watching my team play pickup in McDonough, the door opened and Rayful walked into the gym. He had three guys with him: Bootney; Melvin Middleton, a good basketball player and Bootney's teammate at Spingarn; and another young man who ran the streets with Rayful. My players were shocked—you never saw so many airballs in your life. They already knew I had caught up with their Rayful activities, but his arrival sent a message that I was now one step ahead of them. *Oh, y'all thought it was fun and games when Rayful was in your dorm? Let's see how you like it when I bring him to the gym.* One of our coaches took the visitors upstairs and walked Rayful through the unmarked door into the basketball suite. As he went through the door, Rayful looked back at his guys. I walked him into a private room and shut the door behind us. He and I were going to talk alone.

It was a stressful moment. I didn't know Rayful, and he didn't know me. A lot could go wrong. My program was in extreme danger, and if I could not solve the problem, everything could crumble. The school's reputation could be harmed. It's a lot easier to talk about the experience now than it was to live it.

Rayful was about twenty-three years old, six feet tall, with a solid build. He was handsome and dressed neatly, with a nice polo shirt. He wasn't wearing a hat, long hair, jewelry, or anything flamboyant, which was somewhat surprising to me. Looking at him, you would never think he was a drug kingpin. He did not look like any type of thug. He wasn't running around with a nickname like Fast Shot Willie. Right from the beginning he had a humble approach, which also surprised me. Everything about him was respectful, from his appearance to his demeanor. His overall presentation made me think that he thought I had the upper hand.

I recognized his intelligence right away. He behaved like his mind gave him credibility, not acting tough or violent or speaking a whole bunch of street language. I determined that it would be advantageous to let him know that I recognized his intelligence. I treated him respectfully, and as a result he gave me the same respect, and he answered my questions in what proved to be a truthful manner.

My primary concern was to find out what, exactly, Alonzo and JT were doing. I needed to do this without talking directly about drugs. Rayful had not been convicted of anything. He wasn't sneaking around like a fugitive; he walked into my office in broad daylight. I didn't want him to think I was setting him up or secretly taping him. I also didn't want to be told anything that might incriminate him later, because I was cognizant of the fact that he eventually would be caught. I tried not to ask him questions that would put him in a position of confessing anything. He was too smart to do that anyway.

Our conversation was a bit like pig Latin. We spoke around the elephant in the room. We both knew what it was. I had no need to identify it. The conversation was serious and firm, with no small talk. I got right to the point.

"I don't know what's going on with you, and I don't care what's going on, that's your business," I said. "But I'm hearing things about Alonzo and JT, and what I'm hearing could cause them a lot of problems. It could affect their basketball careers. I don't need anything going on with my players, the school doesn't need it, the players don't need it. I don't get involved with anybody's business, but if there's anything going on, I need you to let me know right now."

Rayful said, "Nothing's happening, Coach Thompson. People are making up a lot of stuff. All we do is play ball, go get something to eat, maybe hang out a little bit."

We went back and forth in this manner as I tried to gather as much information as possible. I was the authority figure and led the conversation, but I knew I had very little leverage. I couldn't control him. If what I had heard about him was true, Rayful had all the money in the world. If he wanted to cause problems for me, that would have been easy. He could simply keep showing up on campus, or keep taking my players to restaurants and nightclubs. He could arrange for something to be left in their dorm room. If he got arrested, he could say they were involved. All these possibilities ran through my mind. But I quickly recognized that Rayful wasn't hostile toward me or my team. This young man loved basketball. We both had an allegiance to Boys Club No. 2 and relationships with people there. He respected what I represented in the game he played every day. He might have been running an operation that made millions, but Rayful was also a Georgetown basketball fan.

I had a level of respect for Rayful, too. I didn't respect or condone selling drugs, and I was probably a bit naïve about the extent of his activities when we first met. I knew he ran the city, but I didn't realize his operation extended up and down the whole East Coast. Still, I didn't look down on him as a human being. I didn't want to judge him, and I still don't. As a Black kid growing up in his neighborhood, his opportunities were limited, which inevitably affected the choices he made. Dr. Anita Hughes taught me to understand the problems of other people. There but for the grace of God go I.

Rayful told me how good a player he was, and how he would have liked to play college basketball. I suggested that it wasn't too late for him to go to college, because he clearly had the intelligence to succeed academically. He said that was something he wanted to do. We talked about that for a while, then I brought the conversation back to the matter at hand.

"So what can we do here?" I asked. "Because I really don't need this kind of stuff in my life. My players' careers could be ruined, the school could be hurt. Can you control this situation? We both know the type of things that should not be happening. Can you make sure they don't happen?"

"Oh, yeah, that's no problem," Rayful said. "You don't have anything to worry about. Not with Alonzo."

Wait a minute. He only said Alonzo.

"What about JT?" I asked.

Rayful tried to be tactful about it. "JT isn't doing anything, Coach Thompson, but he enjoys being around guys who might be, you know, who might be doing something. He's attracted to the lifestyle. I tell him to stay away from all that, but you know how he is."

Rayful shared a detail I found particularly significant. You remember the huge cell phones back in the 1980s, that were the size of a quart of milk against your ear? Rayful said JT carried one of those around, but the service was not activated. He just wanted people to see him with it.

I was sympathetic to why a kid like Turner would feel that way. America worships people with money. Young Black kids had so few examples of wealth in their communities, they naturally gravitated toward drug dealers. Even if they didn't, drugs were so embedded in the culture of the city at that time, it was hard to play basketball and not be associated with someone from that world. That said, JT had to make better decisions. He had to leave the streets alone.

"I'm not asking you to tell me anything," I told Rayful. "I'm just asking for you to handle it. You know what I mean? Because you know some folks want to see us go down in this situation." Exactly what the situation was, we never said.

"I got you, Coach Thompson. You don't have to worry about anything with Alonzo. But JT, I don't know."

Throughout the whole conversation, Rayful was as polite and cooperative as could be. I was polite, too. It would have been stupid to make Rayful angry.

Over the years, many people have said what they thought happened in that room. Everybody says it went this way or that way, but there were only two people in there, Rayful and me. A myth has grown about me threatening Rayful and ordering him to stay away from my players. Some people like to say I stood over him and pointed my finger in his face. That's nonsense. Why would I threaten someone who could bring down my whole program? That myth is based on the perception of me as intimidating and a bully. Like when I argued with the refs, I supposedly scared them. When I met with Rayful, the thinking goes, I had to threaten him. I've always been offended when some people assume our interaction had a physical component. They don't want to give me credit for the fact that Rayful respected me.

My conversation with Rayful was less than what everybody said, and also more. It wasn't like meeting some outlaw in the woods. I thought of Rayful as my neighbor's child, who was exposing my kids to some trouble. I wanted to protect my players, my university, and myself. The conversation was between two Black men from Washington who both loved basketball, respected each other as human beings, and had enough intelligence to work out a solution to our problem.

I was never afraid for my own safety. Someone compared it to summoning Al Capone, but that was based on people transferring their fear of Rayful onto me. They thought violence was the only way Rayful had relationships with people.

We finished talking, walked out of the office, and said goodbye. Rayful went downstairs past the practice court and left with Bootney,

Melvin, and his friend. Bootney and Melvin later got jobs working at Georgetown. I wonder how that happened?

According to Bootney, Rayful smiled the whole drive home. When Bootney kept asking what we talked about, all Rayful said was, "Man, Coach Thompson is cool as hell."

A FEW DAYS after the meeting, my phone started ringing off the hook. It seemed like every branch of the police wanted to know what we talked about. Rayful was under heavy investigation by local and federal authorities, with surveillance and phone taps, and they wanted something from me they could use to arrest him. On the one hand, it was good they didn't know what we discussed, because that meant Alonzo and Turner weren't on their radar. But when they started telling me the quantities of cocaine that Rayful was allegedly distributing, and about the geographic reach of his operation, I started to understand more the magnitude of who this young man was. One cop told me they had information implicating Rayful's organization in thirty murders. That was news to me. I became even more concerned, especially for someone as naïve as Alonzo. After a while, I got frustrated with all their calls. I told one agent, "Look, he didn't sneak in here in the middle of the night. He walked into my office like a normal person. If you have something on this guy, arrest him. If not, I can't help you. I'm not trying to lock him up, I'm trying to protect my kids."

I tried to shift my focus to basketball, because our first game of the season was approaching. We were ranked second in the preseason AP poll, and we cruised through the early part of our schedule, as usual. As the season progressed, Charles Smith was clutch, as expected. Alonzo played extremely well and ended up leading the nation in blocked shots. Jaren Jackson started every game. Turner was solid, averaging seven points and six rebounds per game. But the big surprise was Dikembe Mutombo.

Even though Dikembe played just eleven minutes per game, he had a major impact with his defensive ability, like when he blocked twelve shots against St. John's, which at the time was some sort of record. I brought in Bill Russell that year to tutor Dikembe and Alonzo, and Russ talked to them as much about the mental approach to the game as how to block shots to their teammates instead of out of bounds. I did struggle to figure out how to play Dikembe and Alonzo together, not only offensively but defensively. If you have two seven-footers on the floor, who guards the perimeter? It's not like today where everybody plays like a guard no matter their height. Alonzo got the bulk of the minutes, but Dikembe never complained. He was a great kid to have around, to the point where I could never really get mad at him, even when I was trying to play my role of angry coach. Dikembe would say something in that African accent of his and I would bust out laughing.

One day I was giving the team a scouting report and said, "We're going to have to pay a lot of attention to the opposing center, he's a dominant player, very polished, very tough in the paint. Let's watch the footage." I hit the button on the tape player and it was Dikembe back in Africa, blocking shots on the grass. Everybody had a great laugh, including Dikembe.

But a serious threat still hovered over our program. I got a call from Andrew Johnson, the brother of my buddy Ollie Johnson who got cut from the Celtics. Andrew grew up with me on Benning Road and now worked for the Drug Enforcement Administration. He wanted to talk about Rayful. Drew told me that he and his fellow agents were under pressure to arrest him because of all the murders connected to the drug trade. Washington's homicide rate had almost doubled, and the national crack epidemic was front page news. The new president, George H. W. Bush, had waved a bag of crack on live television during his first Oval Office speech. Drew told me, "We're going to get Rayful."

I asked Drew to come by McDonough. I had some more Pitty Pat in mind. After practice, I asked my team if they knew what the initials DEA stood for. Everybody got nervous. I told Alonzo and Turner the DEA was in my office waiting for them. When they got upstairs, Drew was sitting there with his badge. He grilled them about Rayful and said how dangerous he was. Turner played it cool, but Alonzo was terrified. I repeated my instructions to stop all contact with Rayful and his people. "If you see them in public," I said, "say hello but don't let your feet stop moving."

Alonzo did the right thing. John Turner made a different decision.

15

PROPOSITION 42

The Rayful problem receded into the background as the 1988–89 season progressed. Nobody connected Rayful to us in the media. Frank Rienzo handled the situation with the president's office. In January my team was 11–1 and ranked seventh in the country when a new problem reared its head.

I got a call from Bill Rhoden, the Black *New York Times* columnist. Rhoden organized gatherings of Black journalists and coaches at the Final Four, which I appreciated, and he understood why I did the things I did. Rhoden asked if I had heard about a new NCAA rule called Proposition 42.

I had not. What I learned made me furious.

Proposition 42 made it harder for poor kids, most of them Black, to receive athletic scholarships. Its roots went back to the early 1980s, when a University of Georgia professor named Jan Kemp said publicly that several football players in her classes were close to illiterate but the school kept them eligible anyway. The outcry forced the NCAA to set a minimum standard for athletes to compete as freshmen: a 2.0 high school GPA or 700 score on the SAT. Athletes who took the ACT needed a score of 15. Players who did not meet any of these benchmarks could still receive athletic scholarships but would have to sit out of competition their first year of college, until their grades reached a required level. That rule was called Proposition 48. I could live with that one.

The University of Georgia made things worse by firing Jan Kemp. She sued and got her job back, plus one million dollars in damages. That placed Georgia and the rest of the Southeastern Conference under the microscope, for good reason. The SEC decided as a conference not to give scholarships to players without a 2.0 GPA or 700 SAT. This is the SEC we're talking about, and let's just say they leave no stone unturned in the effort to win ball games. All of a sudden, other schools could recruit athletes the SEC could not. The SEC schools felt that placed them at a competitive disadvantage. So they gathered in the smoke-filled back rooms of the NCAA committees and pushed through a rule that nobody could give scholarships to athletes who did not meet the minimum standards.

That rule was Proposition 42. As soon as Rhoden told me about it, I knew it was unfair for Black kids.

Let's start with the fact that we do not have a centralized education system in this country. Each school district is funded differently. Some have more money, better facilities, and more advanced classes. Some poor schools, meanwhile, don't even have the proper equipment for science classes. Black kids are the most likely to be poor. These kids can't take trips that provide informal educational experiences. The schools my grandchildren go to, they skip off to Europe like it's a field trip to the zoo, while other schools don't even have enough textbooks.

Since we don't have a centralized education system, the vast majority of poor children do not receive an equal education. This is a problem in and of itself. In terms of basic fairness, we should provide the same educational opportunity to everyone. What Proposition 42 did was accept that inequality and compound it. By imposing a centralized test on kids who did not receive a centralized education, the NCAA judged disadvantaged kids by the results of the privileged.

There's a common myth that all privileged kids who earn great grades and test scores do it on their own. Most of the time, they are given more help than everyone else. There's nothing wrong with that. That help is called education. Without the help I received from my mother, Sametta Wallace Jackson, and Dr. Harry Lewis, I wouldn't have been able to read. But a lot of people assume kids with better scores are always smarter, which leads to the false belief that white kids are generally smarter than Black ones. In reality, many of the poor Black kids do not receive an equal education.

I felt the injustice of Proposition 42 deeply, due to my own experiences. I doubt I got 700 on my SAT, but when I got to Providence I passed the same classes as everyone else, even when that professor warned us athletes to get out. I earned a bachelor's degree in economics, a teacher's certificate in social studies, and then a master's degree in counseling and guidance. I've been accused of being a lot of things, but stupid is not one of them. Yet under Proposition 42 I might never even have attended college.

There but for the grace of God go I.

When I got off the phone with Rhoden I knew I had to do something.

Proposition 42 had passed on Wednesday, January 11, 1989. Rhoden called me Thursday. I immediately called Frank Rienzo. This is a good place to mention that the level of advice and support Frank gave me over the years was phenomenal. He had an incredible understanding of the way things worked in sports and education, and how to navigate within those institutions. Frank didn't stand on the sideline, he got into the game. No coach can succeed without a good athletic director, and Frank was a great one.

Frank contacted the NCAA to get clarity on the situation. We learned that the first time Proposition 42 came up for a vote it failed, 151–159. The SEC started leaning on people, another vote was held days later, and it passed, 163–154. Some Black colleges voted for it too; I'm not sure why. Maybe they unconsciously wanted to be accepted. Sometimes we want to sit at the table with white folks so badly, we don't understand the impact of our actions on those who can't sit at that table.

The rule took effect immediately, meaning any kid without a 700 SAT or 2.0 GPA could not receive an athletic scholarship the following fall. This would eliminate an estimated six hundred players, 90 percent of whom were Black. None of my recruits would be affected, but that didn't change how I felt.

I told Frank I was thinking about boycotting a game.

I didn't want the whole team to boycott, because that would have placed an unfair burden on the players and the university. But if I walked out by myself, it would call attention to something the NCAA had done in a secretive way. Frank and I discussed the impact a boycott would have. I had guys on my team trying to make the pros, and I didn't want to hurt their chances. Every game was precious to them, and they wouldn't get any reruns. I also thought about what Georgetown could lose, from a revenue or reputational standpoint. I always tried to be concerned with how my actions impacted other people.

I decided a boycott was the right move. When I told my team, they wanted to walk out with me. That made me feel good about their development as young men, but I told them they should play the game.

I went to see the university president, Father Healy, not to ask permission, but to inform him of my decision. By now we had been working together for a dozen years and had an outstanding relationship. He understood my principles and supported me both privately and publicly. Jack DeGioia was vice president then, and Healy's top assistant. Jack also had a comprehensive understanding of athletics, from both an educational and a sociological perspective. He did not characterize my point of view as militant, like a lot of other people did. I was extremely comfortable with both men.

When I sat down in the Big Irishman's office, I said, "I think I'm obligated to tell you I'm planning to walk out of the next game. There's no question this rule unfairly punishes Black people and poor people. I have to do something. I can't just let it go forward without trying to stop it. I'm going to boycott."

"Christ, John," Father Healy said. "You're a citizen."

I will always love Georgetown, because they never tried to stop me from being me.

Our next game was on Saturday, January 14, at our home arena, the Capital Centre, against Boston College. We let the media know what I planned to do. As the game approached, I felt a certain amount of fear. I didn't know how the NCAA would respond, or if I was getting in over my head. Some people say what I did with Proposition 42 was heroic, but that requires acknowledging fear. The motherfucker who ain't afraid ain't no hero, because he didn't care anyway.

Everyone asked how long I would sit out, but I didn't want to limit my options. The day before the game, I spoke to the media to make sure my actions would not be misinterpreted. "This is my way of bringing attention to a rule a lot of people were not aware of, one which will affect a great many individuals," I said. "I did it to bring attention to the issue in hopes of getting them to take another look at what they've done, and if they feel it unjust, change the rule. I'm looking for a commitment to change."

I went to the Capital Centre and stayed with my team while they warmed up. As the tip-off approached, I told Riley and Esherick, "If everything goes wrong, give the fucking ball to Charles."

After the starters were introduced, I took my mother's towel off my shoulder and gave it to Riley. I walked across the court and through a bunch of waiting cameras. The crowd gave me a standing ovation, with the student section chanting, "Way to go, Thompson, way to go!" I walked into the tunnel, went to my car, and left the arena.

I didn't have any destination in mind, but I soon found myself driving through the neighborhoods I lived in as a child. Anacostia, W Street, 19th Street and Benning Road. I looked at Black faces on street corners and wondered, is this where athletes will end up if they don't qualify under Proposition 42? I listened to the game on the radio but got nervous and turned it off. I still wasn't sure if I was doing the right thing.

We beat Boston College, 86–60. The guys said they were playing for something bigger than themselves.

The next day, my walkout received an enormous reaction in the national media. John Chaney called me and said, "What are we gonna do? Just tell me what we're doing and I'm with you." I love that man. A lot of white coaches also were supportive. We had a game scheduled at Louisiana State in two weeks, and the LSU coach, Dale Brown, wanted to protest with me. I had to talk him off the ledge, because Dale was crazy enough to spit on a flag or something. After a lot of discussion, including conference calls with other coaches, I decided not to ask anybody else to join in—for now. I wanted to see how the NCAA would react. Plus, most other coaches' jobs would have been in jeopardy. One young brother on a conference call, Dwight Freeman, started talking loud about walking out with me. I told him to shut up: "If you do that, you're gonna get fired."

I also knew that fear of the riot is more powerful than the riot itself. Just the idea of numerous coaches boycotting games was a problem for the NCAA. We would waste our leverage if we all walked out right away.

Plenty of people opposed my stance, not all of them white. Some Black people thought I was implying we couldn't score 700 on the SAT. Much of the opposition centered on the idea of exploitation. I had been dealing with this argument since Patrick's recruitment. Some people said that since these athletes were not at the same academic level as other students at their institution, the schools exploited them by bringing them in to play sports and make money for the school. Since I wanted athletes to receive scholarships even if their scores were low, some saw that as an even bigger example of exploitation.

I had two responses to this argument. First, athletes and coaches could refuse to be exploited by making sure the player got an education. Remember how I told my players, "If you want to be a slave, I refuse to be the master"? If my players didn't try to graduate, they had to leave. I would not allow Georgetown to exploit them. This course of action was available to any athlete or coach.

My second answer was that for a lot of poor Black kids, the so-called exploitation of college sports was better than the alternative. Their alternative to being exploited was remaining in a deprived neighborhood, with less opportunity than on a college campus. Being exploited means you're trapped or tricked into a bad deal that doesn't offer something of value in exchange. I'm not saying college athletes don't deserve a share of the money they generate, but don't act like they get nothing. What's the value of a Georgetown diploma? A lot more than a bunch of stories you tell in the neighborhood about how many points you scored in high school.

When people said Proposition 42 led to the exploitation of poor Black kids, they missed the bigger picture. What they called exploitation was really an opportunity *not* to be exploited—an opportunity to get an education.

The root issue was that Black kids performed worse academically due to the residual effect of slavery and segregation. A lot of white people object that that happened many years ago, which is correct. But white people today are still benefiting from it, even if they had nothing to do with what was done in the past. White people benefit from wealth that Blacks were prohibited from obtaining, from not being restricted to living in segregated neighborhoods, from the presumption that they are law-abiding citizens, and much more. So why shouldn't exceptions be made for Black people who continue to suffer from injustices that white people continue to benefit from? Let's make some exceptions for these Black kids instead of just saying they're dumb. If you want to call athletic scholarships reparations, go right ahead. Some of our greatest thinkers grew up in unjust circumstances, and we never would have known their names if exceptions had not been made.

One of the people who strongly disagreed with my stance was the Black tennis champion Arthur Ashe. We had never met, but we shared an agent in David Falk. Ashe called me one night and we talked for several hours. Ashe had already been concerned with the Black community valuing sports over education, so Proposition 42 hit a nerve with him. He told me the standards of a 2.0 GPA and 700 SAT were so low, my protesting those standards sent a dangerous message. He also said that any loss of scholarships by Black athletes would be temporary, because they would rise to the occasion. He kept emphasizing that not every kid who got a scholarship would make the pros, so we had to prepare them for real life. He thought I was lowering standards for Black students and sending a message that we were not as capable as white people.

I told him my main purpose was to protect opportunities for those who have the least. I said it would be tremendously unfair to sacrifice the futures of hundreds of Black kids to prove a point to white people that whites probably wouldn't believe anyway. I also told him I was prepared to test my record as an educator, as a coach or otherwise, against anybody. Our conversation was not hostile or angry. I knew Ashe was intelligent, and I respected the fact that he called to talk to me instead of reacting to someone else's interpretation of my actions. I wanted to hear his point of view, because that would test my convictions. Ashe had that logical, old-school thinking that was true but at the same time untrue. At the end of the conversation, he understood what I was saying, even if we didn't agree.

A lot of people judged my Proposition 42 boycott as coming from a basketball coach, which led to a perception that I acted out of self-interest. Nobody considered that I had earned two degrees in education. They stereotyped me as just a coach and ignored all my training on proper educational techniques.

Our next game was scheduled for Wednesday, January 18, at Providence. As I tried to figure out whether to coach that game or not, Frank Rienzo kept in contact with the NCAA to see if they would reconsider the rule. I also received a letter from the College Board, which administers the SAT. The College Board had explained to the NCAA that the SAT was not supposed to be used as an admissions or eligibility test. The SAT is meant to be part of an accumulation of factors that explain where a kid is academically. Proposition 42 translated the SAT, incorrectly, into a pass/fail measurement. This was a misuse of an educational instrument. I wasn't opposed to the SAT itself, I was opposed to how it was being used. The College Board agreed with me.

I decided to sit out the Providence game and didn't make the trip with the team. The game was close, too close. Rick Pitino knew how to coach. I watched on TV at home. Near the end it was nip and tuck and I yelled at the screen, "Give the fucking ball to Charles!" The little son of a bitch scored and won us the game, 80–77.

Rienzo got word that the NCAA wanted to meet with us. Father Healy chartered a plane and the three of us flew to NCAA headquarters outside Kansas City, Missouri. On Friday, January 20, we met with NCAA president Albert Witte, executive director Dick Shultz, SEC commissioner Harvey Schiller, and Martin Massengale, the president of the University of Minnesota, who was chairman of the NCAA Presidents' Commission.

We delivered our arguments to the group. I didn't make any threats or demands, just explained why Proposition 42 was unfair. They didn't say much, but I got the feeling they were afraid of my protest growing. I had heard people asking "Why is Thompson alone?" The NCAA knew the boycott would snowball. What if all the Black coaches decided to boycott as a group? I sensed that they badly wanted me back on the bench. The fear of the riot was in the air.

We finished the discussion, got back on the plane, and flew home. Later that day, the NCAA put out a press release announcing that they were suspending their discriminatory rule.

We defeated Proposition 42.

There was no time to celebrate. Connecticut was coming to the Capital Centre the next day. That's when I was struck by a thought that stayed with me the rest of my life.

I never had the luxury of just being a basketball coach.

I felt a deep responsibility to use the coaching occupation to open up broader opportunities for Black people. I thought about that responsibility a lot, no question. I didn't have the luxury of not thinking about it, because I've always been haunted by my past.

How many championships could I have won if all I had to do was coach basketball? Think about Dean Smith's seventy percent of factors that affected winning but had nothing to do with basketball. My seventy percent included racist attacks on me and my players, false accusations that I myself was a racist, trying to stop rules that hurt Black kids, being compared with Nazis and Idi Amin. I had to help our players accept and manage how we were being dealt with. Trying to help kids deal rationally with the irrational way they were perceived was a challenge, but it was my job to understand things that were not understandable.

Through it all, I knew I had no choice but to win. I had to be successful to help Black people obtain the right not to be successful.

But you know what? I wouldn't have been satisfied with just being a basketball coach. I needed that extra responsibility, something meaningful to fuss about and fight for. Despite how people tried to portray us, I didn't accept it, nor did I apologize. I didn't change what we were doing or become defensive in my actions. It gave me great satisfaction to challenge situations I felt were unfair. I didn't think about it that way at the time, but I see now that I needed to challenge injustices like Proposition 42, even if the result was my not having the luxury of just being a coach.

My life would have felt empty without it.

AS THE SEASON progressed, I ran into Rayful at Coolidge High School. I was there to watch Curt Smith, Charles's little brother. Curt never made the NBA but became a playground legend in Washington with the nickname Trouble. I was watching the game when Rayful came and sat down beside me. We chatted for a little while about who was better, Charles or Curt. I took Smitty; Rayful liked Trouble. Rayful also told me he and his mother were at the Boston College game when I walked out. He said they were part of the standing ovation.

While we talked, I asked one of my assistant coaches to grab me a hot dog. He came back empty-handed because the line was too long.

Rayful asked, "What happened?"

I explained about the line at the concession stand. Rayful nodded to one of his guys, who had been sitting behind us. The dude cut to the front of the line and ordered a hot dog. Nobody in the line said a word. They all knew who he was with. He came back and handed me the dog. Rayful smiled, and they left.

Pittsburgh beat us at their place in February, and we lost the regular season finale to Syracuse in overtime at the Carrier Dome. In the conference tournament, we bounced back to beat Pitt in the semis and Syracuse in the finals. The Big East championship earned us a No. 1 seed in the East region for the 1989 NCAA tournament.

Our opponent was No. 16 seed Princeton. I was not happy to play them. Nobody liked to play Pete Carril's team, because his "Princeton offense" was tough to deal with. I knew that better than most because my son John had just finished playing there. They were great at taking advantage of pressure defense to cut backdoor for layups, which worked well against a team like mine trained to make steals. Princeton's style also cut the number of possessions and shortened the game, which gave teams with more talent less margin for error. We were one of those teams with more talent.

Princeton sat back in a zone and led 29–21 at halftime. The game was at the Providence Civic Center, and the whole arena was cheering against us. People who were there said they heard a lot of racist stuff from the crowd, but I didn't notice. Nobody roots for Goliath, even when he went to the local university and played for the Celtics.

In the second half we lobbed it inside to Alonzo and he went to work. With 1:45 to go, Princeton was up two points. Alonzo tied the game with two free throws. We stole a pass, then missed a shot, but Alonzo battled for the rebound and was fouled. With the whole arena screaming at him, Zo made the front end of a one-and-one, then missed the second free throw. We led 50–49. Princeton got the rebound and called time-out with 15 seconds left. As Princeton came back onto the floor, the crowd gave them a standing ovation. A No. 16 seed had never beaten a No. 1.

I put my guys in man-to-man defense. Princeton's guard dribbled off a high ball screen and went up for a jumper. Alonzo flew in out of nowhere and blocked the shot. After a scramble, Princeton had the ball out of bounds with one second left. They threw it to Alonzo's man—and Zo blocked the shot again, his seventh rejection of the night.

Game over. We won. As I shook hands with Carril and the Princeton players, the crowd booed our team.

My son John was at that game. He had graduated from Princeton the year before. He says it was the most difficult game he ever experienced, because he loved people on both sides. He got so nervous, he had to leave in the second half and walk around the stadium concourse. Afterward, John told me, "If I was playing, Princeton would have won." But I know he was really rooting for us. Blood is thicker than water.

A lot of people credit our Princeton game for saving the current NCAA tournament format. A movement had been forming to eliminate automatic bids for the lower-level conferences. People thought the fifth- or sixth-place ACC team deserved to play in the tournament more than the champion of the Ivy League. But the huge TV ratings for our Princeton game made it obvious that underdogs make the tournament special.

Nobody ever got more out of losing than Princeton did that game. They deserve a lot of credit for how well they played, though we did win. Years later, I served on the Nike board with Ralph DeNunzio, a Princeton graduate and chairman of the New York Stock Exchange. Ralph and I were close friends. Ralph always talked about that game and would say things like, "That was such a great game, Coach, we almost beat you guys."

I'd tell Ralph, "Yeah, y'all took pride in losing."

Our next opponent was Notre Dame, coached by Digger Phelps. That was the only time Father Healy ever talked to me about a basketball game. The Big Irishman had been an administrator at Fordham while Digger coached there, and Digger had some sort of contractual problem with the school. Before the Notre Dame game, Father Healy came up to me and said, "Kick their ass, John." We did.

In the Sweet Sixteen against North Carolina State, Charles had the flu and scored only one point, but we scratched out a victory. Two days later, we faced Duke, with a trip to the Final Four on the line.

Duke's coach, Mike Krzyzewski, had not yet won his first championship. Danny Ferry was a senior on that team, and Christian Laettner was a freshman. Grant Hill and Bobby Hurley weren't there yet. Duke beat us, 85–77. They led pretty much the whole game. Charles played well with 21 points, but the matchups were in their favor, and they did a good job on Alonzo. Duke deserved to win.

My seventeenth season as Georgetown's coach was over. I had worked nonstop the prior three years, traveling each summer for Olympic scouting and coaching. I went back home to Washington and shut down for some rest.

Three weeks later, on April 15, Rayful Edmond was arrested on federal drug charges and accused of orchestrating three homicides.

NOT LONG AFTER, I got a call from Ted Koppel, from the influential *Nightline* TV news program. He was planning a special town hall episode on the nationwide drug epidemic, to be filmed at my old school, Our Lady of Perpetual Help. Koppel told me he was going to report that my players had been associating with Rayful.

I said I would come on his program to talk about it. In hindsight, I think Koppel was a good journalist who manipulated me into confirming the story. Koppel might not have had more than a rumor, but when I didn't deny it, he knew it was true. Fortunately, the interview turned out to be great for me. I was able to reveal the information on my terms, instead of the media sensationalizing a scoop.

One of the things I did not want to reveal pertained to John Turner. One of the murders Rayful was charged with happened outside the Chapter III nightclub. The police said that Rayful had told an associate named Little Nut to kill a rival dealer, and afterward Rayful gave Little Nut a Mercedes. The next month, Little Nut got ambushed in a barbershop off Benning Road, two blocks from where I grew up. He survived but was paralyzed and had to use a wheelchair. Little Nut was nineteen years old. Several people told me that John Turner was frequently seen driving Little Nut's Mercedes.

On April 27, Koppel broadcast his show live from Our Lady of Perpetual Help. I was nervous. We were on thin ice. Fenlon and I watched the beginning of the show from a nearby house, then headed over to the school as scheduled. When we got into the car, Fenlon said out of the blue, "He's got to go."

I was confused and asked what she was talking about.

"Alonzo," Fenlon said. "He's got to go."

She thought we should dismiss Zo from the team to save the program. Fenlon and Alonzo ended up developing a fantastic relationship, but at that moment she was ready to cut him loose. I put that thought in the back of my mind and focused on what I would say on camera. We were in a large room with several dozen audience members. Mayor Marion Barry was there. So was U.S. Secretary of Housing and Urban Development Jack Kemp, and representatives from the D.C. police and the Drug Enforcement Administration. When it was time for me to speak, I gathered my courage, let my emotions flow, and tried to protect my team and my school.

I told Koppel the basic outline of what happened with Alonzo, Turner, Rayful, and myself. I emphasized that drugs and drug dealers were a problem for everyone in our communities and that we needed to find a way to help young people involved with those things. I reminded everyone that the Rayfuls of the world were our neighbors' children. The revelation that I had met with Rayful deflected media attention from what my players did, and the whole affair was generally perceived as me trying to take care of my kids. People wrote a few articles about what I said, but there was not much fallout after that.

The next problem was whether any of us would be called to testify at Rayful's trial. The summer of 1989 was tense as we learned that Rayful's lawyers planned to call Alonzo as a witness. Through it all, people told me that JT was still driving that Mercedes and hanging out with Rayful's crew. I decided that if Turner wouldn't end those relationships, I had to end his relationship with Georgetown. I told him to have his stuff off campus by morning.

I didn't feel great about that. Turner wasn't a thug or a bad kid, and I liked him as a person. He saw guys his age with cars, money, and clothes, and he couldn't resist the Call of the Wild. But I had given him enough chances, and I had to protect the university. Turner's family accused me of making him a scapegoat and tried to force me to bring him back to Georgetown. His family claimed JT and Alonzo had done the same things, but Alonzo got special treatment because he was a star. No, Alonzo got his act together, while JT rode around town in Little Nut's Benz.

A week after Turner's family complained to the newspaper, he was arrested in a Maryland park and charged with possession and intent to distribute crack. The charges were later dropped on a technicality because the arrests were made by police from another jurisdiction, but that closed the case on his coming back to Georgetown. He ended up making a good life for himself, and he's doing well now. We're on good terms.

My own involvement with the trial was still in question when Bill Butler from Boys Club No. 2 showed up at McDonough one day. He asked me to step outside so we could speak in private.

When we walked out of the gym he said, "Rayful's lawyers are not going to call you as a witness at the trial."

It sounded too good to be true. "How do you know that?" I asked.

"Cornell called me at the club. From Leavenworth."

I did a double take. Cornell Jones was the major drug figure in Washington before getting sent to prison in 1986. After Cornell got locked up, Rayful took over. Cornell also was a No. 2 guy, he hung out at the club and bought equipment for all the kids. I saw him around No. 2 sometimes, and Cornell followed a lot of my players from Washington.

"Cornell told me you don't have anything to worry about," Mr. Butler said. "He said to tell you that Rayful is not going to call you as a witness."

Cornell and Rayful had the same attorney. I found out later that Cornell appreciated how I donated money to No. 2 and helped a lot of kids he knew get degrees. He felt that since I had reached back to the neighborhood and lifted people up, Rayful should not try to bring me down by dragging my name into the trial. Cornell didn't want to give my critics any ammunition, and once he put the word out, it was law. I was amazed that he had the power, all the way from Leavenworth prison in Kansas, to say, "Do *not* put that man on the witness stand."

But think about this for a minute. Where did Cornell call? The Police Boys Club No. 2. That shows how the relationships between people like Cornell or Rayful and the community were often different than commonly portrayed. It was not unusual for hustlers to associate with law-abiding citizens in our neighborhoods. We had some of the same interests. Just because you interacted with someone who broke the law didn't make you a criminal.

When the trial started, Rayful was flown to court each day in a helicopter, and I was shocked to see him sitting behind bulletproof glass in the courtroom. You mean someone could bust in at any moment and shoot him? People wanted him dead that much? It made me think about how close my players came to that kind of danger, and it added a new dimension to Rayful's visit to my office. Perhaps I should have been more concerned. It was a huge relief not to be called as a witness, but Alonzo was not so lucky. He spent about two hours on the witness stand, where he testified that he had visited the homes of Rayful and one of his co-defendants about a dozen times. The defense attorneys asked questions designed to show that Alonzo had never seen or discussed any criminal activity. They wanted to make their clients look innocent. When the prosecution asked Alonzo why he stopped hanging out with the defendants, he started to say, "Coach Thompson put a stop to it." But before he could complete the sentence, Rayful's attorney jumped in to object. My name never came up again.

Thank you, Cornell.

The team left on a trip to Hawaii while Alonzo was caught up with the case, and he had to fly out by himself to join us later. He was still scared to death when he got back with the team. Rayful was convicted and sentenced to life in prison.

One of the reasons I have kept quiet over the years about Rayful, and am still keeping some things we talked about private, is the simple fact that he helped me, even though he didn't have to and I had no way to force him to. He helped me without us even mentioning the word "drugs." My career at Georgetown could have taken a much different course, or ended altogether. But I asked Rayful to separate himself from my players, and he did.

I have some good friends who made bad mistakes in their lives, but they are still good people. I also know bad people who did good things, but they're still bad people. How do we separate the two?

16

ALONZO AND DIKEMBE

Despite all the drama that always seemed to surround our program, we had lots of good times. I didn't always come to practice and curse everybody out. We laughed a lot. I enjoyed being around the coaches and the kids. Sometimes I did things to deliberately lighten the mood, like put on some Motown and dance around the locker room, telling the kids I had better moves than them. I grew up with three sisters, so I was their guinea pig before any dance they went to. If you can't picture me dancing, well, neither could my players before I did it.

Our team discussions continued. I asked what they thought about the TV commentator Jimmy the Greek's statement that Black athletes were genetically superior. Jimmy said on television that during slavery, big male slaves were bred with big female slaves, and as a result a Black athlete had "big thighs that go up into his back," which made us run faster and jump higher. Obviously it was some racist garbage, but I put it out there for the team to talk about. When I got to Mark Tillmon, he didn't have anything to say. I got on his case, told him all he wanted to read in the newspaper was his own press clippings. After that, Mark always expressed his opinion. Alonzo Mourning says that based on our practice conversations, he started reading the newspaper every day.

Early on, Alonzo didn't care much about class. His teammates said he studied the least of anybody on the team, then did better than them on the tests. In the middle of one semester, I reviewed his grades with Mary Fenlon. He had Bs and a few Cs. Fenlon said he had more than enough intelligence to do better. I called Zo into my office and gave him a speech.

"You're wasting your ability, son. Basketball will not be here forever. You feel invincible now, but you never know when the end of your basketball career will come. When it does, you'll wish that you developed your mind more than your body. You'll wish you hadn't wasted your intellectual ability. What if you had some gift for the world inside your mind, like the cure for cancer, but you never pushed yourself enough academically to know it was there? That would be a tragedy."

Alonzo listened. He didn't say anything, because it was a speech, not a conversation. Then he went out and made the dean's list.

I told my players the locker room belonged to them. It was their sanctuary, and they could feel free in there to say whatever they wanted. I knew they liked to make fun of me, call me things like Bighead. Everybody needs a place to blow off steam and be free, so I let them have the locker room for themselves.

But I also told them that when I walk into that locker room, it's mine. They had to know that somebody was in charge, and it wasn't them.

They also knew I was liable to knock on their dormitory doors at any time. And when I knocked, I was coming in. Georgetown basketball was not a democracy, and I didn't need a warrant to enter the premises. I may or may not have had my assistants look through their rooms while they were at practice.

One season, I figured out a particular group of players was drinking beer more often than they should have. I kept getting on them about it, but they kept doing it. I asked Ed Spriggs, who was one of my assistant coaches at the time, "What's the best beer out there?" He told me it was Heineken. I gave him some money and asked him to bring some back to McDonough.

The next practice, I ran the hell out of them before giving them a water break. Every player had his own water bottle with his number on it. I had put Heineken in the water bottles of the beer drinkers.

Some of them tasted it and spat it right out. Other guys tried to play it off like nothing was different. I just sat there staring at them. They looked at me, and I looked back at them. Then somebody said something like, "I think there's something wrong with my Gatorade."

That's when I went off. I hit them with every curse word in the book and might have invented a couple more on the spot. "It's not Gatorade, it's what y'all were drinking last night. Y'all think I'm stupid? I know what y'all are doing, and it better stop!"

I didn't let them drink the beer, of course. It was a teaching moment. I did that kind of stuff to get their attention. Now, how could I do that if reporters were in the gym? There would be headlines about John Thompson getting kids drunk. Some media people thought I kept them out of practice to stop them from doing their jobs. In reality, I was preserving my ability to do mine.

Dikembe missed a class one day. When he walked onto the practice floor that afternoon, I was lying in wait up on the balcony. I went all the way off, kicked him out of practice and sent him back to the locker room. In his locker was a one-way airplane ticket back to the Congo. The flight was leaving that night. Actually, it wasn't a ticket, it was something Dikembe thought was a ticket, and I didn't try to change his mind. Dikembe pleaded for forgiveness, saying he'd had a bad toothache and gone to the dentist. I told him to schedule his medical appointments when he didn't have class. I said if he wasn't going to follow the rules, he could go back to the Congo and fight in Mobutu's army.

Poor Dikembe was scared out of his mind. I didn't let him practice that day, and when practice ended he was crying in my office. I didn't let him off the hook, and left him to be consoled by Fenlon. When we let Dikembe return to practice the next day, he ran harder than anybody I had ever seen. I never saw such rebounding in my life. Dikembe never missed another class at Georgetown and had tremendous success as a student.

The kids knew I cared about them, but it was not my goal for them to know. I was not what some people call a "player's coach." That term is ridiculous to me. You'd better be a "coach's player." Don't get me wrong, I made mistakes. I did and said things I should not have done or said to some of my players. As some of them got older, they understood, and lots of players tell me now they appreciate certain ways I motivated them. But when they were playing, it was more like, "I wish Coach Thompson would leave me alone!"

By this point in my career, my reputation had changed to some degree. More people understood my emphasis on education, character, discipline, and all the other values our program taught. People started saying, "Oh, Thompson is such a great father figure, educating all these poor Black kids." Wait a minute, now. I cared tremendously about being a good coach, too. I spent a lot of time figuring out how to beat Syracuse and St. John's, and it worked. I resented being portrayed as some kind of social worker. Yes, I did feel a strong responsibility to educate kids, based on what I had learned from people like my mother and Dr. Anita Hughes. I always knew the basketball would eventually lose those eight to nine pounds of air. Sometimes I am defined as the person who was mostly concerned about when the ball was empty, but I'll be damned if I wasn't concerned about when the ball was full. When it was full, I beat a lot of good coaches.

In the privacy of my own mind, I was paranoid about being acknowledged too much as an educator. I also was paranoid about being acknowledged too much as a coach. So I was sort of screwed up.

THE PROPOSITION 42 experience awakened a lot of Black college coaches to the fact that we could change the system, and a group of us formed the Black Coaches Association. Rudy Washington, the head coach at Drake, was executive director of the group. The engine was made up of me, George Raveling, John Chaney, and Arkansas coach Nolan Richardson. In 1994, Nolan became the second Black coach to win a national championship. He said his "40 Minutes of Hell" full court press was inspired by my team, which I took as an incredible compliment. But most important, George, Chaney, and Nolan were intelligent men who could articulate our struggle, and we had some of the best teams in the country. The four of us had influence, and we knew how to use it. We needed to, because Black coaches still faced a lot of obstacles. One of my friends went to apply for a job at a Jesuit school, and a high-ranking administrator, who also was a priest, told him, "If you did something like walk out over Proposition 42, I would fire you."

The NCAA was still doing some boneheaded things, which gave us plenty to fuss about. We resisted its attempts to adjust academic standards in ways that would discriminate against poor and Black kids. We tried to keep it from reducing the number of scholarships per team from fifteen to thirteen. We pressured the NCAA on the diversity of its own hiring practices. Another issue was a rule preventing coaches from being in neighborhoods where the NCAA thought all we wanted to do was recruit. In reality, we felt an obligation to interact with youth in these neighborhoods and expose them to the possibilities of higher education, with or without basketball. The rule would have prevented me from going to Boys Club No. 2, or Chaney from stepping into a gym in Philadelphia. It made no sense.

We had the fear of the riot working for us and were able to influence some important issues. The four of us went on the Charlie Rose television show with Bill Rhoden. We went to Capitol Hill and met with the Congressional Black Caucus. Through it all, we operated in a rational and thoughtful manner. Nobody was talking loud or cursing people out. Our leverage was the threat of boycotting games, and we made a difference.

George made a point on the Charlie Rose show that I found incredibly important. He observed that America was built on special interest groups advocating for their needs. Teachers, insurance agents, Italians, Catholics, you name it, each group organizes to voice its concerns.

But when we do it as Black people, let alone as Black coaches, it was perceived to be negative or us discriminating against white people. That's not the case at all. When the Italian coaches in the Big East got together talking about *paisan* this or *goombah* that, I didn't interpret it as them hating me. So there's no reason to feel threatened by a group of Black coaches. No good reason, that is.

We did some positive things, but unfortunately the emphasis of the Black Coaches Association changed over time. It became more of a social organization, putting on games to make money, having conventions at places guys could take their girlfriends and play golf. I started to hear more conversations about tee times than helping kids. They rationalized this by saying a lot of work was done on the golf course, but I believed a lot more got done in a room where people exchanged ideas as a group.

Richard Lapchick was involved with the Black Coaches Association, even though he's white. Lapchick is a great humanitarian and advocate for equality in sports, and he has organized more protests and written more articles to fight racism than most Black people. The BCA had a rotating system for who got to be president, but when it was Lapchick's turn, they refused to give him the office. They said it wouldn't look right for a white man to have the job. I did not agree at all, and said so. It was another sign that we had started to go off track.

I knew that money coming in from games would cause problems with accountability. When I asked questions, people were reluctant to delineate who would manage the funds, how they would be accounted for, and other things that are essential to any properly run organization. That's when I told George, Chaney, and Nolan, "I'm out of here." I wasn't going to give anybody the chance to make accusations against me about misuse of money based on what other people were doing.

The association added football coaches later on and then brought in Black athletic administrators, which diluted our impact. And just as I had predicted, funds became an issue, and soon they didn't have enough money to survive. The NCAA actually stepped in and placed the Black Coaches Association under its corporate structure so it could continue operations. I couldn't think of a worse development. We started out fighting against the NCAA, and now the NCAA controls the Black Coaches Association? That was like giving the Russians the right to vote in our elections.

It made me sad, because we had real leverage, but we lost sight of what we came for. We had nobody to blame but ourselves. We lit the fire, and all they had to do was fan the flames, but they let it go out. It's almost like when a Black man became president of the United States and everybody wanted to believe America was suddenly a postracial society. I won a title, and then Nolan won, so all our problems were supposed to be solved. Clearly that was the farthest thing from the truth, because there are no Black college coaches today with major influence. We took our eye off the ball.

In the 1989–90 season, when Alonzo was a sophomore, he played even better. He wanted to be the next Patrick Ewing, and it was working. Dikembe got more playing time, too, and averaged 11 points and 10.5 rebounds per game. Mark Tillmon had a great season and benefited from all the attention Alonzo got from opposing defenses, putting up 20 points per game.

We had an incident at Connecticut where Alonzo was accused of using anti-Semitic language against a Jewish player on their team. It was a bald-faced lie. I knew it as soon as someone said Alonzo called the UConn kid a "dirty Jew." First of all, we don't think of Jewish people that way. They're just white. In the Black community, if you're white, you're white. We put them all together. Then I asked Alonzo what happened, and I told him I would have a serious problem with any remarks of that nature because of my friendships with Jewish people like the Furashes, Red Auerbach, and David Falk. Zo said he didn't even know the kid was Jewish and denied saying anything anti-Semitic. He did curse him out, but that's part of basketball. Steve Berkowitz from the *Washington Post* wrote that Calhoun acknowledged the whole thing was false. I was relieved to clear that up, because I understand the level of discrimination that Jewish people have been subjected to.

We were 22–4 going into the regular season finale at Syracuse. Jim Boeheim had a strong team with Derrick Coleman and Billy Owens, and more than thirty-three thousand fans packed the Carrier Dome for the largest on-campus crowd ever at a college basketball game. With a few minutes left in the first half, we led by three points when the ref called a reach-in foul on Dwayne Bryant. I argued the call and got a technical foul. I got even angrier and received two more techs, for what they said was leaving the coaching box, and was ejected from the game.

I never liked that box. I thought it was made to protect weak officials. Good referees weren't afraid to have a discussion or listen to what I had to say. They knew how to keep control, and if they told me the discussion was over, I accepted it. If I roamed out onto the court yelling at the refs or my team, certain referees just gave me a certain look and I knew I'd better shut up and get back to the bench. Putting us in a box protected refs who couldn't control the game.

That said, getting ejected at Syracuse was my mistake. It happens sometimes in competition. Contrary to my reputation, I had not received a technical foul that whole season and hadn't been kicked out of a game since 1975. But I let my competitive instincts get the better of me, and it cost my team. Derrick Coleman made seven of eight foul shots from the personal foul plus the technicals. Then Syracuse took the ball out of bounds, and Billy Owens sank a three. It was a ten-point swing in their favor. We went from being up three points to down seven. Of course the crowd loved it when I was ejected, and I waved my arms at them to make more noise as I exited through the tunnel.

We still had the game won, though. Riley and Esherick took over coaching, and we battled back. With four seconds left, Alonzo made both ends of a one-and-one to put us up two points. He had improved his free throw percentage that season to 78 percent, up from 67 percent his freshman year. After Zo gave us the lead, Syracuse inbounded the ball to Owens. As he dribbled toward midcourt looking for a desperation shot, Sam Jefferson fouled him fifty feet from the basket. With one second left, Owens sank two free throws to send it to overtime, where they nipped us, 89–87.

The rest of the season was disappointing. We lost to UConn in the Big East tournament semifinals, then were upset by Xavier, 74–71, in the second round of the NCAAs.

We experienced more heartbreak the following season, 1990–91, when we lost in the Big East championship to Seton Hall. In six previous conference championship games, I had never lost. Then UNLV, the defending national champs, beat us in the second round of the NCAAs. For the second straight year, we didn't even reach the Sweet Sixteen. Duke won it all that year, for Coach K's first championship.

Dikembe had a year of eligibility left, but he was on track to graduate from Georgetown that spring. He went pro and was the fourth pick in the NBA draft. I'm glad we didn't leave him at the airport four years earlier. Dikembe arrived here not speaking English and barely understanding what a zone defense was. He left with a Georgetown degree, and he has done tremendous things with it. The man built an entire hospital in the Congo and named it after his mother. He led a group of players to South Africa and built homes there. He's on the Georgetown board of trustees. He is making a real difference in the world.

Alonzo had one season left and played out of this world in 1991–92, averaging 21 points on only 11 shots, with 11 rebounds and five blocks per game. But we lost to Syracuse 56–54 in the Big East championship, the first time I ever lost that game to Boeheim. And for the third straight year, we lost in the second round of the NCAA tournament. This time Florida State beat us, behind their point guard Sam Cassell. They did everything they could to deny Alonzo the ball, and it worked.

Alonzo's college career ended without a trip to the Final Four. From one perspective, that could be considered a disappointment. But in the broader view, Alonzo got as much out of Georgetown as anyone I ever coached. He learned that he is more than a basketball player. I'm extremely proud of his seven NBA All-Star games and two Defensive

Player of the Year awards. I'm amazed that he returned to the pros after a kidney transplant. I advised him to retire rather than play again. I'm glad he didn't listen to me, because he won an NBA championship in 2006. But as much as I appreciate his basketball accomplishments, I'm equally proud of the youth center he founded in Miami and his numerous other philanthropic activities. Alonzo is driven to make a difference in the world, and he credits Georgetown for exposing him to life beyond basketball.

In Alonzo's autobiography, he perhaps unknowingly repeated something I said to him twenty years earlier. When explaining his passion to help other people, he wrote, "What happens if no one invests in that kid who may be easy to miss but has the cure for cancer in him, or who has a great business mind, or who can be a great musician or teacher or community leader?"

That's Georgetown basketball.

One of the worst episodes of my entire life was when Charles Smith went to prison.

Charles was one of my all-time favorites. Not just because of how good he was, although he did hit more big shots in pressure situations than any player I ever had. But Charles also was a great young man, polite and respectful, his professors loved him, and he was a good teammate. After Charles became the star of the team, which was a surprise because I basically gave him a scholarship as a favor to a friend and didn't expect him to play, he never acted like a big shot in any way. If he went out for pizza, he'd bring back some for his teammates without their asking. I wouldn't say he was humble, because he was confident about his abilities, but he did not carry himself in an arrogant way. He did not seek out attention. He was just a terrific kid. I thought of him as one of my sons.

Charles won Big East Player of the Year his senior season, but he did not get drafted, maybe because of his small size. Charles made the Boston Celtics as a free agent and did fine his rookie year as a backup point guard. In March 1991, Charles was on a ten-day contract and playing well. The Celtics were about to sign him to a guaranteed deal for two or three years. One night, Charles's former Georgetown teammate Ben Gillery came to Boston and they went out together. About one thirty that morning, Charles was driving a van that hit two college students who were walking across the street. Both of the young women were killed. The police said he left the scene of the accident.

I couldn't imagine Charles leaving the scene. I was a character witness at his trial, which was heartbreaking. I told the truth—that Charles was an extraordinarily decent, honest, and trustworthy individual. He was convicted of vehicular homicide and leaving the scene of an accident, acquitted of the more serious charge of manslaughter and being under the influence of alcohol. The judge sentenced him to four and a half years.

He did his time at the jail in Boston. I told him to call me collect every day. The first time he called, I cried. The thought of Charles behind bars was almost unbearable.

Cornell Jones, from the Rayful situation, was still incarcerated at the time. I was told that Cornell sent word to people he knew in the Boston jail to make sure nobody touched Charles. Once again, I was amazed by what Cornell could do from prison. But it was cold comfort, because Charles was still locked up.

The next year, we had a game up in Boston and lost. Afterward, I gave the bus driver the address of the jail. We pulled up and I went inside. I wanted the whole team to visit with Charles, but the people who ran the jail wouldn't allow it, so Fenlon and I went in there by ourselves.

That was the most difficult moment for me. Charles sat on the other side of bulletproof glass from us in one of those booths, wearing a prison outfit. He said he was doing okay, although his face said otherwise. I'll never forget the moment that our visit was over, when they took Charles away and the metal door closed shut behind him. Right before the door closed, Charles looked back at me and Fenlon. I cried then, too.

Charles served twenty-eight months of his sentence, and he played only eight games in the NBA after that. He came home to Washington and started the rest of his life. About ten years ago, there was a story in the news that Charles was shot twice at his house. Charles liked to gamble; I was told that he used to play cards back at Georgetown. He told me he got into an argument with someone who owed him a gambling debt, and the man came to his house and shot him. No charges were ever filed, and the shooter was never apprehended.

Remember when I said that I knew some good people who might do bad things? It's easy to think about that in the abstract, but it's difficult when you love the person who makes a mistake.

It's even harder when you have to watch them suffer.

17

IVERSON

In late 1993 or early 1994, I got a phone call out of the blue from a guy I respect named Boo Williams, who ran an AAU organization in Virginia. He told me some people wanted to come up and talk to me about kid from Hampton named Allen Iverson.

I knew who Allen was because his court case had been national news. I knew he had experienced a tremendous injustice. There was a fight at a bowling alley after groups of Black and white teenagers had been talking back and forth at each other. They arrested the Black kids and didn't charge the white kids with anything. They said Allen hit a girl with a chair, but a video showed him walking out of the bowling alley soon after the fight started. Allen was seventeen years old and a junior in high school. They tried him as an adult, convicted him of "maiming by mob," and gave him fifteen years. There wasn't a gun, knife, or weapon of any kind. Don't tell me that wasn't racially motivated. They wanted to send a message to the Black people down there. They wanted to keep them in their place. I was overjoyed when the governor, Douglas Wilder, gave Allen clemency and let him out of prison. Wilder was the first Black governor of Virginia. Now we start to understand why some white people didn't want him to be governor in the first place.

I remember something vividly from watching the news. After they convicted Allen, when they handcuffed him and put him in the police van, he never showed any emotion. Never shed a tear, nothing. If they gave me fifteen years, I would have been crying and kicking and hollering. I thought to myself, *What kind of cold young fella is this?*

When Boo asked me to meet Allen's family, I had to think about it. Allen's reputation as a player preceded him. He was player of the year in Virginia as a junior, but it wasn't like Patrick where I said right away, "He can help us win the national championship." I was concerned that recruiting someone coming out of prison wouldn't work. I had an obligation to protect the school. But I agreed to have the conversation.

Allen's mother, Ann Iverson, came to my office with a few people close to her family. The conversation didn't go well. One guy kept asking me whether I could coach a guard. Here they are coming to me with hat in hand, asking for my help, and he's implying all I can do is coach big men. I coached Sleepy Floyd, he was All-American and an NBA All-Star. Charles Smith was All-American, John Duren, Michael Jackson, Jaren Jackson, all NBA guards. But I was supposed to be just a big man's coach?

Ann Iverson told me about Allen's court case, her friend questioned whether I could coach a guard, and they both talked about how all the other programs had stopped recruiting Allen. I think Ann sensed the meeting was not going well. She was young—she had Allen as a single mother when she was fifteen years old—but she's a sharp lady. Ann told everybody else to leave the room.

She explained some more about what happened, then looked at me and said:

"If you don't take him, they're gonna kill him."

That hit me. I identified with a young Black mother trying to help her child. Allen's family was very poor. Not wannabe poor, where you put your hat on sideways and say you come from the 'hood. The Iversons had trouble getting enough food to eat. I knew Ann was correct in saying that her son would be at risk. Not that all policemen are bad people, but I know how authorities can react when they think a Black man has gotten away with something. Sometimes they don't even need that much of an excuse, as we see now with all the videos of police killing Black people for no good reason.

I thought about what my mother would have done.

I told Ann that I wanted to talk to Allen. He came in and I gave him a speech. I told him I would consider trying to get him into the school, and I explained what we expected in terms of academic effort, behavior, and our rules. It wasn't a conversation, it was a speech. He sat there and looked at me. Later, Allen said he had never in his life heard a person use "motherfucker" more than I did that day.

After they left, I talked to my staff and to Frank Rienzo. I got some reaction from other people I respected in and out of the school, like Dr. Anita Hughes and Jill Ker Conway, the former president of Smith College, who was on the Nike board of directors. Frank supported the decision to sign Allen. I would not have done it without his agreement. I knew there was some precedent for what I was trying to do, because the president of the university had a guy working in his office who had been in prison, and the president was helping rehabilitate him. Plus, I had a strong track record. The school never had to kick out any of my players, because I did it myself, numerous times. I knew the president and other people would support me if I made a good case for his admission.

I took Allen based on his reputation as a good player and with his mother's words in my mind. I had no idea he would end up doing all the incredible things he did on the basketball court. I didn't know he was *that* good.

ALLEN ANNOUNCED HIS arrival like no one I had ever seen. He did it the summer before his freshman year, in the 1994 Jabbo Kenner League.

Georgetown always had a summer league for college players, and when I got there I named it after Mr. Jabbo from Boys Club No. 2. That resonated with a lot of us old-timers, because growing up we were not allowed to play many places Across the Park. Segregation is why Mr. Jabbo started No. 2 in the first place, and now he had his name up on Georgetown's campus.

The day of Allen's first Kenner League game, people lined up all the way out of McDonough and down the street. Allen lived up to the hype and scored 40 points, in spectacular fashion. The next game was even more of a mob scene—it was hard to even get into the gym. This was before cell phones and the Internet, and it reminded me of when I was in junior high and word swept through the neighborhood that "Rabbit's back." Allen delivered another sensational performance. He was flying across half court at that top speed of his, pulling up and dropping threes, finishing through contact at the basket, everything was going in. He dunked on one of our big guys and yelled, "Remember that name! Allen Iverson!" The attacking style of Allen's game was remarkable because he was so small, about six feet and 160 pounds. All his guys from Virginia were there, because this was Allen coming back to play in his first organized games since he was released from prison. His boys were yelling, waving their arms, and talking junk. The crowd was standing room only, for summer league.

After the last Kenner game, I told our trainer, Lorry Michel, to grab Allen and take him to the training room. I didn't want the media talking to him before he got acclimated to being here. Allen hadn't even started school yet, or been coached by me. I didn't want him to get bombarded with a bunch of questions about prison and say the wrong thing. Now that I know Allen, I know he wouldn't have said the wrong thing, but we were very protective in situations like that. They were giving out trophies after the game, and Allen wanted to be out there. He was upset I wouldn't let him stay on the floor.

That was the moment when Allen understood that someone was in charge, and it wasn't him.

When practice began that fall, Allen battled on every possession and won every sprint. He scored with ease, stole passes, dunked, you name it, against very good players. People can say our program was down all they want, but Othella Harrington, Jerome Williams, Don Reid, and Jahidi White all had NBA careers. Ya-Ya Dia was tough. We had some big, strong guards on that team, John Jacques and George Butler. Nobody could stop Allen. His talent was obvious to everybody on the team. Too obvious, for some people. I got calls from a few parents who questioned why I would sign a "jailbird." Their kids were the ones Allen ran circles around.

One of the walk-ons had worn uniform number 3 the previous season, and Lorry told me she overheard Allen talking about how he wanted that number. We had a new uniform design for his freshman year, with a kente pattern based on African cloth. I thought it would be meaningful to have something on the uniforms that identified with our ancestral homeland. Allen asked me if he could have number 3. He was humble about it, he didn't say he deserved it over a walk-on. He just said, "That number is special to me, Coach. It would mean a lot to me if I could wear it."

"Motherfucker, you'll take the number I give you," I said. Allen didn't respond, but I could see in those big puppy-dog eyes he was hurt.

A few days later, when he went to his locker, number 3 was hanging there. As soon as Lorry told me he wanted the number, I knew I would give it to him. But sometimes it's healthy not to give kids everything they want right when they want it.

Allen and Lorry developed a special relationship. Allen needed a lot of treatment because he took such a pounding on the court, being so small and fearless. He got knocked down more than any other player I've ever seen. Lorry and Allen were definitely an odd couple, a little white lady and a tough Black kid. But they became extremely close, because he trusted her to take care of him, and they remain close to this day. When Lorry was dealing with medical issues recently, Allen telephoned her frequently. He still calls her Ms. Michel, to this day, because we taught our kids to address the basketball staff with respect.

Classes began, and Allen always cooperated with what we asked him to do. He showed up on time to every practice and followed the dress code. Mary Fenlon said he was a responsible student. On the court, he was coachable. If we ran a play for somebody else and Allen thought he should get the ball, he still followed the plan without complaining. I could list a lot of my players who gave me far more headaches than Allen ever did. In the NBA he had a rebellious image, and they say he was the reason the NBA instituted a dress code. At Georgetown, Allen wore a jacket and tie like everyone else, kept his hair cut low, and didn't give me any lip about it.

Sports Illustrated wanted to put Allen on the cover before his first game, with another freshman, Felipe Lopez from St. John's, but I said no. At that time, freshmen were not dominating the way some do now. I thought it would be too much pressure and attention when Allen hadn't even played a game yet. It also could have created resentment within the team. I wasn't punishing *Sports Illustrated* or Allen, I thought he needed to show he could do it first. And he did.

Allen had one tattoo when he got here, of a bulldog with THE ANSWER written underneath it. I didn't have a rule against tattoos, but they were not as popular or accepted then. Allen was probably my first player to have one. Since there was a certain perception of him coming out of prison, I was more conscious of him having that tattoo, and of the possibility he would want more. Consciously or unconsciously, I felt a responsibility to protect Allen from being falsely judged, and to protect the image of Georgetown, which had taken a chance by letting him in. The thing is, Allen did not act like the stereotype of some tattooed gangster coming out of prison. He was not belligerent or uncooperative. He did not resist my authority. He was sensitive and intelligent, and he cared about other people.

Before Allen, my players knew better than to get tattoos or wear braids in their hair. It wasn't something I had to give speeches about. When I was young, we called braided hair "plaits." I told one of my teams that if anybody had their hair in plaits and missed a rebound, I wouldn't see the ball, all I would see is those plaits.

A lot of my concern about tattoos and hairstyles came from how they would be perceived given the identity of our program. The way some people tried to portray my team as thugs, tattoos would have made it easier for them to run with that stereotype. Also, I always told my players that you give your best interviews when you're not being interviewed. I once saw a manager pick up ice off the floor when nobody was watching, and I gave him a full scholarship with tuition, books, and room and board. So I was concerned about a kid with tattoos sitting on an airplane with someone from corporate America who might be in a position to help them after graduation. Back when those things were not as accepted, that person sitting next to you might translate tattoos as a risk. That was one reason we wore ties to our games.

I loved it when we walked into a Big East banquet and other teams were slouching around in sweatsuits. Sometimes I brought my team in late on purpose. It made an impression when we filed in wearing jackets and ties. It said Georgetown has a higher standard.

Today tattoos and plaits are normal. Allen made that happen. I didn't frown on his NBA image. Times change. Music changes, we went from singing to rapping. I prohibited my players from having cell phones, but that would be silly now. In the seventies, I didn't have a problem when the kids started wearing Afros. All of us in life express ourselves differently, especially as we move from youth to adulthood. If I were coaching now, I would adjust to modern styles the way I adjusted to Afros and long shorts.

We opened the 1994–95 season against Nolan Richardson's Arkansas team, which was the defending national champion and ranked No. 1. Nolan had his two best players back, Corliss Williamson and Scotty Thurman. We lost, but Allen scored 19 on them. Then he had 31 against DePaul and 30 against Providence. Nobody had ever scored for me like that as a freshman.

A lot of people made a big deal out of me changing our style of offense, or "loosening the reins," or whatever they wanted to call it. After I got a full grasp on Allen's talent and knew that he understood our system, I absolutely gave Allen more freedom. His ability deserved more freedom, so I turned him loose within the framework of our principles. For example, we had an offense to break the press, but I told Allen, "If you can dribble through the press, forget about the offense. Just go." That's not loosening the reins. That's common sense.

I always said the boy had been wrongfully incarcerated in prison, so I didn't want to incarcerate him on the court. Why should I lock him up again for the sake of my ego or being in control? When you get an Allen Iverson, you gotta let the bird fly.

Part of letting Allen fly was letting him shoot three-pointers. I had to change with the times. Rick Pitino at Providence was the first coach I saw use the three-point line as a weapon, and you had to take what he was doing into account. That said, I'm old school, so I always thought you should get more points for a layup. It's harder to get all the way to the basket. A layup is easier to make, but harder to get. Half the time when people shoot threes, nobody is guarding them. I think they gave players more points for the wrong thing.

Allen was obviously quick and fast, but he had stamina and toughness, too. In the NBA, Kobe Bryant used to bet people on the number of times Allen would get knocked on the floor. Allen had been a great football player in high school—before he was arrested, Notre Dame offered to let him play both sports—so he was used to the contact. Allen was tough as hell on defense and won Big East Defensive Player of the Year twice. He faced all kinds of trick defenses, other teams beat the hell out of him, and the little fella got up and kept playing.

Allen never complained about the beatings he took, but he wasn't Superman. He confided in Lorry a lot. Sometimes she told me that Allen didn't feel well enough to participate in a shootaround or practice, and I'd tell her, "Put an ice pack on his leg so I can sit him out." I knew he had to conserve his energy, and when it was game time, he'd perform. I worked with him, not against him. Sometimes he didn't want to do something, but we made him do it, and he didn't complain. Allen never held us hostage. I probably let Patrick sit out practice twice as much as Allen.

I think people who treat everyone the same are fools. Not everyone requires the same treatment.

Allen's talent and history, on a team with our reputation, made him more of a target. We had an incident his freshman year at a Big East school that almost led me to pull our team out of the game. Their fans were wearing jail suits and handcuffs and holding up some terrible signs. One banner said ALLEN IVERSON, THE NEXT MICHAEL JORDAN, but MICHAEL JORDAN was crossed out and replaced with O. J. SIMPSON. As if Allen had been accused of murder. And this was at a Catholic university, run by priests. I hope they had a deep confession that week.

It's not widely acknowledged that after Governor Wilder commuted Allen's sentence and let him out of prison, the conviction was overturned. There was no good evidence to convict Allen of the crime. The headlines when he came here said CONVICTED FELON, which turned out to be false. But those fans still wanted to compare Allen to a murderer, and just like with Patrick, the administrators from these Christian universities didn't do anything.

I played Allen just ten minutes that game. It was his only time in a Georgetown uniform when he didn't score in double figures.

We had a good team that year, with Othella Harrington playing well as an undersized center and Jerome Williams averaging 10 rebounds per game. Jerome stole his nickname when I told the team they had to play like a bunch of junkyard dogs. Soon I heard Jerome referring to himself as *the* Junkyard Dog, which was a smart thing to do. But even with Allen as good as he was, the Big East was still the Big East. UConn had Ray Allen and Kevin Ollie. Syracuse had John Wallace and Lawrence Moten. Villanova had Kerry Kittles and Alvin Williams. We split with Syracuse and lost twice to UConn. Miami and Boston College beat us during a four-game skid in the middle of the season that dropped our record to 14–7 and bumped us out of the national rankings. Then Allen scored 26 points against Villanova at our place and we thumped them 77–52. ESPN broadcast the game on national television, with President Bill Clinton sitting courtside.

Clinton was a big fan of ours because he had graduated from

Georgetown, and he also had a genuine affection for Black people and felt comfortable around us. One night I was leaving the Verizon Center with David Falk when the presidential motorcade stopped right in front of us. Clinton jumped out of his limousine and gave me a big hug, and we chatted for a while about basketball. I thought the Secret Service was going to shoot Falk when he reached inside his jacket pocket for something. I have to admit, it made me feel good to know the president of the United States stopped his car to say hello to the boy from the Frederick Douglass projects.

I interacted with every president from Gerald Ford through Barack Obama, but the person I most regret not meeting is Mother Teresa. I admire her tremendously. She came to Georgetown to receive an honorary degree, but I missed the opportunity to shake her hand. I did appreciate being able to shake Obama's hand. It made me emotional when he was elected president, and frankly I was surprised that he could get that many white votes. I met Obama and his wife, Michelle, at Georgetown's annual Martin Luther King function at the Kennedy Center. Obama was very nice to me, and I was equally impressed by the First Lady. At one point during the evening I walked over to her and said, "You wear your Blackness well." She responded, "Coming from you, that means a lot."

Getting back to Allen's first season, UConn beat us in the semifinals of the Big East tournament. We made it to the Sweet Sixteen of the NCAAs, where we lost 74–64 to Dean Smith's North Carolina team featuring Jerry Stackhouse and Rasheed Wallace. Allen averaged 20.4 points, 4.5 assists, and three steals per game and was named 1995 Big East Rookie of the Year.

Frank Rienzo made an amusing observation about this time. "When you first came here, John," he said, "people complained to me about how your team ran up and down the floor and didn't have any plays. After you started winning, people complained that you were too regimented, and you should let the kids go. Now they're back to complaining about you not running plays."

Allen just played, man. A lot of people play the game so they can look good. Allen played the game to win, and he thought the best way to win was him. He wanted to win more than he wanted to look good. If Allen scored 30 and we lost he was furious. Jeff Van Gundy once told me he was coaching Allen in the NBA All-Star Game, which is all about looking good. Van Gundy said the East was relaxing their way through the game, and at halftime Allen came into the locker room and cursed everybody out. He told those guys he was tired of losing to the West and they had to play harder. Allen led the East to a win.

The thing is, Allen did look good when he played, no question. He was one of the few players who were entertaining without trying to play with flair or pizzazz. Jordan and Kobe were like that. LeBron is like that. Other guys score all night but are boring to watch. Allen was entertaining from the very beginning. Not to mention a tough son of a bitch.

AFTER ALLEN'S FIRST season ended, all my other guards graduated, and I needed backcourt help. I decided to take a chance on a troubled local kid named Victor Page.

Victor grew up in Barry Farms in Anacostia, the worst housing project in Washington. His father died of a drug overdose when Victor was ten. His mother was also an addict, and she died of AIDS when Victor was in high school, so he lived in his grandmother's apartment with about eleven other people. Victor was a big guard, six foot three and 200 pounds, strong around the basket, with a feathery touch on his jump shot. He destroyed competition at McKinley Tech High School, but his grades were poor, so he spent the next year at two different prep schools. When I decided to recruit him, I got a lot of resistance from the admissions office, but I kept advocating for Victor and they reluctantly let him in. He might have had the most difficult background of any kid I recruited, but I felt that a person coming from his environment deserved an opportunity to grow, and I believed he was willing to put forth the effort to succeed in school. Of course, I only gave him an opportunity because he was the best schoolboy player out of Washington in years.

Victor turned out to be a project unto himself. His abilities in the classroom were more limited than I had anticipated, and he had trouble following the rules. For example, one of the Georgetown parking attendants told me they saw him driving in and out of the gate on Canal Road. Players were not allowed to have cars on campus. I walked into the locker room the next day and said, "Anybody who has a car on campus, stand up right now."

Nobody stood up, which I already knew would be the case. I told Coach Spriggs to go inside Victor's locker and give me his car keys.

Victor tried to act surprised. Who knows where he got that old junk pile, because there was no registration, no insurance, no nothing. I donated it to a charity. As the years went by, Victor loved to tell that story around me. He always ended it with, "Coach, what did you do with my car? I never saw that car again." I never told him.

We began the 1995–96 season ranked fifth in the country. I broke with tradition and scheduled some real games early in the season in the preseason NIT tournament, where we beat No. 25 Georgia Tech and then lost to No. 19 Arizona. Victor had 25 against Tech, then Allen dropped 40 against Arizona. Both of them could defend, too, and I knew I had one of the best backcourts in the country.

Allen's game improved a lot his sophomore year. He shot a significantly higher percentage, especially from the three-point line. He worked hard in practice to get better and develop his game. He was such a fierce competitor. Lorry had a cardiovascular stress test for the players, and when it was Allen's turn, the first thing he asked was, "What's the record?" There were seven stages to the test, three minutes each, and each stage was faster and steeper. Allen told Lorry to put an extra minute on the last stage, and he set a record that still stood when I stopped coaching.

I liked to see who would be in the gym on Friday nights, because that was the start of the weekend and everybody liked to party. Most

Friday nights, Allen was in the gym playing pickup or working on his game. He also liked to play one-on-one after practice. We had a freshman walk-on from Brooklyn named Dean Berry. Dean had perfected a crossover dribble that Allen could not defend. Allen was ten times better than Dean, but still got shook by this move. Allen asked Dean to teach him the crossover, then started using it in games that season.

That's how Allen got his legendary move. He was humble enough to ask a walk-on to teach him.

WE WERE PLAYING at Villanova and Allen went to the hole, made a difficult basket, and drew the foul. I hate to talk so much about Allen with this team, because other guys made important contributions. Othella, Jerome, the big fella Jahidi White. Victor Page had some huge moments. But Allen's talent overshadowed everything else. Anyway, up at Villanova, Allen got the and-one. Billy Packer was announcing on TV. He got excited and called Allen a "tough little monkey."

Viewers immediately called the network, complaining that what Billy said was racist. Billy apologized on the air. Immediately after the game people told me what happened. I knew it had the potential to blow up, so I found Billy in the arena and told him to shut up and let me handle it.

I like Billy, we go way back. I didn't like when he tried to referee our games while announcing, and I didn't appreciate his description of Georgetown players as "rough" or "intimidating" during our championship run in the eighties, but I know for a fact he's not a racist. When he called Allen a tough monkey, he didn't realize Black people would associate something negative with his comment. At my postgame press conference, I started by saying flat out that Billy was not a racist. He might have made a mistake, but don't put that man in a box and play this up for the sake of entertainment. Ninety percent of the time when something racial was brought to my attention, it was another white person looking for more readers or higher ratings. "Allen is not offended,

I'm not offended, so let's leave that stuff alone," I said. It was pretty much over after that.

But think about this for a minute: the people the media should have been calling racist all these years, they didn't.

CONNECTICUT CAME TO our place with a 24–1 record in February 1996; they were undefeated in the Big East and ranked third in the country. We beat them 77–65, behind Allen's 26 points and eight steals. The boy was running around snatching passes like the defensive back he used to be in high school. Early in the second half, Allen dunked it on somebody in traffic plus the foul, just cocked that thing back and *boom!* It was like something Patrick would have done, but from a kid half Patrick's size.

I never heard Allen refer to himself as little. I don't believe he ever conceived of himself that way. In his mind, he was a giant. A great player is not great because he's rational. He's great because he's irrational.

As he got better and better, there was a lot of speculation in the media about whether Allen would skip his last two college seasons and leave for the NBA. None of my previous players had done that, not Patrick, Alonzo, Dikembe, nobody. They all got their degrees. I didn't like the media talk because I felt it encouraged Allen to leave. You put something like that in a kid's mind, it doesn't come out. I wasn't necessarily opposed to his leaving, but I wanted him to make the decision for the right reasons, not because of headlines. We tried to shield him from all the questions, and I said some things to the media strategically, to take some of the pressure off him. "Allen's not going anywhere unless I tell him it's time for him to go," I said in one article. "Tomorrow I may tell him it's time to go, but I doubt it." I said that to keep the wolves at bay.

In the last game of the regular season, Allen scored 37 and we crushed Villanova at home, 106–68. Late in the game, Allen held the ball out past the three-point line and dribbled the shot clock down to ten seconds. Allen and Victor were so effective against man-to-man defense that when I wanted to cut the clock, instead of passing I would tell them to keep the ball and then attack the basket. Allen dribbled down the clock and then took off like he was shot out of a gun. The whole Villanova defense collapsed on him and Allen still scored. Our student section went crazy and chanted, "Two more years! Two more years!" That made me angry. The newspaper said I yelled "Shut up!" at our students and threw my towel in their direction. I don't remember all that, but it sounds like something I would do. See, they didn't know why Allen was thinking about leaving. His family had nothing. His sister needed medical treatment, but they couldn't afford it. They didn't have enough food. The fans weren't concerned with any of that. They pressured Allen out of their own selfishness.

In the Big East tournament, we played Villanova again in the semifinals, and this time it was a battle. Rollie Massimino had retired by then, Steve Lappas was the coach, and Kerry Kittles was in the conversation for the best player in the Big East. Allen got into foul trouble, but Victor put us on his back and dropped 34, and we won, 84–76.

The Big East championship game at Madison Square Garden was a rematch against Connecticut. Allen committed his third foul in the first half, then his fourth early in the second. I had to sit him down. Victor started cooking and kept us in the game. I should have let Victor keep going, but I sent Allen back in and put the ball in his hands. That was a mistake.

With about five minutes left we were up 74–63. Then we couldn't score down the stretch. Nothing went in, literally. We were clinging to a 74–73 lead when Ray Allen went up for a jumper with 13 seconds left. He had missed fourteen straight shots at that point. Allen played great defense on Ray and forced him to look for a pass, but we had everybody covered. Ray threw the ball up over his shoulder, it went in, and UConn took the lead, 75–74.

Allen brought the ball upcourt and pulled up at the free throw line for a fadeaway with six seconds left. He had two guys on him. It was the kind of shot Allen made all the time, but it didn't go in. The Junkyard Dog got the rebound under the basket but missed the putback. UConn won by one. After the game, Ray Allen said he got a lucky roll on his winning basket. Allen finished with only 13 points. Victor Page had 20 and was named tournament MVP. It was a tough loss, but with the NCAAs coming up, we had a great chance to reach the Final Four or even win another championship.

I'VE SPENT A lot of time in Las Vegas over the years and have made a lot of friends there. I like to hang out in casinos and play slot machines next to the old ladies. I don't play golf, I don't go hunting, I don't have any hobbies to relieve stress other than playing those machines. They don't talk to me, and I don't talk to them.

During a coaches' convention one year we stayed at the Barbary Coast casino, across the street from Caesars Palace. A bunch of us were sitting in a booth in the back and the owner, Michael Gaughan, came over to say hello. He and I got to talking and over time became close friends. Michael is one of the many white people who became colorless to me once I got to know them. Martin Luther King said we should judge people by the content of their character and not the color of their skin, and he was right. But he was also wrong, because when you first meet somebody you can't help but see their color, and you have no idea about their character.

A few years after I met Michael, his son Brendan came to Georgetown. Brendan is a NASCAR driver now, but in college he was a kicker on the football team, and he started messing up in school. In the fall of 1995, I called Brendan to my office and said, "Take your ass to the locker room and put on a practice jersey. You just joined the basketball team." I made him a walk-on, which allowed Fenlon to supervise him academically. Brendan's job was to beat up Allen in practice, whack him and foul him like the other teams did. Allen was so small, that was a common strategy other teams used against him. It didn't work.

One day Michael Gaughan and I were walking through McCarran Airport in Vegas. I asked Michael, "How many Black people own licenses for these slot machines in the airport?"

"None," Michael said.

"Then I want one."

In addition to the opportunity to make money, what attracted me to it was that Blacks hadn't been permitted to have the opportunity. This door is closed to us? I'm gonna try to open it. I went to Carson City, the capital of Nevada, and applied for a license to buy a 10 percent interest in Gaughan's airport slot concession. I never kept it a secret, it was part of the public record and reported in the Carson City newspaper. It was not against any NCAA rules. The gaming people investigated me thoroughly, sent people to knock on my neighbor's door, looked at what felt like every check I'd cashed in my entire life. My gaming license was about to be approved when the national media decided to write about it during the 1996 NCAA tournament. I don't think it's a coincidence that the story came out at that time.

Some people went crazy, which in my opinion exposed a deeper truth. I knew what the perception was, but perception had never scared me. I knew I wasn't doing anything wrong. I wanted to own slot machines at the airport, not a sports book. It had zero connection to betting on games. Cedric Dempsey, the executive director of the NCAA, said, "It is ill-advised for anyone connected to college sports to be involved even peripherally with gambling interests." What was ill-advised was for a Black man to initiate it. It was ill-advised for me to have the audacity not to ask permission. Thomas Boswell is a *Washington Post* columnist I love to pieces, he'd been covering me since St. Anthony's. Boswell started his column with, "John Thompson has lost his mind." I didn't conform, that's how I lost my mind.

When I applied for that gaming license, I didn't think I was being rebellious. I was being free. I could break down another door for Black people.

But look at the big picture. What it came down to for some white people, consciously or unconsciously, was the idea that this nigger was out of his element. I exceeded the range of that chain they tried to put us on. I hadn't asked permission. I could be wrong, but again my so-called paranoia led me to think "*Something is holding me back / Is it because I'm Black?*"

The furor put a lot of pressure on Georgetown. Father Healy had moved on and the president was Father Leo O'Donovan. I think my pursuit of the license scared Father O'Donovan to death because of how some alumni or faculty perceived it. I don't think the Big Irishman would have been scared. I had the right to get the license, but perhaps it was not fair to the school. Georgetown had given me an opportunity to be me and had trusted me with a lot of things. Even though I never saw more bingo than in the Catholic Church, starting in elementary school when Our Lady of Perpetual Help gave perpetual bingo money to itself, I had to respect the school's position. I heard about Father O'Donovan's apprehension and called to ask him if he wanted me to withdraw my application. He said yes, so I did.

I say this on my father's grave: a big part of why I went after that license was because Black people hadn't done it before. How many other Black people could ask a friend who owned casinos to help them own slots at the airport? How many Black coaches got opportunities after I won the national championship? When Black people come up to me now and say thank you, they're not thanking me for beating St. John's.

Still, all these years later, I feel I made the right decision to walk away from the license, although it amuses me how widely accepted gambling is today. I was ahead of my time.

WE WON OUR first three games of the 1996 NCAA tournament, including an extremely physical contest against Texas Tech. In the Elite Eight, we faced John Calipari's Massachusetts team with the center Marcus Camby, who would be named national player of the year.

UMass blew us out, 86–62. Allen shot 6 for 21 from the field. Victor took only five shots and missed them all, and he had four turnovers too. Our team didn't play well, but UMass was the reason for that. They had an excellent team. What I remember more than anything else is after they won, Calipari told his players, "Do not embarrass Coach Thompson." His kids weren't jumping all over the place and acting like fools; they came over politely and shook our hands. He told them to treat me respectfully based on what I represented and everything I had done for the game. That meant a lot, because it was an embarrassing loss.

Isiah Thomas, the Detroit Pistons legend, was the first person who made me truly believe that Allen should leave school for the NBA. Isiah was one of the best point guards of all time and won two championships. We were having dinner one night, and I was nervous about Allen. I asked, "If Allen left school, how high would he go in the draft?"

Isiah looked at me and held one finger up in the air. Didn't say a word. Just held up one finger.

I was like, "What? You gotta be kidding me."

Isiah said, "Coach, he will go number one."

I didn't make the decision for Allen to leave. He told me he wanted to go, and I agreed with him. He told Fenlon, "Look where me and my family are living." I know his mother definitely wanted him to leave. How could he turn down all that money? Jesus and I would have had an argument about that.

From a basketball standpoint, Allen was more than ready. I worried about the twenty-two hours of the day when he wasn't playing basketball. Allen was twenty years old, from a troubled background, about to have millions of dollars. My concerns about those other twenty-two hours made me think he might benefit from another year in college. But I supported his wishes because you can't get drafted higher than No. 1, and there's always a danger that the NBA will fall out of love with you. Also, it would have been wrong for me to educate a young man to make judgments, then discourage him from doing what he felt in his heart he should do. I was conscious of the fact that I had built my career on education, and that none of my players, even Patrick and Alonzo, had left school without graduating to go pro. But at the same time, I did not want to be a prisoner of my own reputation.

Later that spring, when I heard Allen was driving a Mercedes around Washington, I was very angry. I went to the dealership and told them a few things, but at the end of the day, they're trying to sell cars. What happened at the car dealership was an example of what could happen in those twenty-two hours. But I might have done the same thing in Allen's position if I'd known I was leaving school. Might as well get me a car, ride around, and have a good time.

I encouraged Allen to sign with David Falk as his agent, which he did, the same as almost all of my players. Some Black agents got mad at me for sending my players to a white agent. This was especially the case with Allen, because he represented Black youth culture in a new and very strong way. Some Black agents said Falk couldn't "relate to" a kid like Allen. I responded that with all the money Falk would get him, Allen could hire whoever he wanted to "relate to." I knew Falk was the best in the business. He represented so many players, including Michael Jordan, that he had enormous leverage over the teams he was negotiating with. Falk got his players more money than anybody else, and he influenced the draft and trades to put players on teams where they could have the most success. I didn't think it was wise for my players to experiment with unproven agents. My kids had only one chance to get it right. If I needed a medical operation and knew a great white doctor, I wouldn't go to a surgeon I'd never heard of.

Allen's leaving early was an inevitable sign of the times. In today's climate, there's no way Patrick or Alonzo would have stayed four years. They might not even have gone to college at all, which is not necessarily a bad thing. Money never stopped anybody from getting an education. In fact, it makes it a lot easier.

Another thing is, not everybody who drops out of school leaves campus. A lot of athletes stayed in college but just went through the motions of being educated. They should be counted as dropouts too.

Allen did the right thing. He was the first pick and Rookie of the Year. He had that famous moment his first season when he crossed up Michael Jordan. I was excited by the move, of course, especially because I knew how good a defender Michael was. I also knew that Allen adored Michael, absolutely worshipped him. That said, I was not surprised by the crossover, because I knew what Allen could do.

Let's keep it in perspective, though. How many championships did Michael win? Six. Let me repeat: the man won six championships. Allen can have his crossover. It's like, I dunked on Bill Russell in practice. Russ still has eleven rings for ten fingers. At the end of the day, Allen's crossover don't mean shit.

The whole time he was at Georgetown, Allen never complained once about being sent to prison. I never heard him say, "They did me wrong," even though they did. As a person who is haunted by my past, I'm absolutely amazed that Allen never brought up that injustice, even in the many private moments we shared. He shook it off and kept going. Very few of us have experienced the path he had to walk to get where he is. I'm not certain John Thompson would have been different from Allen Iverson if I had his history. I'm not certain I wouldn't have had the tattoos and the attitude.

Not all of Allen's persona came from the injustice he was subjected to. Part of it was generational, and connected to hip-hop culture. I liked the attitude those young rap guys were showing. They took no shit from anybody, and they ran their own world. I love that boy Sean Combs or Puffy or whatever his name is, even though we've never had so much as a conversation. He cursed out David Falk one day because he didn't like how Falk dealt with him. As close as I am with Falk, I liked how Puffy put him in his place. Now every time I see Puffy on TV, I say, "That's not an apologetic Black man." And I don't always say "Black man," either.

Allen was one of the leaders who changed the way an entire generation dressed, even beyond basketball. The way he dribbled the ball literally changed the way basketball is played around the world. A guy brought some kids to Georgetown recently and they took a picture with me. One little boy looked up at me and asked, "Did you teach Allen

Iverson the crossover?" There's no way that boy was old enough to have seen Allen play in the NBA. That shows Allen's impact. I respect that he stayed true to himself. I like people who are not afraid to cross that bridge.

Lorry Michel once heard Allen say he wanted to be the first guy to play in the NBA with braids. He didn't grow them here, though. It was never a discussion. Early in his pro career, when he started to get more tattoos, someone asked in an interview, "What would Coach Thompson say about all your new ink?"

Allen paused and said, "If he was here, I wouldn't have all these tattoos."

I tell Allen he should have trademarked the phrase "You talking about practice." People say that all the time now. It has come to define him, but it's always taken out of context. I talked to Allen about it after that news conference. He was addressing rumors that 76ers coach Larry Brown wanted to trade him out of Philadelphia. Allen wanted to explain that they had patched up their relationship, but the media kept asking him about practice. He was not saying he didn't care about practice. He meant, I came here to talk about something else, and you're asking me about practice. Of course Allen cared about practice. He wouldn't have achieved what he achieved without practice. He learned the crossover doing extra work after practice. At the same time, he knew when it was more important to save his energy. Allen could be great without practice. So could Bill Russell.

Allen would not have been greater if he'd practiced more, because he had "It." Whatever you think It is, that undefinable quality that makes some players truly special, Allen had It.

He still calls me on my birthday, or just to say hello. He likes to say, "Thanks for saving my life. No other college wanted me." He might have ended up like one of these playground legends, the guys I saw in the park who had all the talent in the world but who never got the opportunity or were derailed by some injustice.

When I think about Allen now, I realize that I brought him to Georgetown because he was a challenge. He was the kind of challenge that coincided with who I am. He represented bigger issues off the court. He was a young Black kid in trouble, with a young Black mother who needed help. I'm the kind of person who needs something to fight for. That's why I took Allen. I needed his kind of challenge.

You have to remember, I didn't know he was *that* good.

18

NIKE

The first time I met Sonny Vaccaro, he tried to give me a soul brother handshake. This happened in 1971 at the Dapper Dan all-star game in Pittsburgh. Sonny was a schoolteacher and basketball promoter before he started the Dapper Dan, which became the first big-time game for the best high school players in the country. I took Donald Washington there when I was coaching at St. Anthony's, and this short white man with an Afro tried to grab my hand by the thumb, the way young Black people greeted each other in those days. I always resented when white people tried to shake my hand that way, to show they were sympathetic to Black folks.

I told Sonny, "You better cut that out. If you try that with the wrong person, you might get your hand cut off. The sum total of Black people is not a handshake."

Sonny laughed it off and was not bothered by my comment, which I found interesting. As I observed him, I noticed he really cared about the kids. Dozens of college and NBA coaches were hanging around, but I saw Sonny more concerned with making sure the players had enough to eat or the right size shoes. The more I got to know Sonny, the more I liked him, especially after the NCAA started trying to crack down on him. Our relationship kept developing after I began coaching at Georgetown.

In 1977, Sonny thought he'd invented a basketball shoe and took it out to a new company in Oregon called Nike. The Nike guys laughed at his shoe but hired Sonny to sign college basketball coaches to endorsement deals. That's when Sonny called me.

Georgetown had a deal with Converse at the time, the same lousy deal that was in place before I arrived. We paid for our shoes, clothing, socks, everything. Maybe we got a bit of a markdown on the retail price, or some free wristbands now and then. I didn't personally receive a penny. Converse had a major presence in basketball then, especially in the NBA because of their deal with Julius Erving. Adidas had Kareem Abdul-Jabbar, plus many of the top college programs, including Dean Smith and North Carolina. The main way sneaker companies paid college coaches was for speaking at camps or clinics. The fees were peanuts, about fifty or a hundred dollars. It reminded me of the jelly beans I got for giving speeches back at Providence.

Sonny flew me out to Portland to introduce me to Nike CEO Phil Knight and his deputy Rob Strasser. Phil was quiet and did a lot of listening. He had started his company in 1962 by distributing the Japanese shoe brand Tiger in the United States. In 1972, the year I started at Georgetown, Phil launched his own Nike brand. When we met in 1977, Phil had not yet taken Nike public. The company was surviving month to month on Japanese loans and shuffling money from one account to another. This was the trip when we met in a hotel suite with clothing hanging on racks. I specifically recall Rob saying they did not believe in advertising. Phil thought ads didn't help sales and that the quality of his product should speak for itself. I later found out it was convenient for Phil not to believe in advertising, because he didn't have enough money to pay for it.

I don't remember how much they offered me, but it couldn't have been much more than $5,000 per year, plus free shoes. When I told Frank Rienzo, he said it was not a problem for me to get paid as long as

Thompson and his teams were gracious in victory as well as defeat. (*Above*) They won the NCAA championship in 1984, behind the great Patrick Ewing. (*Below*) In 1985, after losing to Villanova, they stayed on the court to applaud their opponent.

© GEORGETOWN UNIVERSITY

The deflated basketball that Thompson kept in his office was a constant reminder to his players of the importance of education, because "you never want the sum total of your value to be the eight or nine pounds of air inside a basketball." The first staff member Thompson hired was Mary Fenlon, who supervised his players' academics and became his most trusted assistant.

COURTESY OF THE THOMPSON FAMILY

Thompson with University of North Carolina coach Dean Smith, his mentor and dear friend, who taught him one of his most important lessons: "Seventy percent of coaching doesn't have anything to do with basketball. But that seventy percent affects whether you win or lose."

Thompson was awarded the President's Medal by Georgetown president Father Timothy Healy in 1982. "I called him the Big Irishman," Thompson said. "He called me the Boss." Thompson's basketball teams played a primary role in lifting Georgetown from a regional school to a top-ranked national university with a $1.6 billion endowment.

COURTESY OF THE THOMPSON FAMILY

© NATIONAL ARCHIVES (75853739)

© GEORGETOWN UNIVERSITY

Thompson with a few of his fans: Presidents Gerald Ford (*top left*), Ronald Reagan (*top right*), and fellow Hoya Bill Clinton (*above*).

"I rejected the implication that I was the first Black coach with the ability to win a championship. Barack Obama wasn't the first Black man with the ability to be president."

(*Above*) Allen Iverson often thanked his coach for saving his life, and Thompson soon recognized that with a player as gifted as Iverson, "you gotta let the bird fly." His coaching often was delivered with the quiet touch of a parent—until a louder approach *(below)* was needed.

In a defining moment of his career, Thompson walks off the court at the beginning of a 1989 game to protest the NCAA's Proposition 42, which would have discriminated against Black athletes.

Georgetown, which once owned hundreds of slaves, erected a larger-than-life statue of a descendant of slaves in its new athletic center. "I tell young people not to let the fear of failure keep them from pursuing their dreams," Thompson said. "I lost far more big games than I won, and still ended up with my statue on campus."

COURTESY OF THE THOMPSON FAMILY

Thompson with his children—Ronny, Tiffany, and John—at the 2016 dedication ceremony of the John R. Thompson Jr. Athletic Center.

© JESSE WASHINGTON

The shadow of John Thompson, reflected in a window as he drives past Maryland fields where his ancestors were once enslaved.

Georgetown got something out of the deal too. It didn't take me long to decide to sign with Nike. I liked Sonny. Georgetown would save money and get free shoes. Nike was more of a track and field company at that time, almost an afterthought in basketball, and you know how I like underdogs. Phil had run track at Oregon, and the school's defining athlete was Steve Prefontaine, a distance runner who had died young in a car crash. The way Phil talked about Prefontaine reminded me of how I felt about Elgin Baylor.

Sonny sensed the growing influence of basketball, which was not obvious in 1977. The NCAA tournament was only thirty-two teams. The NBA Finals aired on tape delay. Outside the inner city, almost nobody wore sneakers for fashion. Sonny's genius was to embrace the Black element of the game, and to recognize that Black kids set trends for what is cool throughout America. That's what Sonny's handshake was all about.

When I told Dean Smith about my move, he was surprised. I think he saw Nike like that sport coat with no lining I used to wear. Not in a mean way, but as an accurate observation, because Adidas was first class. Later, after Nike became dominant, I got the idea that Dean wanted to come over with us. We never discussed it, but in my mind it made me laugh.

The first time Phil came to see me in Washington, we went to a restaurant for lunch. This is when I really learned that Phil is not a loquacious person. He did a lot of listening again, and took notes. That made an impression on me, because he was not one of those white people who were only comfortable in a teaching position with Black people. I listened to Phil, too, and started to understand his offbeat way of looking at the world. His viewpoint was different from mine, but we both enjoyed going against the mainstream. Phil had had to fight and claw like hell to get Nike going, and his company had a rebellious nature. I empathized with that, and it became the foundation of our relationship.

I was one of eighty coaches Nike signed in 1977. They did a good job of sending people to Georgetown's campus for feedback on their products. They sent us shoes before they came on the market and asked players what they liked or disliked about them. Phil learned that strategy from when his college track coach, Bill Bowerman, experimented with shoes on his athletes, and Phil was not so arrogant as to force things on you. I recall telling Nike they should put the name on the bottom of the sneaker, because the players are always getting photographed in the air, or falling down on TV, and we see the soles of their shoes. I don't know whether that was the reason Nike started doing it, but I did bring it up.

Nike went public in 1980, and I was lucky enough to be in on the ground floor. Mary Fenlon was the first person to advise me to take stock as compensation instead of salary. Soon, Nike recognized that I was different from their other seventy-nine coaches. Phil actually liked when Georgetown was vilified, because it meant that people were paying attention to a Nike team and not to an Indiana or Carolina.

When Patrick Ewing was a freshman, in 1981, he caught a cold before the start of the season. Lorry Michel suggested that Patrick wear a T-shirt under his uniform to keep him warm. Patrick is the one who made that style popular. I said, "Why don't we have Nike make us a shirt with the swoosh on the sleeve?" As soon as the NCAA saw the swoosh on Patrick's shirt, they said we were not allowed to advertise on uniforms. Today there are swooshes all over the uniforms, socks, headbands, you name it. The Nike swoosh is on the basketball itself. I'm happy about how things have developed because I like Phil, and I own a lot of Nike stock. But that's what I mean about some white people only wanting to accept us in a learning role. The NCAA called what I did a sin because I initiated it, and they were not the ones who conceived of getting money from it.

I DEFINITELY NOTICED when so many young Black kids started wearing our hats and clothing. A lot of Black people assumed Georgetown was a historically Black university because of the complexion of our team. They especially loved our sneakers, the gray and blue Nikes with a big HOYAS on the heel. Nike sold a version of those with NIKE on the heel and couldn't keep them in the stores. Phil's people kept an exact count of how many sneakers were being sold every day, and when my team really got rolling in 1983 the sales shot up.

I'm not into fashion, but I knew that some white people go to the ghetto to watch Black people and figure out how to sell stuff. What I did not realize in the early 1980s was that young Black and Hispanic kids were creating a whole new culture called hip-hop, and that sneakers were a huge part of it. I heard kids rapping, of course, and I saw the change in the way my players dressed, but I had no idea this new hip-hop culture would take over the world. These days, it's nothing for someone to own twenty or even fifty pairs of sneakers, and the real collectors own hundreds. This is a big reason why Nike now does almost $40 billion in sales per year. Businessmen wear sneakers with their suits. That seed was planted in the 1980s by young Black kids, and one reason they loved Nikes is because of Georgetown basketball. Michael Jordan took it to a whole new level, of course, when he came out with his Air Jordans in 1985. Michael deserves as much credit as anybody, maybe the most credit, for how big Nike became. But Georgetown was in the mix too.

PHIL SAYS THAT as a white guy from Oregon, working with mostly other white guys, he didn't think much about race back then. But Phil did understand that Black America had a special connection to our program, and how that translated into sales. Phil understood what I told Morgan Wootten: where you come to get players, I live.

By the time Patrick got to Georgetown, Nike was paying me a lot more than $5,000 per year. After I won the national championship, I made it clear that I didn't want any coach to be paid more than me, not even one dollar more. Phil invited me to lunch one day and ripped up my contract, then gave me a new deal because another one of his coaches had surpassed my salary. He didn't have to do that, because my contract was a few years away from expiring, but Phil was a man of his word.

Sonny traveled with our team during the Final Four and became part of the Georgetown family. He was one of the few people I let travel on our bus and stay in the team hotel, which shows how much I loved him, because the big joke was I never let anybody know where our hotel was. I even let Sonny watch us practice. Despite my affection for him, Sonny did things that drove me crazy. Once we sent a couple of players down to get breakfast with their own meal money, but Sonny insisted on paying for the food. That could have become a big NCAA violation based on his working for Nike, so we made the kids give Sonny back the money, which amounted to twenty or thirty dollars.

Sonny was the most softhearted guy in the world. Once we were in Utah and he heard that we had to drive over some mountain pass to get to the arena. Sonny told me that we had to leave early because the pass would get snowed over. I hated to deviate from my routine on game days, but Sonny drove me nuts. "John, you're a Black coach," he said. "What will they say if you don't show up?" I cussed him out all kinds of ways, but we left early. Sonny stood in the aisle in the front of the bus until we made it through the pass. It wasn't even snowing hard. But I loved the guy and let him roll with the team.

People tried to say Sonny was a crook or selfish, which was a big lie. He was what Fenlon called a "bleeder," someone who truly cared for the kids. He thought every Black kid was poor and the school should pay for everything. The NCAA has now made a lot of adjustments that addressed exactly what Sonny was saying. Parents can now get certain privileges, and kids get a stipend. Many of the rules the NCAA has now, Sonny proposed first.

The 1985 Final Four was big for Nike because they had all four teams: us, Villanova, St. John's, and Memphis State. Sonny and Phil attended the games together. Before the championship game, Sonny warned Phil not to root openly for Georgetown because the TV cameras might catch it, and that could cause problems for Nike's relationship with other programs. Phil bit his lip through the whole game to keep his emotions in check. After we lost to Villanova, Phil turned to look at Sonny, and tears were streaming down Sonny's cheeks.

By now, Phil was changing his mind about advertising. He put up a huge Nike billboard in Washington to advertise the fact that Georgetown was a Nike team. Well, Lefty Driesell over at Maryland was with Nike too. Lefty told Sonny he was upset that we had a billboard and he didn't. So Phil put an ad on a bus stop by Lefty's house. Things had changed from when Maryland used to kill us every year.

As we all know, Nike quickly became as innovative with its advertising as with its products, which created a mystique around the company that set us apart. A lot of that connects back to Michael Jordan, although Nike promoted other Black athletes as well. One of the things I respect the most about Phil is that he was not afraid to advertise Michael and other Black athletes in abundance. That was extremely unusual in the 1980s. As phenomenal a player as Dr. J was, Converse did not put him in a lot of commercials. At that time, Black people were mostly confined to ads for products that were targeted at other Blacks, though sometimes there was a sprinkle of token Blacks in ads for the general population. Phil broke that mold, first with Michael, then with other athletes. The important thing is that he did it in abundance, which made it safe for companies outside the world of sports to do the same thing. Other companies may have wanted to do it; Phil had the balls to actually do it. Michael's charisma and basketball greatness were special, but don't think for a second that every company would have featured him so prominently. Phil's promotion of Michael also had a trickle-down effect, like when Nike brought in Spike Lee to direct and co-star in some of Michael's commercials. Today we see ordinary Black people in ads for insurance, soap, cereal, or whatever else, and there's no special reason for us to be there. We don't have to be as great as Michael Jordan to be in a commercial, we can just be ourselves. Phil deserves a good deal of credit for that.

In the summer of 1990, the Reverend Jesse Jackson and his civil rights organization, Operation PUSH, came after Nike. Today's young people may not know how famous and influential Jesse was at that point in history, but he had real power. Jesse started saying publicly that Nike did not use any Black banks, had no Black people as vice presidents or on its board of directors, and used no Black advertising agencies. Jesse observed that Black people were responsible for a lot of Nike's success, from Georgetown to Michael Jordan to all the Black kids who paid big money for Nike sneakers. All of this was true.

I understood and respected what Jesse was doing. He was a brilliant person. Nike was not the only big company Jesse targeted. He had studied the white man and was attacking his system by confronting the most well-known and successful businesses. Nike had about $2 billion in annual sales by then. I also knew that although Jesse's accusations were true, they were also untrue. The situation for Black people at Nike was improving. Few people knew that Phil was already considering me for a position on the board of directors, and I had attended the previous board meeting as a consultant. Nike's progress may not have been apparent to those outside the company, or it may not have been happening as fast as Jesse thought it should happen. Phil was like a newer version of Red Auerbach, who did more to help Black players than any other coach but still had to operate under the quota system. Phil went as far as he could, given the obstacles of that time. He had to dance to the music that was being played. Jesse and I were philosophically aligned, but I did not agree with his approach as it applied to Phil and to Nike. That's why I defended Nike in good conscience.

Nike opened talks with Operation PUSH about Jesse's demands. Some other companies had immediately given Jesse what he wanted, but Nike noticed that PUSH was negotiating with Reebok at the same time, and Nike resisted. That's when PUSH called for a nationwide boycott of Nike products. Nike announced that it would put a minority person on the board of directors, promote more minorities as department heads within a year, and name a minority vice president within two years. That wasn't enough for Operation PUSH, and the boycott continued.

I had been advising Phil throughout the process, but now it was time to get more deeply involved. I arranged for Phil and Jesse to meet in my Georgetown office. When Jesse arrived outside McDonough, he had somebody with him who burned a Nike shoe in front of our gym. Phil and I were watching. I became more convinced that even though I understood the bigger picture of what Jesse was trying to do, I thought there were other avenues he could have taken to do it.

Phil tapped me on the arm and pointed at Jesse's feet. Jesse had on some nice dress shoes.

"Hey John, look. Jesse is wearing Cole-Haans," Phil said. "He doesn't know I own that company, too."

When Jesse and Phil came into my office, I was sitting behind my desk with a baseball bat on top of it. The bat was an attempt to lighten the mood. "We're going to bring you two guys together," I said. It didn't happen. Jesse demanded that Phil buy ads in Black magazines and spend money with certain companies. I was not knowledgeable about Nike's advertising policies then, because rightly or wrongly I was focused on trying to win games. I had Alonzo and Dikembe and was trying to get back to the Final Four. This Nike boycott was part of my never having the luxury to just be a basketball coach.

At one point, Phil told Jesse, "John Thompson isn't our best Black coach. He's our best coach, period." Phil was saying that he would not pander by promoting a Black token. He would promote a qualified Black person because he understood what had happened in the past.

When people complain about affirmative action, I respond that there's nothing more unequal than the equal treatment of unequals. If we run a hundred-yard dash, and I'm at the starting line while you begin at the fifty, and they want to measure who finishes first? That's the equal treatment of unequals. I did not believe in that, and neither did Phil.

I did not want Phil to be publicly vilified by Jesse. I also respected the greater good of Jesse's mission, the message he wanted to send to corporate America in general. Jesse went after the big fish, which I would have done in his shoes, and it wouldn't have been personal. The whole scenario was a struggle for me. I had to straddle the divide between two good men. Back in the day, the funny papers had that guy Dagwood in the *Blondie* comic, and he'd be running to catch the trolley car while reaching back for his coat. That's how stretched out I felt.

Phil thought Jesse was trying to make money for himself in the negotiations to end the boycott. Well, I tried to make money for myself, too. You can never pay me to compromise what I believe in, I've proven that. But if I believe in something, then you can pay me and I'll enjoy the money, because it's mine. I got paid more money than Big House Gaines and Cal Irvin. I got a Nike contract and had the audacity to be a Black person who insisted on being their highest-paid coach. I took advantage of my position to make sure the name of the Wilson basketball was on the cover of *Sports Illustrated*. Were those things so much different from what Jesse was doing? He needed money to maintain his platform. You can talk about white and Black all you want to, but without green you got nothing. A lot of things I did were selfishly related to me. I wanted to be rich. I won't wag my finger at Jesse for not taking a vow of poverty, because I know what good he did, too. Some people said he was crazy when he ran for president in 1984 and 1988, but he opened up the political process and made it possible for a lot of other Black people to get elected, including Barack Obama. His activism was powerful. Poor Blacks who faced injustice could just mention Jesse's name, like, "You don't want Reverend Jackson coming over here." Jesse improved a lot of lives. At that time, he was probably the only Black person that white America feared.

But I had to defend Phil. If Phil could be attacked after stepping outside the norm to embrace Black people and culture as much as he did, other companies would be more reluctant to work with us. My stance was questioned by some Black people, including some who had praised me a year earlier for walking out over Proposition 42. They said, "Why are you defending Nike? Nike should be doing more." I responded that everybody should be doing more, there are Black institutions that should be doing more, but it's not always feasible from a business or political standpoint. We had to go through steps to achieve these goals. These kids today wouldn't be where they are if somebody hadn't made that first step happen. People look back and say, "Why didn't you take steps two, three, and four?" They look at a Stepin Fetchit and say we shouldn't have let that happen. Stepin Fetchit stepped and fetched it so you young people don't have to step and fetch right now.

Yes, I have respect for Stepin Fetchit. I have respect for Pebbles, too.

Phil and Jesse left my office without coming to any resolution. The boycott continued. Jesse was quoted as saying some things about me and Michael Jordan in the newspapers, like calling us "shoe salesmen who seem more interested in making money than fighting for equal opportunity." None of that bothered me, and I couldn't be sure Jesse really said it. Either way, I wasn't going to let the media goad us into attacking each other. Black people always pursued progress on different paths, which sometimes led to their calling each other names or acting like enemies. That even happened with Martin Luther King and Malcolm X. Jesse and I pursued the same goal.

But let's be clear about one thing: Black people were not about to stop buying Nikes, nor should they have. Phil, Michael, and I knew that. Jesse probably did too. Jesse was PUSHing. I think the boycott helped us, because Nike's sales increased more than 50 percent during that time. Meanwhile, Operation PUSH ran so low on funds, it laid off all twelve of its employees. Jesse had very little leverage.

When Phil told me he wasn't getting anywhere in the negotiations with Jesse, I replied that he was thinking too much like a white man. I suggested that Michael and I meet with Jesse alone. We needed to have the type of candid conversation that Black people have amongst ourselves. We needed to talk the way we talk. I set up the meeting, and we gathered in Sonny Vaccaro's hotel suite in New York City. Spike Lee was also there. Sonny was the only white guy in the room. Think about the kind of respect Sonny had, to be accepted by us in that setting.

We didn't make any agreements in the meeting, but we weren't at each other's throats, either. We dealt with one another on a personal basis, totally different from what our relationship appeared to be in some of the media. Everybody in that room shared the same goal, but many roads lead to Rome. Sometimes our people want us all to take the same road. Michael had his own road, and he cared deeply about Black equality, even though there is a perception otherwise based on that joke he made about Republicans buying sneakers too. I know from personally dealing with him that he has done amazing things behind the scenes to help Black people, to give them jobs and create opportunities. Michael did a lot more to lift up our people than some others who are praised for being champions of Black progress.

We had some laughs in the meeting, like when I told Jesse, "You're fucking with *my* money now." I could say that because he knew I respected him. I left the meeting with a sense that the conflict would not continue indefinitely. Jesse was moving on to other things. His point had been made.

A month later, I sent Jesse a pair of Nikes for his birthday. He claims he never took them out of the box.

Operation PUSH didn't announce an end to the boycott, but in the spring of 1991 Jesse stopped talking about it, and it fizzled out.

That March, Phil put me on Nike's board of directors.

My getting on the Nike board was similar to how I got the job at Georgetown. Even though I was well qualified, it would be naïve to say my Blackness was not a major factor. But I also had to be successful. White people who are not successful are still offered opportunities. As Gandhi said, we won't be truly free until we have the freedom to make mistakes.

Phil cared about diversity and was moving to improve his company in that area. Maybe what Jesse did influenced Phil to move faster, but not because he was afraid. It influenced Phil based on what was right or wrong. A lot of what Jesse said was right.

If Jesse did play a role in my getting a board seat with Nike, I'm not apologetic about that. I'm grateful to him and all the other Black people, famous or not, who helped create that opportunity. They made sacrifices to open that door for me. Once the door was open, I could handle the rest. As James Brown sang, "I don't want nobody to give me nothing. Open up the door, I'll get it myself."

Jesse and I both played the long game with Nike. Like that book where the Black guy infiltrated the CIA, I was "the spook who sat by the door."

Years later, I saw Jesse while I was broadcasting an NCAA tournament game. He was sitting across the arena from me, and I asked one of our production assistants to go tell Jesse I said hello. Jesse came all the way over to talk to me. We messed around for a little while and then Jesse said, "I respect the fact that you spoke up for Black people early in your career. A lot of people wait until they are comfortable and safe. But you spoke up when you had something to lose."

A FEW PEOPLE on the Nike board questioned Phil's plan to bring me in. Phil said they thought I would be a "disruptive force." But Phil told the board to trust him and pushed my selection through. Years later, board member Tim Cook, the CEO of Apple, pulled Phil aside and told him, "John Thompson is much more than a basketball coach."

I was not the type of Black person they usually invited into corporate America, but Phil looked beyond my reputation and saw the real person. Based on the way I was portrayed, how many other white people would have put me on their board? Phil didn't fall into the trap I resented so much over the years, of making assumptions based on my size and color. That's why I love the man. He also made me a decent piece of change.

I was suspicious of the board, too, because I'm haunted by my past.

I didn't go in there trying to get along with them. I thought, *They haven't been around Black people at the level that I have, I wonder how they think about us,* and all that. But I ended up making some great friends that I love to pieces. This group came from the absolute pinnacle of corporate America, but they weren't a bunch of starchy people and I genuinely enjoyed being around them. We could laugh and joke together. Tim Cook gave me a special Apple credential, and when I pulled it out at the Apple Store near Georgetown's campus, the staff almost fainted. I learned from a lot of the board members, and I hope they were willing to learn from me, too. All of us were exposed to something new.

I mostly listen during board meetings. I can go for hours without saying a word. When the other members are speaking on their areas of expertise, I shut up and pay attention. I'm sensitive to human resources issues because of what I've seen Black people and women go through. I enjoy discussions about marketing. As one of the few people in the room who participated in sports, when I do have something to add, I think they value my contributions. We talk much less than people think about sneaker designs or which player is coming out of college early. It always amuses me how many people think we focus on the NBA draft in board meetings. It's more things like factories and government regulations.

I do like the shoes, though, and my players loved them. Whenever I went to the Nike headquarters in Oregon, they let me go into the warehouse and take all the gear I could carry. One off-season, with my team back at Georgetown, Fenlon and I brought more than a dozen duffel bags to the airport. The baggage agent at the curb outside the terminal was dumbfounded by the amount of luggage we had. You can't just check that many bags for two people without special permission and all kinds of extra fees. I looked at the man with a straight face and said, "Have you seen my team yet? I got all their bags. Thanks for helping out. The team is coming!"

It was a big deal in the late 1990s when Nike got attacked for the pay and working conditions in our international factories. Protesters burned Phil in effigy outside the Nike store in Portland. Not all the accusations were fair, but we took them seriously. Phil genuinely cared about treating everyone as well as possible. He asked me and my fellow board member Jill Ker Conway to visit our factories in Vietnam, Indonesia, and India and report back on what we saw. I wanted to know if we were exploiting people like the critics said. I took George Raveling and Fenlon along, because I trusted their discernment and opinions.

Most Nike products are made in factories owned by foreign companies, and these factories make products for other American companies besides Nike. We still have an obligation, though, to make sure our subcontractors treat their workers fairly. When we went on the factory tour, we knew they would clean up and make everything look good for us. That's what I did when I worked for 4-H and the Agriculture Department people who funded our program came around. But there were still useful things that Jill, George, Fenlon, and I could observe. As soon as we came through the factory doors, we split up and headed in opposite directions. We talked to workers and their bosses and looked through the dormitories where women workers lived. Jill was a huge champion of women's rights and extremely concerned with how the women were treated, how they cared for their children, and what kind of family lives they had. I saw a suggestion box on one wall and looked inside. It was empty, which made me laugh, because even the best companies in the world have employees who complain. We observed what it took to put together shoes and how fast employees had to work.

We found some things to correct, and other people in the company did too. We reported back to the board and Nike made significant changes. We also concluded that some of the critics were judging these factories and the wages we paid by American standards. Nike could not pay American wages in a lot of places, because doctors in those countries didn't make that kind of money. Not that Nike shouldn't do better, and we did, but the situation reminded me of people saying that college basketball players were exploited. For these foreign factory workers, the so-called exploitation was better than the alternative, because making Nikes was considered good employment where they lived.

Jill and I became great friends during these trips. People might not expect the president of an all-female college to become so close to someone with my reputation. I enjoyed defying the assumptions that people like me did not belong in elite and intellectual circles. After I got older, I was at a meeting standing around talking to Phil and Tim Cook and some other folks. Jill came into the room, and we hadn't seen each other for a while. She ran up and hugged me, but since she's a short lady she had to jump up to give me a hug. I was old at that point, and she knocked me right over. I almost took out about three or four other people on the way down. I like to say that little Jill Conway is the last person ever to knock me down.

When I turned seventy-two, which is the mandatory retirement age for Nike board members, I called Phil to talk about the transition. He said, "Get back to me when you're eighty," and he has kept me on the board ever since.

By now I've been with Nike for more than forty years, since before they believed in advertising. Phil and I became so close because we both needed to challenge the status quo. We lived by Saint Augustine's motto: "An unjust law is no law at all." Phil always stood up for what he believed was right, regardless of what the media, Jesse Jackson, or anybody else said. And he was extremely loyal. Phil could have abandoned me when people said I was a racist and a bully. When I walked out over Proposition 42, Phil asked what kind of support I needed. He stuck by Tiger Woods and other athletes who got in trouble. After Colin Kaepernick got blackballed from the NFL for protesting during the national anthem, Phil signed him to a new endorsement deal and put out a commercial supporting him. I privately thought, *Uh-oh, what's that gonna do to my stock?* A lot of white people boycotted Nike over the Kaepernick ad, which I found ironic given what we went through with Jesse. But Phil supported Kaepernick when it wasn't clear what the reaction would be. A lot of people asked me if I had something to do with that, but it was all Phil. The stock went up after the ad came out, too, and reached an all-time high.

Back when I was being criticized so heavily, Phil didn't cut me loose or say, "You're giving my product a bad name." People like to coach results and judge what Phil did in the context of what I did later, or how legendary Nike is now. But Phil stuck with me when he was still struggling to climb the ladder. He did it when he had something to lose.

19

TIME TO GO

After practice one day, Mary Fenlon asked Victor Page for his Social Security number.

"Which one?" Victor replied.

That sums up the Victor Page experience. The kid had NBA talent, but his upbringing was so problematic, he had difficulty functioning on a day-to-day basis. He was always getting into something back in his old neighborhood, and it was a constant project to make sure he did what he was supposed to do. The thing was, Vic was so respectful and likable that when he messed up, which was often, it was hard to get angry at him.

One of Vic's teammates missed a test or a class assignment. Fenlon came through the office looking for the other kid and called out, "Where's that idiot?" Victor overheard and said, "You looking for me, Ms. Fenlon?"

How could you stay mad at a kid like that?

In our 1996–97 season, with Allen, Othella Harrington, and Jerome Williams departed for the NBA, Victor averaged almost 23 points per game. Ya-Ya Dia and Jahidi White were also good, but halfway through the season we had a 5–6 record in the conference. Then we upset

Villanova, Vic hit a game winner at St. John's, and we won eight of our last nine Big East games. The progress was an illusion, though. We lost to Boston College in the Big East tournament semifinals, then got beaten in the first round of the NCAAs by North Carolina–Charlotte.

When we got back to campus, I called Victor into my office and told him, "It's time for you to declare for the NBA draft." People thought it was his decision, but in reality he had become persona non grata. I knew he wasn't going to get drafted, but he had the ability to play professionally somewhere. There was no sense in sending him to another school because it was clear he could not succeed in a university environment. Like Michael Graham, Victor could never escape the Call of the Wild. I understood it, but I didn't accept it. He had an opportunity to walk through the door that was opened for him, an opportunity to change his life. But it's hard to understand you can change if you're conditioned to being in that type of life.

Looking back, I don't think I made the right decision bringing Victor to Georgetown. He was a gamble, and not the only one. I knew everybody I brought in wasn't an altar boy. I thought Victor could potentially respond well to being here, that he could grow and develop. Part of my mistake came from my selfishness in wanting a good player. I probably had too much confidence in my own ability to change him, and a lot of that came from my rationalizing based on how talented he was. After Victor got here, some people said he was functionally illiterate, which I don't think is true, but he had problems in class. His jump shot sure fell, though.

Victor made the Continental Basketball Association and played well there for a little while. He said in a newspaper article that he blew an NBA shot with the Timberwolves when he got in a fight outside a hotel and hurt his arm. After that, he came back to Washington, to the streets. He got shot in the eye and had to wear a patch over it, got arrested a bunch of times, and went to prison for a while. I didn't condone his actions by any means, but I supported him through his troubles. The last time he got out of prison, I took him some clothes and gave him a piece of change. I also told him, "Vic, if you get arrested again, don't call me." He said he had found God, and I think he meant it, but drugs are a difficult thing to overcome. In 2019, Victor was convicted of sexually assaulting a seventeen-year-old girl. The judge gave him twenty years. I had to step away from him at that point. When I got my counseling degree, they taught what you can't counsel, too.

I would have felt guilty if I hadn't tried to help Victor as best I could. I'm not without sin in some of these situations.

I still think about another decision I made, about a player I don't want to name. He committed to us out of Dunbar Baltimore, but some of his street associates got into his head and persuaded him to enroll at a Los Angeles junior college instead. Things didn't work out there, and the junior college coach sent him home, which I did not think the kid deserved. Not only that, but the coach made him ride home on a bus, all the way across the country.

The kid asked me if he could have his spot back on my team. I no longer had a scholarship available, but even if I had, I was angry and disappointed. I had been counting on him, and he'd left us high and dry late in the recruiting cycle. I said I couldn't do anything for him.

Not long afterward, the kid committed suicide.

Should I have taken him back? I mean, we weren't running a charity. He gave up a Georgetown education and put me in a bad spot because foolish people got visions of sugar plums dancing in his head. Even if I did have a spot available, I don't think I would have taken him back. I probably should have been more considerate, though, maybe gotten involved to help him in some other way. But I do my social work during my free time. When I'm working, I'm the basketball coach. I'm dedicated to the kids that I have. I didn't feel the need to forgive him because those people in California let him go. He didn't reject them and come back to me. They rejected him and sent him back. I didn't know the kid was going to end up dead.

A few years later, I was at a meeting in California with Smokey Gaines and George Raveling, and we saw the coach who sent that kid home. Smokey and George had to physically restrain me. That may be the only time in my coaching life I felt violent.

IN THE SUMMER of 1997, three kids left the team, or were asked to leave. One was a very good player who sped away from police because he had marijuana in his car. He sped right out of Georgetown, too. When the season began, freshman guard Kenny Brunner from California played well, but he had some emotional problems I had not recognized when we recruited him. After we lost at Seton Hall, I had someone pick Kenny up from the team hotel, and he became the fourth kid to leave that team. Jahidi and freshman center Ruben Boumtje-Boumtje both had season-ending injuries. We lost in the second round of the Big East tournament, did not get invited to the NCAAs, and lost in the second round of the NIT. Our final record was 16–15.

That's when I knew it was time for me to go.

That 16–15 record was my fault, not my players'. I no longer had the energy that was needed for the job. I was no longer hungry for the challenge of winning. I was no longer capable of the huge personal investment it took to do things the way they should be done. For me, coaching at Georgetown came with an extra layer of responsibility, because Georgetown was not an easy place academically or socially for the type of kids I liked to work with. I spent most of my time in McDonough. I'd show up at a kid's room at two o'clock in the morning, or follow a kid as he returned from somewhere he wasn't supposed to be. If I asked Georgetown to take somebody in, I had to fulfill my commitment to properly supervise the kid. At the end of the 1997–98 season, I realized I no longer had the desire to make that commitment. I was fifty-six years old and had been coaching Georgetown for almost half my life.

I also was in the middle of a divorce from Gwen. I've always kept my personal life private, and I'm not about to change that now, but some of what happened is public knowledge. In September 1996, our house on Colorado Avenue Northwest burned down. Georgetown had given me the house when we started going to the Final Four and other schools were wooing me. After the fire, Gwen and I separated, and the divorce negotiations were difficult. Court filings, dealing with lawyers, arguing back and forth, all that was almost worse than the pain of the breakup itself. It was stressful, as it should have been, especially since I still cared about Gwen. I felt that I owed it to my family to focus on resolving this problem.

Back in 1972, when Georgetown offered me the head coaching job, I asked Gwen for her opinion. "You should take the job, you will do it well," Gwen said. "But what will it do to our relationship?" She was one hundred percent right about that. She got caught smack in the middle.

That said, no single thing told me it was time to stop coaching. I made the decision the same way I decided not to play pro ball anymore. I didn't have a master plan. One thing I did know was not to resign during the off-season. I wanted to choose my replacement. When Dean Smith retired, he did it during the season, and as a result he chose his assistant Bill Gutheridge to succeed him. I decided to take the same course. So even though I knew I was about to step down, in the fall of 1998 I began my twenty-seventh season as Georgetown's head coach.

I probably was not as grouchy or demanding as I had been in the past. I didn't consciously ease up, but due to human nature that happens. We opened the season against John Chaney's seventh-ranked Temple team in Madison Square Garden and lost 65–49. Right after New Year's, I started informing my closest friends of my decision. On January 2, 1999, we got blown out at Connecticut, who would go on to win the national championship that year. The following Monday, we lost at Seton Hall, 72–61, in the last game I ever coached.

We returned to Washington that night. In the morning, I drove to Craig Esherick's house and told him he was taking my place. I shared my decision with my team, and shed tears in the process. I spoke with all the other people who needed to know. Some of them tried to talk me out of it, some were worried about my well-being, some urged me just to take a leave of absence and then return to the bench. None of them could change my mind. People told me I should win four more games to reach six hundred for my career and then leave. I couldn't care less about winning six hundred games. I cared about knocking down a wall that had hindered Black people, about defying the structure that had denied us opportunities. I had conquered those things.

We called a press conference. Patrick, Alonzo, and Dikembe were there, along with more former players, my three children, and many other people I loved. I explained that I was not retiring, because retirement means you don't want to work anymore. I was resigning as head coach. I intended to remain involved, with Georgetown and with whichever players needed me. I was not too proud to admit that I also needed my players.

"We make young people think that responsibility goes only one way," I told the crowd. "I'm John Thompson, who is fragile and weak and has to address problems too."

It was over. I left with 596 victories, 239 losses, and a .714 winning percentage. Twenty-seven of my players were drafted into the NBA, including eight in the first round. Patrick and Allen went No. 1. Of the seventy-eight players who stayed four years, seventy-six earned a degree. Some of the ones who left I failed, but I do not regret refusing to be their master.

In the weeks after I resigned, I felt like I was coming down off drugs. As time went on and people asked me if I missed coaching, I said no. That was the biggest lie I ever told. There was an emptiness, a hollowness, in my life that took a long time to fill back up. You don't devote that kind of time, energy, and emotion to something and not feel its absence. I missed teasing Patrick. I missed talking to Steve Martin. I missed cussing out Michael Jackson or calling Lonnie Duren a dirty name. I missed the competition. I missed teaching in my classroom, the court. I missed the seventy percent of things that had nothing to do with basketball, all those things that prevented me, thank God, from having the luxury of just being a coach.

I dealt with it. I had always tried to be considerate of what my players were experiencing off the court that affected their ability to play well. I had to think about myself the same way, too.

I WAS NOT chosen for the Naismith Memorial Basketball Hall of Fame when I first became eligible in 1997. Dean Smith, who was involved with the Hall, told me my name never came up for serious consideration. I assumed my reputation was the problem.

In 1998, Dave Gavitt called and broke the news that I had been passed over again. This time, I was so furious that tears stung my eyes. Coaches I had regularly beaten got inducted on their first try. Mike Krzyzewski called our office and spoke to Fenlon about how wrong he thought it was. I could see only one explanation for why I was denied: payback. Enough people on the selection committee didn't like the positions I had taken or the way I'd challenged people. In other words, they didn't respect what I stood for. My past was haunting me once again.

The Hall of Fame finally voted me in a few months after I retired. I think Dean and Dave made it happen in the game behind the game. I always used to say, "I don't seek approval from man, I seek approval from God." But even though I didn't care about being validated by others, I did want to be chosen for the Hall of Fame. Both of those things were true. I wanted and needed to be in the Hall. It felt more personal.

AS I WAS finally being inducted, the Washington radio station WTEM 980 AM asked me to come on the air during the 1999 NCAA tournament to discuss the games. It was fun, and I think people were surprised to hear the human side of the big scary guy who supposedly hated the media. After the tournament ended, the station asked me to host a daily talk show, along with former Washington Redskins tight end Doc Walker and the broadcaster Al Koken. I did the show for the next thirteen years.

Al and Doc were great to work with. I knew Doc from when he covered my team for local TV news in the early 1980s, as one of the young Black guys I thought were integrating the media through my reputation. I let Doc into practice one day with a cameraman, and the ball bounced off Horace Broadnax's leg during a weave drill. I walked up to Doc and politely asked, "Can you turn that camera off, please?" Then I went ballistic on Horace, and the rest of the team too because they had to take the weight together. I cussed them out to such an extent that Doc, who spent his life in football locker rooms, says he got scared. After I made my point, I went back over to Doc and calmly said, "Let's continue," and they turned the camera back on.

Al's radio nickname was Smokin' Al Koken, but I called him the Hanging Judge because he went after people with strong criticism. We had some intense debates, especially about Bobby Knight.

I had a lot of respect for Bobby because he never cheated, his kids graduated, he had discipline, and I can attest from playing his team that he was one of the best coaches the game has ever seen. Bobby had a bad reputation because he yelled and cursed and coached his kids hard. That sounded familiar to me. During one of our games, before they had the coaching box, I ran down by Indiana's bench to yell at one of my players. On the way back I turned and said to Bobby, "I bet you never got on a kid like *that*." The point is, there was a method to both our madness, a side the public did not see. I was at a Final Four and saw Bobby in a back room where nobody was watching, feeding an old coach in a wheelchair. Bobby was literally feeding this man with a spoon. People talk about the video of Bobby supposedly choking that kid in practice, but what was the context leading up to that? Did it really happen the way they said it happened? My sisters got mad at me once because I grabbed a player to get him subbed out of the game, and they interpreted it as me yoking the kid. Way more coaches were more detrimental to kids than Bobby ever was.

Al Koken didn't like a lot of things that Bobby did. My arguments with Al about Bobby might have sounded serious on the air, but I understood enough about radio to know the audience didn't want to hear two guys agreeing with each other all day. In real life, Al and I became great friends. I sat to his left in the studio, Doc sat to his right, and Al played a traffic cop role. He also did a huge amount of research and preparation on topics for me to talk about on the show. I was a novice coming into Al and Doc's realm, and their program became "The John Thompson Show," but they were extremely generous in teaching me about radio.

When we first started, I talked into the commercial breaks. Al had to pull me aside and say, "This is when we get paid." That was all I needed to hear. After that I stopped early for commercials: "Is it time to get paid yet?" Since I was no longer coaching, my primary responsibility was not to protect the kids or the school, but to entertain and inform people. I could let my guard down and act like Joe the Fan. Instead of being interpreted through sound bites chosen by other people, I directly communicated my own views, at length, every weekday. People learned that I liked telling jokes and laughing, that I cared about the rights of women, that I liked the country musician George Strait. They found out I didn't hate white people. I enjoyed blowing up a lot of the assumptions people had about me.

Early on, the people who owned the station asked a consultant to give us advice on how to improve the show. They brought us into a conference room where the consultant was standing in front of a blackboard. He began by saying that a three-man program was different, because shows usually had only two hosts. "Let's think about this like *Seinfeld*," the consultant said. He wrote SEINFELD on the board. "John, you are Jerry."

That was all I needed to hear. I hit him with my favorite profanity and said, "I've never watched *Seinfeld*, and I don't plan to watch *Seinfeld*. Doc, Al, and I will just get together and do our thing." Then I walked out.

People liked how we did our thing, because the ratings were good and they kept giving me new contracts. Eventually my contract said I could do the show by phone from anyplace I wanted. I did one show from the high roller room at the Aladdin hotel in Las Vegas, and when I hit the jackpot on the slot machine, Al interviewed the casino manager.

Doing radio made me sympathize more with people in the media, because I understood the pressures they faced to get interviews. I did get a lot of big names to talk to us on the show: Red, Dean, Bill Russell, Coach K, Spike Lee, Bill Cosby, Michael Jordan, Kobe Bryant, Tiger Woods and both of his parents, LeBron James when he was still in high school. Lefty Driesell came on and we had a ball. Everyone expected Lefty and me to tear each other apart, but that was one of the times I showed people that I wasn't who they thought I was. We had Allen Iverson and Charles Barkley on the air at the same time, for about an hour. We had a lot of fun.

We ranged beyond sports, too. Sometimes I asked Doc and Al "What's going on in the world today?" like I used to do at practice. A few months after I started the show, Jesse Jackson made front page news when he negotiated the release of three American soldiers who had been captured in Yugoslavia. I gave our producer Jesse's information and told him, "That motherfucker owes me a favor." We interviewed Jesse on the show his first day back in America.

Another time I was on the air talking about how some Black people look down on those of us who achieve success and accuse us of forgetting where we come from or trying to be like white people. The studio phone rang, and it was Supreme Court Justice Clarence Thomas. We spoke privately on the phone, not on the air. He said my comments resonated with his experiences. I respect Clarence Thomas, regardless of the decisions he has made on the court, which some feel have hurt Black people. Too many of us don't accept differences in one another. I don't have to agree with somebody to respect him. I hope that at least some of my radio audience felt the same way about me.

MARY FENLON RETIRED from Georgetown and moved to Las Vegas shortly after I stopped coaching. In September 2001, I was planning to fly out to her birthday party when Jim Rome asked me to appear on his show in Los Angeles. I gave them my very specific travel requirements, because I wanted to get to Vegas the day before Fenlon's party, and they booked me the flight. A few days before I was scheduled to leave, the producer called and asked to change the flight, because there were problems with studio availability. I gave them a flat no, but the producer was insistent. He wanted me to leave a day later than planned, fly in to Los Angeles, do Rome's show, then fly to Vegas the same day. I was extremely resistant. After a whole lot of back-and-forth, he persuaded me to accept the new itinerary, which shows how good he was at his job because I did not usually relent in those situations.

A few days later, on September 11, I was in my house in Arlington, Virginia, when I heard a noise outside, and felt a rumble. Fenlon called me a few minutes later and said, "John, are you watching the news? Airplanes crashed into the World Trade Center and the Pentagon." I had felt the impact from the plane that hit the Pentagon. I got scared and went outside, then drove around for a while. Later that day Fenlon called and said, "The plane that crashed into the Pentagon, it was headed from Washington to Los Angeles. That's the plane you were supposed to be on today."

I should have died on 9/11. I think about that all the time. I would have been on that plane if that kid producer hadn't persuaded me to change the flight. I sent him a huge box of Nike gear, but that didn't begin to repay him for saving my life. I argued and argued to stay on the flight that hit the Pentagon, but he made me change my mind.

Later on, Frank Rienzo joked that it might have been good if I was on the plane, because I could have talked the hijackers out of what they did. But on 9/11, it wasn't funny at all. I was terrified.

WHILE I DID my radio show, I also worked for Turner Sports, doing feature interviews and color commentary for NBA broadcasts. I got the job from one of my former players.

My point guard Michael Jackson had an exceptional academic career at Georgetown and graduated with a degree in political science and a minor in sociology. Michael also sacrificed more of his game than anyone else who ever played for me, in proportion to his ability. He could score almost at will and could easily have averaged more than 20 points per game, but he gave up most of his scoring in order for our team to win a national championship. Michael sacrificed so much of his offense, it affected his NBA opportunities to a significant degree. Coming out of Georgetown in 1986, he was a second-round draft pick and also got accepted to graduate school at Harvard. I told him, "Son, you can go to the Kennedy School of Government at any age, but how often do you get an opportunity to play in the NBA?" Michael played in the league for three seasons, at which point he secured his pension. Then we had another talk, and I told him it was time to give up the dream and contribute to the world with his mind. I basically told him to retire, and he did. He was the perfect example of my old saying that far more money is made sitting down than standing up.

Michael went to work for the U.S. Olympic Committee, then got a job as assistant to the president of Turner Sports, where he assembled the *Inside the NBA* show that is now recognized as one of the best sports programs ever on television. When Michael arrived, the show was just Ernie Johnson doing highlights. Michael knew there was a hunger for more than that, based on the way he and other pros talked about and understood the game. He also was determined to give Black people an opportunity in front of and behind the camera. Michael is the one who hired Kenny Smith and Charles Barkley, plus a lot of people you never heard of who make the show happen. There was not an abundance of Black people doing NBA television when Michael arrived at Turner. Now it's normal, and Michael helped bring about that change.

One day Michael called me up and said I should come work for Turner as a color commentator. I didn't want to do it. It seemed out of my element. This wasn't like the radio, where I did what I had always done in private, which was sit around and shoot the bull with my friends. Becoming a color commentator and interviewer was like being an official member of the media. Michael is the kind of person who had enough gumption to urge me to change my mind: "No, Coach, you'd be really good. I think you should give it a try." He persuaded me to do it. That is when the pupil became the teacher.

One we got started, I liked it. It was a way for me to stay around basketball. I enjoyed working with guys like Kevin Harlan, Marv Albert, Dick Stockton, Danny Ainge, Craig Sager, and the producers and camera people who did the dirty work. My radio show was local, but this was national. A lot of people didn't realize I was such a talker, because of the reputation I had from my public coaching persona. Michael Jackson had experienced me in a different realm. He remembered those long conversations in practice and all the lessons I taught. At Turner, Michael was a few levels above me. He was an outstanding administrator, and he supervised the producers who ran my broadcasts. He and I also had conversations that were helpful to me as I found my footing in that business.

Kenny Smith was there when I arrived. He always had a brilliant basketball mind. I can't believe that no NBA team has hired him, because he has a tremendous amount of knowledge and understanding of the game. Charles Barkley and I got there about the same time. I always liked Charles, from when he was a player. I was at an Olympic workout where I saw him get clobbered by someone on the other team. The ref called the foul, and Charles told the ref *not* to call fouls on the other guy. That was a new one for me. Then, as a commentator, Charles was not afraid to say what needed to be said, regardless of what other people thought about it. Charles did not seek approval from others, which is a quality I appreciate.

Michael brought me in to do color commentary, but soon he figured out that I should interview players one-on-one. That came naturally to me. I had been talking to players all my life, and they were more likely to let their guard down with me than with someone who was strictly a reporter. Michael also knew I could obtain interviews that might be difficult for some other media people to get. I got Russ, Wayne Embry, and Oscar Robertson on the same program for a Martin Luther King Day roundtable discussion. When I interviewed Michael Jordan, as soon as he came into the room he announced to everybody, "The only reason I'm here is because John asked me."

One of my most memorable interviews was Kevin Garnett. He was playing for the Timberwolves and his coach Flip Saunders had just been fired. He was the reigning MVP of the league, coming off a trip to the conference finals, but now his team was losing. I knew he was hurting, emotionally and physically. Halfway through the interview I told Kevin, "Give me a straight answer on this one. I don't want anything politically correct. How healthy are you now?"

Kevin is a warrior. He said, "I suit up every night. A hundred percent, thirty percent, ain't no numbers. It's my heart, and you can't measure that."

"What's driving you?" I asked.

"That I'm losing. I'm losing. I'm losing." I could see tears forming in Kevin's eyes. He motioned to the camera and asked to stop taping.

"These are tears of pain," he said when we came back.

"Tears of pride, too," I said.

The tears kept flowing, and we put them on the air. I respected and empathized with him for allowing himself to be vulnerable. Kevin felt his tears showed weakness, but I told him they were actually a sign of strength, a sign of the confidence he had despite stereotypes of what a man or a dominant player is supposed to be. Most people never knew that I am quick to cry, too. Maybe on some level Kevin knew he could trust me with his pain, because losing hurt me the same way it was killing him.

Other times, I was not so sympathetic. I sat down with J. R. Rider, a talented guy who had run himself out of the NBA by getting into all sorts of trouble off the court. Normally, before an interview starts, you sit down across from the guest and make small talk while they set up the cameras and microphones. This time, I sat there with my arms folded, silently looking at him. I didn't say a word. When the tape rolled, the first thing I said was, "Boy, what the fuck is wrong with you?"

I knew that part wasn't going to be on television. Sometimes you just have to let 'em know.

20

TO BE A COACH

Craig Esherick was a good coach: smart, knowledgeable, hardworking, could communicate and get along with the kids. But he was in an extremely difficult position, based on the success and expectations of a program he helped build in four years as a player and seventeen years as an assistant.

After he took over midway through the 1999 season, I made it a point to keep my distance. At games, I sat way up high in the arena. But because people saw me around the gym or on campus, and because of my personality, they thought I had more of an influence than I did. It was extremely hard, for both of us, to deal with the perception that I was coaching Craig's team. I didn't know how much I could or should advise Craig. I certainly cared about Craig and the program. I was torn. Our relationship became difficult because comparisons were made between us, and I pulled back out of an abundance of caution. Maybe he did too.

In Craig's first full season in charge, his team finished 19–15 overall, 6–10 in the Big East, and went to the NIT. For the next season, Craig recruited Mike Sweetney, a big power forward and future pro. With Sweetney, Kevin Braswell at guard, and Boumtje-Boumtje at center, the team started the season 16–0 and climbed back into the national rankings. They lost in the first round of the Big East tournament but received an at-large bid to the NCAAs. In the first round, they nipped Arkansas on a buzzer beater, then beat Hampton to make the Sweet Sixteen, where they lost to Maryland and finished with a record of 25–8. All things considered, a very good season.

That was as good as it got. Craig's team did not make the NCAAs in 2002, and he declined an invitation to the NIT. Craig said the players would have had to miss too much class time with the distance the NIT wanted them to travel. The next season, 2002–3, Sweetney averaged 25 points per game but the team missed the NCAAs again. Craig accepted the NIT bid this time and made it to the finals before losing 70–67 to St. John's.

Craig received a six-year contract extension in 2003. Then Sweetney left early for the NBA, the team finished 13–14 overall and 4–12 in the Big East, and Craig got fired in 2004.

When Craig went to the Sweet Sixteen, I was Joe the Fan. I watched the games along with everyone else, I wasn't giving Craig instructions in the middle of the night. When Craig's team wasn't doing well and I kept the same distance, some people interpreted that as me not supporting him or the program. Both of us were in a no-win situation, but it was worse for Craig. It got to the point where he was defending himself about my actions, and I was defending myself about his coaching. It was painful and hurt our relationship.

Craig was a very good coach, but that was not the issue. A lot of bad coaches kept jobs for years. It was about winning, and winning at Georgetown is harder than at a lot of places Georgetown wants to compete with. Georgetown is not committed in the same way as those other schools. Those other schools are committed to winning at any cost. They do things we don't, including but not limited to paying for players. For example, other schools would not have permitted me to get rid of Michael Graham. I would not have been allowed to make that decision. Georgetown alumni, people on the board of directors, other influential members of the university community, they got used to having the Patricks and Alonzos, and going out on the town at the Final Four, and living it up in New York City at the Big East tournament. They got used to making money. When Craig faltered, they didn't care about his graduation rate.

Craig Esherick is a better coach than a lot of guys who are still coaching, and he's a good man. Unfortunately, a lot of good coaches don't get a second chance.

I ALWAYS TRIED to give my sons a realistic perspective on being a basketball coach. I told them about the pressures, the daily grind, how losses eat at you, how your livelihood depends on eighteen-to-twenty-two-year-old kids. I also made it clear, as I did with every player I had, that basketball is a fantasy world, much different from the world of work. I required my sons to educate themselves in preparation for making contributions to something besides basketball. Their lives had more value than the eight to nine pounds of air in that ball. Before I coached my first game, I worked for 4-H and the poverty program. That experience taught me how to supervise people, how to understand the larger forces at work in an organization, the financial motivations behind various decisions, how to follow rules and processes, all those kinds of things. I felt that type of experience was necessary before they made decisions about going into coaching. So I was pleased when John graduated from Princeton and decided to work for a Ford training program, learning how to operate and own car dealerships. He did that for a few years but didn't feel a passion for cars the way he felt for sports. He went to work for a sports marketing company, then got a call from Pete Carril at Princeton. John took a job as an unpaid assistant coach, then worked his way up and became Princeton's head coach in 2000.

John won immediately, with an Ivy championship three out of his four seasons. In year four the Tigers won twenty games and led Texas at halftime in the first round of the NCAAs, but lost 66–49. John was standing outside the locker room after that loss when a reporter said, "The Georgetown job just came open, what do you think about the possibility of coaching there?" That was a bad time to ask that question, because John and his team had just lost a tournament game they thought they could win. John was more than happy at Princeton, and he had almost his whole team coming back the next season. It was not an easy decision for him to make, but when he did take the Georgetown job I was glad.

Jeff Green and Roy Hibbert were freshmen on John's first Georgetown team in 2004–5. Green was a versatile forward and Hibbert a classic big man, and both went on to have outstanding NBA careers. John led his team to the NIT his first season, then made the Sweet Sixteen in the NCAAs the following year. In 2007, his team won the Big East regular season and conference championships, then went all the way to the Final Four. They lost in the national semifinals, 67–60, to the Ohio State team with Greg Oden and Mike Conley Jr.

John reaching the Final Four was one of the proudest moments of my life. He and I were the only father and son ever to coach in the Final Four, until Virginia coach Tony Bennett, the son of Dick Bennett, went in 2019. I wear John's Final Four ring every day, not any of mine. But in retrospect, I think John had too much success too quickly. People don't understand how hard it is to reach the Final Four. Even with a great team, so many things have to fall into place. A significant amount of luck is involved. I lost a lot of games in the early rounds of the tournament, and I lost three times in the Elite Eight. When John went to the Final Four in his third season, it created an unreasonable level of expectation among some people who did not know the game.

I still had to deal with the perception that I was coaching John's team. In reality, John invited my input, and even asked for my opinion on some things, which was the intelligent thing to do. A smart person uses all the resources at his or her disposal. And then John did whatever he felt was best, which a lot of times was not what I suggested. He was secure enough to make his own decisions. I taught him to be his own man. That didn't make it easy, though, for either of us. It was difficult for me to see him not take my advice. I have strong opinions about basketball, and on some level I did want to coach his team. I sat there chomping at the bit, but I also knew he had to make his own way. The whole thing was painful, as it was with Craig, but even more so because John is my son.

Some people criticized John for bringing what they thought was the Princeton offense to Georgetown. At times, I agreed with them. What John actually did, especially after Hibbert graduated, was try to put five skilled, unselfish guys on the floor who could dribble, pass, and shoot. He didn't walk the ball up the court or milk the shot clock. Since John played and coached at Princeton, his system was perceived as an old-fashioned offense for non-athletic players, but it actually was similar to how the Golden State Warriors play now. John adapted what he learned from Pete Carril to create a system for more talented and athletic players. Even if I wasn't always on board with it, that was one of the areas in which John made his own decisions. He turned out to be ahead of his time, but back then, the phrase "Princeton offense" was a stigma he could not escape.

Another issue was that some people didn't think Black kids could run a read-and-react offense. They thought all we were capable of was running a set pattern, instead of making decisions according to the options in real time. That was one factor in the criticism John received.

In 2008, the year after his run to the Final Four, John's team was upset in the second round of the NCAAs by Davidson and Stephen Curry, before anybody realized how great Curry was. John got no further than the second round for the next seven years. In each of those seasons, things happened with players, injuries, illnesses, or academic problems, and John kept it all secret. Some students and alumni started getting impatient, and a lot of the media piled on. Locally, some talented high school kids left the area to attend other colleges. This connects back to Georgetown being different. We didn't cheat, we didn't pay for players, but our success or failure was judged against those who did. Compared with when I coached, there was much more money flowing through basketball. NBA salaries were much higher, the college TV contracts were into the hundreds of millions of dollars, all the shoe companies were pouring money into AAU summer basketball. There was more incentive and opportunity for kids to be paid, and the amounts they received under the table were greater.

John was recruiting one kid who was a future NBA player. His AAU coach asked for money, so John stopped recruiting him. A while later, the mother called John to ask why Georgetown had stopped recruiting her son. John didn't tell on the AAU coach. Then the mother asked him point-blank, "Did he ask you for money?" She said her family wasn't about that and they had moved on from the AAU coach. The kid ended up coming to Georgetown, but that type of outcome was rare. Most of the time, they took the money.

John recruited another kid who chose an SEC school. Not long afterward, the coach was caught on tape talking about how much he paid the kid to get him to sign. After the tape came out, the SEC coach kept his job.

Georgetown's facilities posed another disadvantage. McDonough was more than fifty years old. We shared it with the volleyball team and whoever else. Facilities have a tremendous effect on recruiting. Some colleges have nicer locker rooms than the pros. Georgetown finally accepted the fact that we needed a new athletic complex. In the fall of 2016, twelve seasons after John became head coach, Georgetown opened a $62 million facility with all the practice courts and bells and whistles that players love. They named it after me—the John R. Thompson Jr. Intercollegiate Athletic Center.

My son barely got to use it.

One of his best players was diagnosed with multiple sclerosis, which John kept hidden at the request of the kid's parents. Several other key players had illnesses and injuries. In March 2017, less than a year after they unveiled my statue in the athletic center bearing our family name, John finished the season with a 14–18 record and was fired.

This was a new kind of hurt for me. I thought it was tremendously unfair. President Jack DeGioia did not want to fire John, but he works for the board of directors, and some of the board members stuck their nose into something they didn't know a damn thing about. I understand that I set a high bar for success at Georgetown, and I don't blame the school for wanting that standard to be met. John had two bad years, for reasons that the board chose to ignore and that had nothing to do with his coaching ability. He made mistakes, like all coaches do, including me. But in seventeen years as a head coach, John won six conference championships, including three Big East championships when it was really the Big East. John chalked up victories over the best coaches in the game, including Jim Calhoun, Roy Williams, Jim Boeheim, Jay Wright, Tom Izzo, John Calipari, and Mike Krzyzewski. If it sounds like I'm being biased and pissed off, you're damn right I am, but you can't argue with the truth. John went to the NCAAs eight of thirteen years and took us to the Final Four. Hell, I never made it back to the Final Four after Patrick left, not with Alonzo, not with Dikembe, not with the legendary Allen Iverson. That shows how hard it is to get there.

There is more to a coach's win-loss record than wins and losses. Is Georgetown first and foremost an educational institution, where we care about what goes on with these kids outside the gym? Are we truly concerned when their bodies hurt, or when they struggle in the classroom or have problems in their personal lives? Or is Georgetown more like professional sports, where winning is the only thing that matters? Part of what hurt so badly is that I built the program to educate the kids at all costs, not to win at all costs.

After he got fired, John said to me, "Dad, I thought Georgetown was different."

There were a lot of things I could not say at that time, because it could have affected John's future opportunities. Black people are often the last to get jobs because people think they can't fire them without getting attacked. But I can say this now. In John's final ten seasons, he had the twenty-eighth-best record in college basketball. Of the twenty-seven coaches with better winning percentages, thirteen had been placed on probation for violating NCAA rules.

A lot of schools that don't cheat actually encourage cheating, because they fire coaches who don't beat the cheaters. Think about what I'm saying. If you don't win, they fire you. To win, you have to beat schools that cheat. But hardly any universities are willing to let a coach ride out a few down seasons. That puts pressure on more coaches to break the rules.

The NCAA likes to "vacate" the wins of schools that are caught cheating. They rewrite the record books and act like those games were never won. They punish the coaches, take scholarships away from the schools, and take down banners from the rafters.

But they never vacate losses, do they?

College sports has a lot of hypocrisy. These are supposed to be educational institutions, but for too many schools, their self-worth is tied to winning. Nobody cares about the graduation rate if they lose. When you win, you make more TV money. The school receives more alumni donations and student applications. Local businesses fill up with more customers. Enrollment increases, which brings revenue up. The NCAA is run by universities, so it has a conflict of interest between education and money. We all know how that conflict turns out. I once spoke to a meeting of athletic directors and told them, "All you administrators preach education, but you vote money. When it's time to make rules, you vote for the rules that will make everybody the most money."

I'm not saying that voting money is bad. I'm saying let's call it what it is. Capitalism is the system we operate in. College basketball is subject to the laws of supply and demand. The amateurism of big-time college sports is antiquated and needs to be redefined. We shouldn't act like going to college is a religious experience for everybody. The best players right now are not going to college for an education. They are going to college for a few months to make millions in the pros, which can be a smart decision. Pretty soon, very few of the best players will attend college at all. Most of them will go straight to the NBA or the G League, or overseas, or just stay home and work out. The problem is, there aren't enough jobs for all the high school kids who think they are pro material. These kids won't care about academics, because they think they're going to the League. The ones who don't make it, which will be many if not most of them, would have been much better off with a college education.

But the world is changing, and college athletics needs to adapt. For many years, I resisted the idea of paying players. I felt it would be too hard to change the system, and that paying players would create more problems than it solved. I thought we had dug our own grave so deep, we couldn't throw the shovel out. But recently, watching how the NCAA is refusing to enforce its own rules, I changed my mind. I've been joking for years that whenever a blue-blood school commits a violation, the NCAA puts an Alcorn State on probation. Now those jokes don't sound so funny anymore, because some big schools are on federal wiretaps talking about paying kids and the NCAA doesn't do anything about it. Everybody knows which schools are buying players, the whole system is filthy with it, but somehow the NCAA can't find or penalize the worst cheaters. Since the NCAA won't hold everyone accountable, paying players might as well be legal. Schools that don't pay for players have an extremely hard time competing for championships, and coaches who don't cheat can barely hold on to their jobs, because their losses against the cheaters are counted against them. The NCAA is also teaching young athletes that the way to succeed in life is to break rules, not follow them. We are abdicating our responsibility to act on the rules we make and corrupting the educational mission that universities are supposed to have. It seems like the NCAA is making players into thieves. It feels like entrapment.

If I were coaching right now, I would cheat too. I would pay for players, because if I didn't I would lose to the cheaters and get fired. The NCAA has almost given coaches no other choice but to cheat if they want to compete for championships.

I don't condone how adults who control the high school kids use them to make money, and a lot of these kids are not innocent either. Most of the kids who take money make a conscious decision to take it. I'm sick and tired of hearing that helpless kids are being taken advantage of by unscrupulous adults. These kids know their worth on the black market, and they decide to cheat. They are not innocent, and they should be penalized when they break the rules. But the people who run the NCAA are more guilty than anybody, because they ignore their own rules. They go after petty violations like having too many coaches at practice, but turn a blind eye to buying five-star recruits who bring in millions of dollars' worth of ticket sales and TV ratings.

On the rare occasions when there is an investigation, what happens too often is the Black assistant coaches take all the punishment and the white head coaches escape accountability. Schools hire the Black guys to recruit Black players, to be the natives with the spears up ahead in the jungle. The Black assistants say they have a hard time getting promoted to be head coaches, but when a violation occurs, they're treated like they're in charge. And don't even get me started about the NCAA putting historically Black colleges on probation for low graduation rates while Power Five schools are on tape paying for players but receive no punishment.

Coming to the conclusion that players should be paid was not an easy step for me to take. I've always been bothered when some people say college athletes make money for schools but get nothing in return. A free education is not nothing—ask someone with student loans about that. Ask someone stuck in a low-wage job if a college degree is nothing. It does make sense to say that college athletes should receive more, but don't devalue education.

Paying players would not be easy. A lot of difficult questions would need to be answered. For example, when Allen Iverson was at Georgetown, he would have believed that he should be paid more than everybody else, and he would have been right. How do you set up a fair compensation system? How would we ensure that female athletes are treated equitably under Title IX? How would it change our responsibility to educate players? What about the majority of schools whose football and basketball teams do not make money? If we are basically hiring kids to play college sports, does that mean we can fire them, too? I haven't heard anyone satisfactorily explain how all this could work. But that doesn't mean it's impossible, or worse than the alternative.

A wise person once told me that love is not a word, it's an action. The same concept applies to fairness and justice. Without action, we cannot have fairness and justice in college basketball. Since the NCAA is clearly hurting kids and coaches by refusing to act on its own rules, let's end the charade and allow college athletes to be paid.

AFTER JOHN WAS fired, I told Patrick he should apply for the job.

Patrick had been an assistant coach in the NBA for thirteen years without getting close to a head coaching position. I considered this an example of the bias against big men in coaching, and how big people are stereotyped as not smart. How many former centers have you seen coaching at the top levels of the game? Patrick humbled himself after a superstar playing career, did all the little things and dirty work required of an NBA assistant coach, and still got passed over time and time again. I told Patrick it was obvious that the NBA owners wouldn't give him a fair shot, and he should try for the Georgetown job. I thought he deserved it, not because of what he did here when he was a player, but because he's an intelligent man who knows the game and would be able to recruit and win.

Of course I advocated for Patrick, but I couldn't make Georgetown give him the job. I never had as much influence or power as people thought, and I sure don't have it now. If I did, they never would have fired my son.

Patrick was hired in April 2017, and after his first few games, people thought they were saying something nice by telling me "Patrick can coach, he runs good plays and everything." To me, that was insulting. It was based on the presumption that he was incompetent. I think he's done a good job so far, but he has to keep recruiting at a high level, he has to deal with kids transferring like they change their socks, and he has to take Georgetown back to the NCAA tournament. He and I talk fairly often, and I give him advice, but by now I can accept when Patrick wants to do things his own way. I made it very clear to him that I'm not going to be offended if he doesn't do what I suggest. I've learned.

Despite what happened to John, I still love Georgetown for allowing me to be me, and for taking a chance on a lot of players who were not superstars but still deserved an opportunity to be educated. I appreciate Georgetown's transformation since they hired me in 1972 to bring some Black people Across the Park. I'm glad I was able to contribute to those changes.

But some things still haven't changed.

Black coaches still aren't fairly represented in college basketball. We actually have less influence than when John Chaney, Nolan Richardson, George Raveling, and I were on the bench. Only four Black coaches have won a national championship: me, Nolan in 1994, Tubby Smith at Kentucky in 1998, and Kevin Ollie at Connecticut in 2014. Of those four, I'm the only one who didn't get fired or forced out.

When I talk these days with Chaney, Nolan, and George, we call ourselves the Final Four, and it doesn't have anything to do with the NCAA tournament. It refers to the environment for today's Black coaches. Their challenges are an updated version of the obstacles that I faced. Almost fifty years after I came to Georgetown, after Black coaches won four national championships, after Georgetown erected my statue in a building that carries my family name, most Black coaches still do not have the freedom to not be successful.

21

DO NOT FORGET

I'm more satisfied by things I did other than winning basketball games, probably because I never intended to be a basketball coach. I'm fulfilled by the fact that I learned how to read after the nuns said I was "retarded." Experiencing that kind of hurt and disappointment at a young age prepared me for the road ahead. It prepared me to lose a championship game before I won one. Then I lost another championship game, and then I lost in the Olympics. I tell young people not to let the fear of failure keep them from pursuing their dreams. I lost far more big games than I won, and still ended up with my statue on campus and a decent piece of change in my pocket.

I'm gratified that I could contribute to the cause of higher education, even beyond our school. I hope that I helped more young people discover the value of college. My players rarely tell me I was a great coach. They say I taught them a lot about life, and I love that, because that's what education is all about. For me, coaching was more than getting kids to put the ball through the hoop. Coaching was when Alonzo got mixed up with Rayful, when Victor Page broke curfew, when Derrick Jackson tried to play with a bleeding ulcer, when Allen's mother was in tears in my office. Coaching was about building relationships with players most people never heard of. We did win a lot of games, which encouraged white people to bring more of us into their schools, including Black kids who are not athletes. We are far less of a rarity on campuses today than in 1972. Opening that door was one reason I had to win. Nobody pays attention if you lose.

Georgetown's endowment is now $1.6 billion. The ranking of the school and the grade point averages and standardized test scores of incoming students are far higher now than when the basketball team went 3–23. Basketball gave Georgetown a national reputation. And still, for a long time, Black people here were made to believe that we were guests. I felt that way long after I won the national championship.

I also am proud of the fact that I won championships in junior high school, high school, at Providence, with the Boston Celtics, with the United States Olympic team, and at Georgetown. I don't know how many players from my hometown of Washington, if any, have won at all those levels. But as good as it felt to add that final championship in the 1984 NCAA tournament, it felt better to kick down the door that had kept us from being recognized for using our intelligence. I didn't want to prove something to white people, which is why I rejected the implication that I was the first Black coach with the ability to win a championship. Barack Obama wasn't the first Black man with the ability to be president. I wanted to communicate to Black people that we can think our way to greatness. I wanted to kick down the door in our minds.

I knew I carried a different burden than other coaches, and I felt the weight of that responsibility. The payoff comes in my retirement, when young people walk up to me and say "Thank you." The next generation is who I did it for. I'm not ashamed to say I did it for the money too.

My sense of responsibility to speak out and resist is why people said, "John Thompson is hard to get along with. He walks around with a cloud over his head. He makes everything racial." Everything *was* racial, due to what I had seen and experienced. Don't make me sit in the back of the church, don't subject me and my team to the abuse we experienced, and then wonder why I see the world through the lens of heredity, environment, and time. Some people expect too much of you. They expect you to forgive and to forget.

How you react to not forgetting is a separate issue. I think not forgetting makes you strong. It bestows certain accolades on those who experienced what you remember. To hell with winning games, or dunking backwards, or making three-point shots. The real heroes are the ones who lived in bondage, or scrubbed toilets when they couldn't teach school, or went to work instead of learning how to read. When Georgetown spent $62 million on a new athletic center, I said, "That's my father's name on this building." The real heroes are the ones who took a lot of shit so I could talk a lot of shit.

I'll say it one last time. Despite its flaws, I will always love Georgetown because once they discovered who and what I was, they allowed me to be me. None of my bosses ever told me to quiet down or stop speaking my mind. There also were plenty of people associated with the school—alumni, professors, students, staff—who strongly opposed what I did and said. A lot of people who had never won anything in their lives were extremely judgmental. It wasn't a smooth trip where everybody at Georgetown was glad they'd hired a Black man. The antagonism was communicated to me, verbally and nonverbally. But that's the Black man's burden. It could be hurtful or disappointing, but I took most of it as a challenge.

Those were still the best times of my life. The fight gave me strength to keep going. I have no complaints, because a whole lot of people paid a far higher price than I did. Pebbles. John McLendon. Levern Tart. My parents. The list goes on. Compared with them, I had it made, flying in nice planes and eating good meals. I had so many great times.

Today I have a tiny, windowless office in the athletic center, far away from the basketball floor because I don't want to get in their way. Pictures of my heroes hang on the walls: Martin Luther King, Malcolm X, Rosa Parks, Nelson Mandela. Barack and Michelle Obama. Red Auerbach, Dean Smith, Dave Gavitt. Next to a photo of me with my children is a statuette of the Virgin Mary. I wear three emblems on my necklace: a cross, the Blessed Mother, and a pair of dice. Because if the first two don't help you, then roll the dice.

I asked Georgetown to put a full-size statue of the Virgin Mary in the courtyard of the athletic center, because I have always leaned on her for strength, assistance, and forgiveness. When the workers lowered her statue into place, I slipped a photo of my parents underneath.

I live right across the Potomac River from campus. In my bedroom, I have a small statue of a female slave that Mary Fenlon gave me. The statue is staring out the window, across the river and at the school. I keep her there to remember what had to take place in order for me to become the coach at Georgetown. The slave woman is telling me, "Don't feel like you did this yourself. Don't forget those who picked the tobacco, scrubbed the floors, endured unspeakable abuse, and sacrificed their lives. Do not forget."

I STILL VISIT St. Mary's County, Maryland, where my father grew up, where as much as I loved my aunts and uncles and enjoyed playing in the fields with my cousins, Black people sat in the back of the church. A place where, when it was time to take the body and blood of our Lord Jesus Christ, all of us Black people went last. I bought some property down there, to remember my past. To get there, I take the same route as the old Greyhound bus, fifty-six miles southeast from Washington. The Waldorf rest stop is now a strip mall, but then the stores thin out and it's the way I remember: thick woods, wide open fields, country lanes, and that church.

St. Francis Xavier Catholic Church is a historic landmark now, dating back to 1662. It looks basically the same as when I was a boy, the brick entrance leading to a small sanctuary with eleven pews. Outside, the church is surrounded by fields where slaves once worked. It's easy to close my eyes and see the ghosts of my ancestors here. My father was born only forty years after slavery ended. His father could have been a slave. His grandparents almost certainly were enslaved in the same fields where I once thought it was so much fun to frolic through the corn and watch my cousins pick tobacco.

But my connection to that land cuts even deeper. It all revolves around that church.

The Jesuits established huge plantations in St. Mary's County, to support Catholicism in their so-called New World. They made all the slaves Catholic and named a lot of them after saints. Jesuit priests lived on the plantations and controlled the slaves. The money earned from slavery helped pay priests' salaries, build churches, homes, schools, seminaries . . . and Georgetown University.

The same Jesuits who founded Georgetown owned my father's ancestors.

I can't prove it, but there is no doubt in my mind. My father's whole family is Catholic. His people are from St. Mary's County, where the Jesuits owned everything. They must have owned my father's people. Why else would we be Catholic instead of Baptist or African Methodist? Why else would so many of my family members be named Mary or John?

When Georgetown was founded in 1789, slaves helped lay the first stones. As students arrived, slaves emptied their chamber pots and cooked their food. Money from Jesuit plantations paid for Georgetown's food, books, the priests' robes, the bread and wine for Mass.

In 1838, when growing debt threatened to shut down Georgetown, the Jesuits sold 272 enslaved Black people. Women, men, children, even a two-month-old baby. Families were torn apart. Most people were forced into their worst nightmare, the Deep South, the sugar and cotton plantations of Louisiana. The university collected more than $3 million in today's dollars from the sale, and survived.

When the sale came to light a few years ago, I felt concerned. I felt angry. I felt hurt. I experienced a lot of emotions I can't describe. I also felt puzzled. I had not been naïve about the school owning Black people, but the magnitude of the sale surprised me. I was knocked off balance by the fact that the people they sold were from the place where my father grew up. It made me wonder whether any of my relatives were sold, and it brought back childhood memories of being in that church.

More than ever, I am haunted by my past.

What Georgetown did during slavery is indefensible. We were whipped and tortured, treated like horses and pigs. They sold our babies. We heard our wives being raped. Georgetown profited from all that. Georgetown would not exist today without it. Some white people never want to admit that even though they did not personally participate in slavery or discrimination, they still benefit from it today. They pretend that everyone is treated equally now, but they have a fifty-yard head start in a hundred-yard race. They aren't walking backwards to come start the race with us.

Georgetown is not one of those deniers. After the news of the slave sale came out, I was proud of how the school, and especially President Jack DeGioia, faced it head-on. They investigated, uncovered all the facts, and publicized it. The school is now raising money to help the descendants of the people they sold and is giving them preferential access in admissions. The student body voted to charge themselves a fee that would pay for reparations to the descendants. All of this is highly unusual for our society. When Black people talk about slavery and reparations, we are often defined as aggrieved or militant, or accused of playing the race card, even though a hand full of spades is all we were ever dealt. Jack made sure the university exposed its own sins, then went about trying to heal the damage. Which is impossible. The Jesuits started buying slaves in the 1600s. How can you heal wounds that deep?

Georgetown hired me as part of that effort to heal itself. Why would an all-white school want a Black coach in 1972? To revisit what they claimed they stood for, because they had strayed from the mission of higher education, not to mention the principles of the Jesuits and Catholicism itself. Georgetown was not practicing what it preached, even more than a century after selling all those slaves.

Georgetown didn't cause slavery to happen. The school participated in it, but at some point they accepted what they had done and felt the need to make amends. That's how they ended up hiring a Black man from the same place they had kept his family in bondage.

Georgetown, too, is haunted by its past. That past is me.

I came as a shadow,
I stand now a light;
The depth of my darkness
Transfigures your night.

ACKNOWLEDGMENTS

I originally wanted to write this book so my grandchildren, and their children, would know the good, the bad, and the ugly of who Poppy really was. Now you can paint your own picture.

My parents, Anna and Rob Thompson, made everything possible for me. I can never thank them enough.

Thank you to my children, Tiffany, Ronny, and John, for encouraging me to do this book.

Many of the people who helped me the most in life have passed away, and I wish they were here to share my reflections about what we did together. I hope that Sametta Wallace Jackson, Jabbo Kenner, Julius Wyatt, Bill Butler, Red Auerbach, Dean Smith, Dave Gavitt, Frank Rienzo, and Mary Fenlon know how much they meant to me.

To Dr. Anita Hughes: I'm still your student, trying to utilize the education you gave me. I did my best to make you proud. Thank you to David Falk, a great lawyer and friend. Lorry Michel's feedback and memories were extremely helpful on this project. Jack DeGioia made me finally feel at home at Georgetown.

Anybody who has seen me these last few years has seen *my* shadow, my head of security, and my friend, Greg Roberts. I appreciate all you've done for me.

I'm extremely grateful to my players for their commitment and loyalty. It's always portrayed like I lifted them out of poverty or saved somebody's life, but in reality they deserve the credit. I could not have accomplished anything without them believing in me. Thank you for giving me the honor of coaching you.

I'd like to conclude by offering thanks to the Blessed Mother, for always providing me with strength and comfort. Like I told my players as they left the locker room before games: Always remember to "say one for the Lady."

—John Thompson

Coach Thompson: Thank you for sharing your story with me, and with the world. Not bad for two guys from the projects.

I'm thankful that John Skipper, Tiffany Thompson, and John Thompson III believed I should write this book. Tiffany's idea for the title was inspirational. I appreciate the support of Steve Reiss and Kevin Merida at *The Undefeated*. David Black, your guidance and knowledge was invaluable.

Emanuel Reid, your countless acts of assistance may not show up on the stat sheet, but we would not have won this game without you.

The passion and skill of the Henry Holt editor Paul Golob elevated our work, and I appreciate the Holt team that saw this project through: Sarah Crichton, Conor Mintzer, Natalia Ruiz, and Chris O'Connell.

Many thanks for the assistance of Ronny Thompson, Michael Jackson, David Falk, Dr. Anita Hughes, Charlie Deacon, Jack DeGioia, Patrick Ewing, Dikembe Mutombo, Steve Martin, Derrick Jackson, Lonnie Duren, Felix Yeoman, Bill Stein, Sonny Vaccaro, Diana Pulupa, Lorry Michel, Bill Rhoden, Doc Walker, Al Koken, Scooter Vertino, Tim Kiely, Cornell Jones, and Phil Knight.

Finally, I could not have done this without the support and patience of my wife, Alaina, and our children, Zora, Zachary, Corinne, and Coletrane. I love you.

—Jesse Washington

INDEX

AAU (Amateur Athletic Union), 58, 250, 309–10
Abdul-Jabbar, Kareem, 84–85, 274
Adams, Michael, 172
Adande, J. A., 149
Adidas, 171, 274–75
Ainge, Danny, 302
Albert, Marv, 302
Aldridge, David, 149
Alexander, Lewis Grandison (uncle), 11–13, 111, 161, 201
Ali, Muhammad, 148, 207
Allen, Ray, 258, 264–65
All Saints High School (*formerly* St. Anthony's), 197
Altobello, Dan, 100
American Basketball Association, 63
American University, 131
Amin, Idi, 155, 230
Anders, Benny, 178
Anderson, Willie, 206
Archbishop Carroll High School, 33–38, 43–44, 84, 127, 133
Arizona, University of, 178, 261
Arkansas, University of, 242, 256, 306
Ashe, Arthur, 183, 227–28
Asher, Mark, 147–48
Atlanta serial killer, 106
Atlantic 10 Conference, 199
Atlantic Coast Conference (ACC), 139, 156, 232
Auerbach, Red, 39–41, 46–47, 50–52, 57, 61–74, 79, 85, 87, 107, 110, 120, 127, 152, 154, 177, 187, 244, 280, 299, 319, 325
Augmon, Stacey, 206
Augustine, Saint, 288
Austin, John, 36, 84
Australia basketball team, 207

Baker, Allen, 80
Ballou High School, 200
Barkley, Charles, 299, 301–2
Barrett, Charles, 80
Barry, Marion, 234
Bavaro, Dick, 175
Baylor, Elgin "Rabbit," 28–31, 33, 38–39, 42, 46, 72, 189, 275
Bennett, Dick, 308
Bennett, Michael, 80
Bennett, Tony, 308
Berkowitz, Steve, 244
Berry, Dean, 262
Berry, Walter, 189
Bias, Len, 209
Bickerstaff, Bernie, 92
Big East, 139–41, 153–54, 165, 167, 172, 185, 188–91, 198, 243, 256, 258, 259, 311
  tournaments: (1980), 141; (1982), 155; (1983), 167–68; (1984), 173–76; (1985), 190; (1987), 197; (1988), 198; (1989), 231; (1990), 246; (1991), 246; (1992), 246; (1995), 259; (1996), 264; (1997), 291; (1998), 293; (2000), 306; (2007), 308
Big Ten, 139
Bird, Larry, 64
Black Coaches Association (BCA), 241–44
Black referees, 134, 142, 178

Blaylock, Mookie, 204
Blaylock, Ron, 132, 150
Boeheim, Jim, 111, 139, 175–76, 188, 245, 246, 311
Boston Celtics, 30, 39, 46, 50, 52, 61–67, 70–74, 129, 151, 180, 187–88, 210, 219, 247–48, 318
Boston College, 46, 117, 139–40, 153, 172, 189, 225, 230, 258, 291
Boswell, Thomas, 147, 266
Bouie, Roosevelt, 140
Boumtje-Boumtje, Ruben, 293, 305
Bowerman, Bill, 276
Bowie, Sam, 177
Bowman, Blanche, 92
Bradley University, 63
Braswell, Kevin, 305
Brazil basketball team, 203, 206
Broadnax, Horace, 162, 170, 179, 185, 196, 297
Brooks, Greg, 80, 97
Brown, Dale, 226
Brown, Fred, 150–52, 159–60, 162, 167, 170, 179, 185, 192
Brown, James, 65, 285
Brown, Larry, 271
Brown, David "Lieutenant," 33
Brown, Walter, 61, 67
Brown Junior High School, 27–29
Brown v. Board of Education, 24
Brunner, Kenny, 293
Bryant, Dwayne, 197, 245
Bryant, Kobe, 257, 260, 299
Bucknell University, 197
Buckner, Quinn, 124
Bullis, Jeff, 133
Burwell, Bryan, 149
Bush, George H. W., 219
Butler, Bill, 31, 51, 53, 98, 235, 325
Butler, George, 254
Butler, John, 80

Calhoun, Jim, 244, 311
California, University of, LA (UCLA), 58, 139, 154, 183
California, University of, Riverside, 92
California State University, Hayward, 92
Calipari, John, 199, 267–68, 311
Cambridge Rindge and Latin School, 143
Camby, Marcus, 267
Campanelli, Lou, 133
Canada basketball team, 206
Canisius College, 54
Cardozo High School, 37, 85, 115
Carlesimo, P. J., 188
Carnesecca, Lou, 139, 154, 176, 189–90
Carr, Kenny, 124
Carril, Pete, 202, 232, 309
Cassell, Sam, 246
Catholic Church. 18–19, 46, 267. *See also* Jesuits
Catholic league (high school), 36, 37, 87
CBS News, 200
Central Michigan University, 118–19
Chamberlain, Wilt, 29, 70–71
Chaney, John, 190, 199, 226, 242–43, 294, 316
Chapman, Rex, 203
Cheyney State College, 199, 212
Chicago Bulls, 74
China basketball team, 206–7
Cincinnati, University of, 46
Civil Rights Movement, 54–55
Cleveland Indians, 10, 27
Clinton, Bill, 258–59
Coleman, Derrick, 245
Coles, Bimbo, 206
Combs, Sean, 270
Community Scholars program, 100
Compton, Maryland, 7, 16–18
Congressional Black Caucus, 242
Conley, Mike, Jr., 308
Connecticut, University of, 139, 229, 244, 246, 258–59, 263–64, 294, 316
Connors, Fran, 187
Continental Basketball Association, 291
Converse, 111, 171, 279
Conway, Jill Ker, 252, 287–88
Cook, Tim, 285–86, 288
Coolidge High School, 230
Copeland, Reggie, 119
Cosby, Bill, 299
Cosell, Howard, 148
Counts, Mel, 64
Cousy, Bob, 50, 64
Cullen, Countee, 41
Curry, Stephen, 309
Cushing, Richard, 46
Czechoslovakia, 124

Dalton, Ralph, 152–53, 169–70, 177, 179, 185, 190, 196
Dantley, Adrian, 86, 109, 124
Dapper Dan all-star game, 45, 273

Dartmouth College, 115
Daugherty, Brad, 191
Davidson, Joe Dean, 126–27, 168
Davidson College, 81, 309
Davis, Benjamin, 7
Davis, Walter, 124
Dayton, University of, 177
DC Teachers College (*formerly* Miner), 7, 201
Deacon, Charlie, 88–90, 100, 103, 169
Dean, Harold, 85
deflated basketball metaphor, 4, 91–92, 241, 307
DeGioia, Jack, 122–23, 224, 310, 322, 325
DeJesu, Denny, 48, 51–52
Dell, Donald, 183
DeMatha High School, 84–88, 115, 202
Dempsey, Cedric, 266
DeNunzio, Ralph, 232
DePaul University, 172, 256
Detroit Pistons, 268
Dia, Ya-Ya, 254, 290
Dickinson College, 115–16
DiMaggio, Joe, 66
Doby, Larry, 10, 27
Doherty, Matt, 158
Douglass, Frederick, 11
Drake University, 241
Drew, Charles, 7, 29
Drexler, Clyde, 178
Driesell, Lefty, 109, 115, 130–32, 140–41, 152, 279, 299
Drug Enforcement Administration (DEA), 219, 234
Duke University, 233, 246
  secret game vs. North Carolina Central, 56–57
Dunbar High School (Baltimore), 140, 168, 292
Dunbar High School (DC), 7, 126–27, 152, 164, 168, 211
Dunn, David, 170
Durant, Kevin, 30
Duren, John "Bay Bay," 126–30, 132, 136, 141, 170, 183, 251
Duren, Lonnie, 113, 126, 136–38, 295
Dutch, Al, 127
Dwyer, Bob, 33–39, 44, 84–85, 89, 133

East Coast Athletic Conference (ECAC) tournaments, 133; (1975), 118; (1977), 130; (1978), 130; (1979), 132
Easter, Luke, 10
Eastern European tour, 56–58
Edmond, Rayful, III, 209–21, 230–37, 317
education, xii, 2, 22, 76, 89, 90, 92, 104, 122, 127, 145, 148, 150, 162–63, 184, 227–28, 242, 268, 311–14, 317, 322
  exploitation and, 26, 227
  importance of, 12, 104, 163
  informal, 48, 77, 107, 194
  origin of Thompson's coaching as instrument of, 82–83
  Thompson's at Providence college, 52–53
  unequal access to, 100–102, 222–23
Edwards, Johnathan, 196
Edwards, Mark, 107
Ellison, Pervis, 203–4
Elmore, Len, 109–10
Embry, Wayne, 303
Emerson, Ralph Waldo, 4
Ernst, Vinnie, 52
Erving, Julius "Dr. J," 152, 274, 279
Esherick, Craig, 115, 130, 162, 169, 180, 187, 209, 225, 245, 294–95, 305–7, 309
ESPN, 139–40, 148, 258
Eunice, Sister, 15, 147
Ewing, Carl, 144–45
Ewing, Dorothy, 111–16, 162, 169, 181
Ewing, Patrick, xi, 4, 69, 111, 113, 128, 138, 143–59, 162–73, 177–79, 182–85, 192–96, 198, 203, 226, 244, 251, 257–58, 263, 268–69, 276–77, 295, 311, 315–16
  academic ability of, 143–44, 146
  character of, 146–47, 194
  as Georgetown coach, 315
  NBA draft and, 162, 184, 196
  recruitment of, 143–46

Fairfield University, 56
Fairleigh Dickinson University, 117
Falk, David, 183–85, 196–97, 227, 244, 259, 269–70, 325
Federal City College (*later* University of the District of Columbia), 76
Fellowship of Christian Athletes, 122–23
Fenlon, Mary, 82, 90, 97, 100–103, 111–16, 119, 136, 139, 144–51, 162, 164, 173, 178–79, 187, 189, 197–98, 202, 204, 234, 239–40, 248, 255, 265, 268, 276, 278, 286–87, 290, 296, 299–300, 320, 325

Fentress, Lee, 183
Ferry, Danny, 233
Florida State University, 246
Floyd, Eric "Sleepy," 131–32, 140, 142, 148, 150, 158–59, 162, 183, 251
Floyd, George, 3–4
Flynn, Ray, 52
Ford, Gerald, 259
Ford, Phil, 124
Fordham University, 232
4-H programs, 77, 92, 287
Franklin, Alvin, 178
Frederick Douglass projects, 8–11, 22
Freeman, Dwight, 226
Freeman, Ellsworth "Sandy," 27–29, 31, 37
Fresno State University, 155
Furash, Harold, 52, 71, 183, 244
Furash, Marty, 52, 71

Gaines, Clarence "Big House," 131–32, 180, 282
Gaines, Smokey, 292
Gallagher, Mark, 109
Gandhi, Mahatma, 2, 204, 284
Garnett, Kevin, 303
Gaughan, Brendan, 265
Gaughan, Michael, 265–66
Gavitt, Dave, 51–52, 138–39, 141, 149, 172, 179, 203, 296, 319, 325
Georgetown Prep, 81
Georgetown University
  academics and, 99–101, 103, 293
  all-Black team of, 170, 174, 185
  alumni, 99, 174, 267, 306, 309, 319
  basketball team segregated, 45
  board of directors, 306, 310
  educational vs. basketball mission, 311
  endowment, 318
  hiring Thompson because he was Black, 88–89
  John R. Thompson Jr. Intercollegiate Athletic Center, xi, 310, 316–17, 319
  negative image of team, 109–11, 145, 147, 154–55, 165, 176, 187
  "Nigger Flop Must Go" banner and, 116–18
  1984 national championship game, 178–81
  1985 NCAA championship loss, 191–94
  sale of slaves and, xi, 321–22
  seasons: (1972–73), 97–98, 107; (1973–74), 108–10, 140; (1974–75), 113–19; (1976–77), 126–30; (1977–78), 130; (1978–79), 132–33; (1979–80), 139–42; (1981–82), 146–60; (1982–83), 161–68; (1983–84), 168–82; (1984–85), 183–95; (1985–86), 196–97; (1986–87), 197; (1987–88), 198–99; (1988–89), 208–33; (1989–90), 244–46; (1990–91), 246; (1991–92), 246; (1994–95), 253–60; (1995–96), 261–68; (1996–97), 290–91; (1997–98), 293; (1998–99), 294–95; (1999–2000), 305–7; (2001–2), 306; (2002–3), 306; (2003–4), 306; (2004–5), 308; (2005–6), 308; (2006–7), 308
  student body votes for reparations, 322
  Thompson's love for, 91, 225, 315, 319
  thought to be historically Black college, 171, 266–67
George Washington University, 118, 131, 137, 201
Georgia, University of, 170, 221–22
Georgia Tech, 190, 261
Gibson, Josh, 27
Gill, Slats, 58, 74
Gillery, Ben, 209, 248
Glenn, Ed, 116
Golden State Warriors, 309
Gonzaga High School, 162, 202
Goss, Fred, 92
Graham, Ernie, 140
Graham, Michael, 168–70, 173–79, 182, 291, 306
Grant, Gary, 204
Grayer, Jeff, 206
Green, Clarence "Bootney," 212–13, 217–18
Green, Jeff, 308
Greene, Petey, 200
Grier, Bob, 27–29, 31, 33, 37
Grunfeld, Ernie, 124
Gutheridge, Bill, 124, 294

Hackett, Rudy, 140
Hadnot, Jim, 50, 52
Hall, Tom T., 122
Hampton University, 306

Hancock, Mike, 132, 150–51, 162
Harlan, Kevin, 302
Harlem Renaissance, 41–42
Harrington, Othella, 254, 258, 262, 290
Harrison Elementary School, 20–22, 24
Havlicek, John, 63–64, 71
Hawkins, Andre, 175
Hawkins, Connie, 45
Hawkins, Hersey, 206–7
Hazzard, Walt, 58
Healy, Timothy, 126, 169, 182, 224, 229, 232, 267
Heath, Walter J., 59
Heinsohn, Tommy, 66–67
Henle, Robert, 88, 90, 92, 100, 109, 116–17
Henning, Herman, 208–9
Henry T. Blow elementary school, 72
Hibbert, Roy, 308–9
Highsmith, Ronnie, 185, 196
Hill, Grant, 233
Hirshey, Steve, 149
historically Black colleges, 168, 180–81, 185, 199, 223–24, 314
Holland, Terry, 81
Holy Cross College, 50
Hoover, Tom, 36, 39, 45
Hopkins, Ed, 103, 127, 130
Houston, Charles Hamilton, 7
Houston, University of, 178–79
Houston Rockets, 184
Howard University, 201
Howell, Jimmy, 134
Huggins, Bob, 118
Hughes, Anita, 76–78, 82–83, 107, 153, 159, 215, 241, 252, 325
Hughes, Langston, 41
Hurley, Bobby, 233

illegal payments to college athletes, 45, 127, 144, 309, 313
Illinois State University, 92
Indiana University, 124, 132, 139, 154, 297
Indonesia, 287
Inside the NBA (TV show), 301–4
Iona College, 141
Iowa, University of, 142
Irvin, Cal, 180–81, 282
"Is It Because I'm Black" (Johnson), 119, 267
Iverson, Allen, xi, 4, 113, 198, 250–72, 290, 295, 299, 311, 314, 317
Iverson, Ann, 251–52, 268
Ivy League, 232
Izzo, Tom, 311

Jabbo Kenner League, 252
Jackson, Derrick, 114–15, 117–18, 127–28, 130, 132, 317
Jackson, Jaren, 196–97, 208, 218, 251
Jackson, Mark, 172, 189
Jackson, Michael, 69, 141, 162–63, 170, 175, 179, 185, 196, 209, 251, 295, 301–3
Jackson, Reggie, 132
Jackson, Jesse, 280–85, 288, 299
Jackson, Sametta Wallace, 20–22, 25–26, 34, 105, 107, 113, 159, 223, 325
Jacques, John, 254
James, LeBron, 4, 30, 260, 299
James Madison High School, 133
Jarvis, Mike, 143–44, 146, 168
Jefferson, Sam, 246
Jelleff Boys Club, 43, 86
Jesuits, 18, 321–23
Jim Crow, 16, 119, 174
Johnson, Andrew, 219–20
Johnson, Ernie, 301
Johnson, Ollie, 71–74, 219
Johnson, Syl, 119
Jones, Anthony "Red," 132, 103–04, 109
Jones, Cornell, 235–36, 248
Jones, K. C., 63–64, 67, 70, 72
Jones, Sam, 63–64, 71–72, 151
Jones, Wil, 38
Jordan, Michael, 30, 38, 62, 84, 152, 156–58, 171–72, 183, 203, 260, 269–70, 277, 279–80, 283–84, 299, 303

Kaepernick, Colin, 3, 4, 288
Kansas, University of, 56, 198, 202, 206
Kemp, Jack, 234
Kemp, Jan, 221–22
Kenner, James "Jabbo," 31–32, 51, 53, 79, 94–95, 98, 127, 253, 325
Kentucky, University of, 119, 177–78, 183, 203, 316
King, Albert, 132, 142
King, Martin Luther, 35, 55, 80, 148, 163, 265, 283, 319
  assassination of, 81, 88
Kirkpatrick, Curry, 173–77, 184
Kittles, Kerry, 258, 264
Knight, Bobby, 124, 154, 182–83, 203, 297–98

Knight, Phil, 171, 188, 274–89
Knights of Columbus tournament, 86, 91
Koken, Al, 296–99
Koncak, Jon, 177
Koppel, Ted, 233–34
Krzyzewski, Mike, 233, 246, 296, 311
Kupchak, Mitch, 124
Kurtinaitis, Rimas, 207
Kutsher's resort, 39–41

Laettner, Christian, 233
Lancaster, Maurice, 88
Lansky, Meyer, 166, 212
Lapchick, Richard, 243
Lappas, Steve, 264
Las Vegas, 166, 169, 205, 212, 265, 299–300
Lee, Spike, 279, 284, 299
Leftwich, George, 36, 39, 89, 97, 111
Lehigh University, 190
LeRoux, Buddy, 62
Lewis, Harry, 21–22, 223
Liberia, 65
Little, Paul, 143
Lloyd, Earl, 58
Long, Aaron, 80, 97, 197
Long, Larry, 113–15, 117
Lopez, Felipe, 255
Los Angeles Lakers, 71–72
Los Angeles Times, 205
Louis, Joe, 10, 42, 55, 207
Louisiana State University (LSU), 199, 226
Louisville, University of, 65, 156, 203
Loyola University, 190
Lucas, John, 105, 109, 110
Lynn, Billy, 97–101, 103–4, 117

MacArthur, Douglas, 142
Madison Square Garden, 104, 141, 153–54, 175, 188–90, 264
Majerle, Dan, 206
Malcolm X, 55, 58, 87, 121, 148, 163, 283, 319
Malloy, Monk, 36
Mandela, Nelson, xi, 319
Manhattan College, 117
Manley Field House (Syracuse), 140
Manning, Danny, 206–7
Maravich, Pete, 64
Marciulionis, Sarunas, 207
Martin, Bill, 152, 170, 179, 185
Martin, Steve, 113, 127–28, 295
Maryland, University of, 85–86, 89, 109, 115, 130–32, 140–42, 183, 279, 306
Massachusetts, University of, 199, 267–68
Massachusetts General Hospital, 144–45
Massengale, Martin, 229
Massimino, Rollie, 139, 172, 188, 191–93, 264
Mateen, Grady, 185
Mathis, Fred "Doc," 200–201
May, Scott, 124
Mays, Gary "Bandit," 38
McClain, Dwayne, 192
McDermott, Mike, 109
McDonald, Perry, 185, 196, 198
McGuire, Brian, 187
McKinley Tech High School, 151–52, 260
McLain, Gary, 192–93
McLendon, John "Coach Mac," 56–58, 104, 110, 180, 185, 319
M Club Classic tournament, 85–86
McMillen, Tom, 109–10
Medley, Raymond "Pebbles," 94–97, 283, 319
Memphis State University, 168, 278
Meyers, Eddie, 162
Miami, University of, 54, 258
Micheaux, Larry, 178
Michel, Lorry, 153, 187, 253–54, 257, 261, 271, 276, 325
Michigan State University, 197
Middleton, Melvin, 213, 218
Miles, Leo, 33
Miner Teachers College (*later* DC Teachers College), 7, 201
Minnesota Timberwolves, 291, 303
Morehouse College, 201
Morgan State University, 152
Most, Johnny, 71
Moten, Lawrence, 258
Mourning, Alonzo, 4, 128, 204–5, 208–20, 231–39, 244–47, 263, 268–69, 281, 295, 311, 317
Mullaney, Joe, 46, 50–51, 54, 138, 174–75
Mullin, Chris, 172–73, 175, 189, 191
Murray, Jim, 205
Musial, Stan, 27
Mutombo, Dikembe, 4, 208–9, 218–19, 240–41, 244, 246, 263, 281, 295, 311

Naismith, James, 56–57
Naismith Memorial Basketball Hall of Fame, 4–5, 50, 57, 131, 141, 191, 203, 206, 296
National Association of Basketball Coaches, 121–22
National Association of Intercollegiate Athletics (NAIA), 56
National Basketball Association (NBA), 39, 41, 46, 58, 63–64, 104, 114, 124, 138, 141, 152, 156, 158, 189, 197, 204, 207, 246–47, 249, 255–57, 263, 268, 274, 290–91, 301, 309
- All-Star Game, 260
- draft, 150, 162, 170, 183–84, 196, 198, 204, 206, 246
- Eastern Division Finals: (1965), 70–71; (1966), 72
- Finals, 275; (1965), 71; (1966), 72–74

National Collegiate Athletic Association (NCAA), 32, 90, 98, 127–28, 192–93, 198, 273–74, 276, 278
- BCA and, 242–44
- education vs. money and, 311–15
- Final Four, 178, 311; (1982), 155–60; (1984), 177–81; (1985), 190–95, 278–79; (2007), 308, 311; (2019), 308
- hypocrisy and, 276, 312
- Presidents' Commission, 229
- Proposition 42 and, 221–30, 241–42, 283, 288
- Proposition 48 and, 221–22
- racism and, 167
- rule violations, 32, 127–28, 165, 192–93, 198, 242, 311–14
- tournament, 50, 133, 155, 232, 275, 311; (1964), 56; (1966), 190; (1975), 118–19; (1977), 130; (1978), 130; (1979), 132; (1980), 141–42; (1982), 152, 155–60; (1983), 168, 178; (1984), 176–81, 318; (1985), 190–95; (1986), 197; (1987), 197–98; (1988), 198–99; (1989), 231–33; (1990), 246; (1991), 246; (1992), 246; (1995), 259; (1996), 266–68; (1997), 291; (1999), 296; (2000), 306; (2004), 307; (2006), 308; (2007), 308; (2008), 309

National Football League, 288
National Invitation Tournament (NIT), 90, 141; (1959, 1960), 50–51; (1963), 54; (1964), 63; (1977), 130; (1978), 130–31; (1995), 261; (1998), 293; (1999), 305; (2003), 306; (2005), 308
Naulls, Willie, 64, 67, 72, 73
Naval Academy, 203–4
Negro Leagues, 27
Nevada, University of, Las Vegas (UNLV), 169, 177, 246
New York Knicks, 196
New York Times, 149, 221
"nigger," use of word, 134
Nightline (TV show), 233
Nike, 44, 163–64, 171–72, 183, 188, 232, 252, 280, 274–89
- advertising, 274, 279
- Air Jordans and, 277
- board of directors, 44, 232, 252, 284–86
- factory working conditions, 286–88
- hip-hop culture and, 276–77
- Jesse Jackson boycott of, 280–85

"Nocturne Varial" (Alexander), 42, 323
Nolan, Tom, 45
North Carolina, University of, 83–84, 120, 124, 131, 139, 144, 156–60, 183, 191, 202, 259, 274
North Carolina, University of, Charlotte, 291
North Carolina A&T, 181, 185–86
North Carolina Central, secret game vs. Duke, 56–57
North Carolina State University, 124, 131, 178, 232–33
Notre Dame, University of, 36, 46, 109, 124, 202, 232, 257

Oakland Raiders, 167
Obama, Barack, 259, 282, 318–19
Obama, Michelle, 259, 319
O'Connell Christmas tournament, 86–87
Oden, Greg, 308
O'Donovan, Leo, 267
Ohio State University, 197, 308
Olajuwon, Hakeem, 178–79, 184, 196
Old Dominion University, 130
Ollie, Kevin, 258, 316
Olsen, Lute, 142
Olympics, 301, 318; (1964), 58–59, 74, 124; (1972), 203; (1976), 123–26, 180, 203; (1984), 182–83, 203; (1988), 203–7
Operation PUSH, 280–84
Oregon, University of, 58, 275
Oregon State University, 155

Orr, Louis, 140
Our Lady of Perpetual Help School, 13–14, 20, 147, 233–34, 267
Owens, Billy, 245–46

Packer, Billy, 165, 262
Page, Victor, 113, 260–65, 267, 290–92, 317
Pan Am Games (1987), 203, 206
Parks, Rosa, xi, 319
paying college athletes, 312–15
Pebbles. *See* Medley, Raymond
Perkins, Sam, 156–57
Perry, Tim, 204
Phelps, Digger, 232
Philadelphia 76ers, 70–72, 271
Phi Slama Jama (Houston), 178
Pinckney, Ed, 192–93
Pitino, Rick, 198, 229, 257
Pittsburgh, University of, 139, 206, 231
  fights with, 198
Plummer, Ronald, 80
Police Boys Club No. 2, 31–32, 51, 79, 98, 126, 135–37, 142, 200, 212, 215, 235–36, 242, 253
Portland Trail Blazers, 184, 206
Power Memorial High School, 84–85
Prefontaine, Steve, 275
Pressley, Harold, 192–93
Price, Kenny, 36
Princeton University, 202, 231–32, 307–9
Proposition 42, 221–30, 241–42, 283, 288
Providence College, 46–56, 59, 76–77, 83, 99, 127, 138–39, 172, 174, 180–81, 188, 198, 223, 228–29, 256–57, 274, 318
  seasons: (1960–61), 49–50; (1961–62), 50–51; (1962–63), 52–54; (1963–64), 56
Puerto Rico, 124, 185–86

quotas, racial, 63–64, 72, 74, 81, 280

racism, 18–19, 43–44, 63, 65, 91, 93, 116–18, 135, 148–49, 165–67, 173–74, 176, 230–31, 238, 262–63, 318–19. *See also* Jim Crow
  in American society, 19
  among opposing fans, 153, 167, 231, 258
  false accusations of, against Thompson, 87, 109, 148, 149, 174, 230
  at Georgetown, 91, 109–10, 116–17, 319
Ramsay, Jack, 89
Rather, Dan, 200
Raveling, George, 89–90, 130, 145, 204, 242–43, 287, 292, 316
Reagan, Ronald, 185
Reebok, 280
Reid, Don, 254
Reid, J. R., 206
Rhoden, Bill, 149, 221–23, 242
Richardson, Nolan, 242–44, 256, 316
Richmond, Mitch, 206
Rickey, Branch, 44
Rider, J. R., 303–4
Rienzo, Frank, 90, 100, 130, 139, 155, 174, 186–87, 210–11, 221, 223–24, 228–29, 252, 259, 274–75, 300, 325
Riley, Mike, 115, 118, 127, 131–32, 162, 187, 209, 225, 245
Roberts, Greg, 325
Robertson, Oscar, 46, 303
Robinson, David, 203–4, 206
Robinson, Jackie, 10, 44, 55
Robinson, Will, 92
Rome, Jim, 300
Rose, Charlie, 242
Rose, Jalen, 56
Rupp, Adolph, 119, 190, 194
Russell, Bill, 30, 38, 62, 64–66, 69–73, 87, 189, 219, 270–71, 299, 303
Rutgers University, 132
Ruth, Babe, 27

Sabonis, Arvydas, 206–7
Sager, Craig, 302
Sampson, Ralph, 164–65, 184
San Antonio Spurs, 197
Sanders, Tom "Satch," 30, 64, 66–67, 69, 72, 145
San Diego University, 92
San Francisco, University of, 71
Saunders, Flip, 303
Scates, Tom, 127, 136–37
Schayes, Danny, 140
Schiller, Harvey, 229
Schmidt, Oscar, 203, 206
Schulz, John, 176
Score, Herb, 27
Scott, Rip, 37
Seattle University, 38
segregation, 7–9, 16, 18–19, 24, 31, 44–45, 64, 119, 227, 253
Seinfeld (TV show), 298

September 11, 2001, attacks, 300
Seton Hall University, 139, 188, 197–98, 246, 293–94
Shapland, Bill, 186–87
Shelton, Craig "Big Sky," 126–27, 130, 132, 140–42, 183
Shultz, Dick, 229
Siegfried, Larry, 74
Simpson, Harry "Suitcase," 10
Simpson, O. J., 258
Skinner, Walt, 36
Skipper, John, 326
slavery, xi, 16, 18, 26, 65, 91, 94–96, 102, 107, 118, 226–27, 238, 320–23
Smith, Charles "Smitty," 113, 197–99, 206, 208, 218, 229–33, 247–49, 251
Smith, Curt "Trouble," 230
Smith, Dean, 57, 83–84, 87, 104, 110, 120–25, 129, 131–32, 139, 148, 156–60, 179, 183, 191, 202–3, 229, 259, 274–75, 294, 296, 299, 319, 325
Smith, Eric, 132, 140, 142, 150–51, 158–59, 162
Smith, Gene, 113, 115, 151–52, 170, 175, 177–79, 185
Smith, Jonathan, 80, 97, 107, 113–15, 117–19
Smith, Kenny, 191, 301–2
Smith, Tubby, 316
Snowden, Fred, 178
Solomon, George, 147
Southeastern Conference (SEC), 119, 222–23, 229, 310
Southern California, University of, 204
Southern Methodist University, 176–77
Soviet Union basketball team, 124, 203, 206–7
Spectrum Club, 54
Spingarn High School, 28–29, 33, 71, 97, 168–69, 200, 212–13
Sports Illustrated, 28, 149, 173–74, 176, 184–85, 192, 255, 282
Spriggs, Ed, 132, 150–51, 162, 239–40, 261
Stackhouse, Jerry, 259
Staggers, John, 92
Standard Art and Tile factory, 11
St. Anthony's High School (*later* All Saints), 78–91, 97, 105–6, 117, 134, 147, 273
State Department, 56
Stein, Bill, 50, 52, 97, 100, 102–3, 111, 114–15, 143–44, 162, 187, 204
Stepin Fetchit, 283
Stewart, Patsy, 15
St. Francis University, 117
St. Francis Xavier Church, 18, 43, 320–21
St. George, Raymond, 51
St. John's University, 109, 139–40, 149, 153–54, 166, 172, 175, 189–91, 219, 241, 255, 278, 291, 306
St. Joseph's University, 117
St. Louis Post-Dispatch, 149
St. Mary's County, Maryland, 16–18, 43, 320–22
Stockton, Dick, 302
Stokes, Mike, 97
Stone, Jimmy, 52
St. Peter's High School, 91
St. Peter's University, 162, 204
Strait, George, 298
Strasser, Rob, 171, 274
summer league games, 128, 152, 252–53
Sursum Corda cooperative, 137–38
Sweetney, Mike, 305–6
Syracuse University, 46, 111, 132, 139–41, 167–68, 172, 175–76, 188–90, 198, 231, 241, 245–46, 258

Tart, Levern, 63–64, 73–74, 319
teaching, 1–2, 77, 83, 106, 113, 121, 163, 194, 240
television, 139, 149, 164–65, 167, 172, 180, 232, 301
Temple University, 51, 190, 199, 294
Tennessee, University of, 124
Tennessee State University, 56, 127, 185–86
Teresa, Mother, 259
Texas, University of, 307
Texas Rangers, 114
Texas Tech University, 267
Texas Western University, 190
Thomas, Clarence, 299
Thomas, Fred, 37
Thomas, Isiah, 268
Thompson, Anna Alexander (mother), 7–8, 11–14, 19–22, 31, 37, 41, 45–47, 78–79, 149, 159, 161, 241, 325
  death of, 161–62
Thompson, Barbara (sister), 8, 18, 22
Thompson, Eddie (nephew), 169

Thompson, Gwen Twitty (wife), 45, 50, 71, 74, 83–84, 116, 135, 161, 179, 293–94
Thompson, Inez (sister), 8
Thompson, John Robert, Sr. "Rob" (father), 7–8, 10–19, 27–28, 35–37, 42, 47–48, 108, 144, 202, 319–21, 325
  death of, 108, 161
Thompson, John Robert, Jr., xi
  birth of, 8–9
  Black empowerment and, xii, 18–19, 24, 44, 55, 59–60, 92–93, 108, 111, 116–17, 134–36, 148, 154–55, 174, 187–88, 217
  Boston Celtics and, 61–66
  broadcast career of, 296–304
  Catholicism of, 13, 18–33, 46, 81, 122, 321
  childhood and early youth, 8–18, 22–38, 212
  city youth program and, 91–92
  closed practices of, 105, 147, 163, 205, 240
  coaching style and, xii, 26, 67–70, 80, 83, 87, 104–7, 112–15, 119–22, 131, 136–37, 147–50, 163–67, 170, 177, 229–30, 317–18
  death of, xi–xii
  death of Auerbach and, 70
  death of father and, 108
  death of mother and, 161–62
  death of son Lewis and, 43
  deflated basketball and, 4, 91–92, 241, 307
  early mentoring by Auerbach and, 39–41, 69
  Eastern Europe tour and, 56–57
  education of, Archbishop Carroll High, 33–37, 45
  education of, early, 12–14, 20–22, 25–28, 113, 317
  education of, Federal City College masters', 76–78, 82–83, 212
  education of, Providence College, 45–46, 50–53
  Elgin "Rabbit" Baylor as inspiration for, 4–5, 28–31
  eyeglasses and, 104, 111
  family life and, 135–36
  Georgetown career of. *See* Georgetown University
  Georgetown emeritus position and, 319–20
  Georgetown hires, as coach, 88–92
  Georgetown retirement and, 293–96
  Hall of Fame and, 4–5, 296–97
  honors and, xi, 4–5, 59, 122, 203, 296–97, 310, 316–17, 320
  house burns down, 293
  intimidation and, 111, 154–55, 165, 187–88, 217
  Kutsher's resort and, 39–41
  Las Vegas gaming license and, 265–67
  marriage to Gwen Twitty, ends in divorce, 293–94
  NABC and, 121–22
  NBA finals of 1966 and, 72–74
  NCAA boycott by, 224–30
  NCAA championship of 1984 and, 180–81
  Nike and, 163–64, 171–72, 274–89
  9/11 and, 299–300
  Olympics and, 58–59, 123–25, 203–7
  pride in career and, 317–19
  profanity, use of, 78, 84, 105, 252
  Rayful Edmond confrontation and, 209–37
  recruiting methods of, 100–104, 126–28, 131–32, 143–46, 151–52, 168–69
  relationship with media, 114, 144, 146–49, 176, 180, 205, 240, 262–63, 299
  son John's coaching career and, 307–12
  sons and, 202, 307–8
  as St. Anthony's coach, 78–91
  statue of, xi, 310, 316, 317
  towel worn over shoulder, 80, 190, 225, 264
  Uncle Lewis and, 41–43
  United Planning and, 74–75, 77
  Villanova championship loss and, 192–94, 207, 279
  Virgin Mary and, xi, 78, 122, 319–20
  Wilson basketball deal and, 185, 282
Thompson, John Robert, III (son), 32, 43, 74, 135, 179–80, 202–3, 231–32, 325–26
  as Georgetown coach, 308–12, 315
  as Princeton coach, 307–8
Thompson, Lewis Grandison Alexander (uncle), 43

Thompson, Mark, 113
Thompson, Roberta (sister), 8, 22, 28, 117
Thompson, Ronny (son), 2, 32, 43, 83, 135, 179–80, 202, 208, 325
Thompson, Tiffany (daughter), 135–36, 325–26
Threet, Fannie, 205
Thurman, Scotty, 256
Till, Emmett, 24
Tillman, Mark, 113, 238, 244
Title IX, 314
Toll Brothers, 138
Trigg, Kermit, 27–28, 33–34, 53, 79
Turner, Booker, 178
Turner, John "JT," 209–20, 233–35
Turner Elementary School, 13
Turner Sports, 300–304
Turpin, Mel, 177

United Planning Organization, 74, 77
Unseld, Wes, 131
USA Basketball, 205
USA Today, 149

Vaccaro, Sonny, 273–75, 278–79, 284
Valvano, Jim, 141
Van Gundy, Jeff, 206
Vietnam, 287
Villanova University, 49, 139, 172, 176–77, 189, 191–94, 201–2, 258, 262–64, 278–79, 291
Virginia, University of, 131, 164–65
Virginia Commonwealth University, 130

Waddy-Lewis, Jackie, 169
Wade, Bob, 168
Wagner, Paul, 80–81
Wake Forest University, 165
Walker, Chet, 71
Walker, Doc, 296–99
Walker, Jimmy, 56
Wallace, John, 258
Wallace, Rasheed, 259
Walters, Tom, 80
Walton, Bill, 154
Washington, Donald, 79–80, 83–84, 86, 273
Washington, Norman, 145–46
Washington, Pearl, 172, 175
Washington, Rudy, 241
Washington Bullets, 131
Washington Capitols, 40
Washington Daily News, 24, 212
Washington Post, 28, 133, 147, 149, 152, 244, 266
Washington Senators, 27
Washington Star, 149, 176
Weber, Rick, 133
Wennington, Bill, 189
West, Jerry, 64, 72
Western Kentucky University, 150
West Virginia University, 118
White, Jahidi, 254, 262, 290, 293
Wideman, John Edgar, 184–85
Wilbon, Mike, 149
Wilder, Douglas, 250, 258
Wiley, Ralph, 149
Wilkens, Lenny, 50
Williams, Alvin, 258
Williams, Boo, 250–51
Williams, Buck, 132, 142
Williams, Jerome "Junkyard Dog," 254, 258, 262, 264, 290
Williams, Reggie, 69, 168, 170, 179–80, 185, 196–98
Williams, Roy, 311
Williamson, Corliss, 256
Wilson, Merlin, 88, 97, 109, 113–15, 117
Wilson basketball, 185, 282
Wingate, David, 162–63, 169–70, 178–79, 185, 196
Winslow, Rickie, 178
Winston-Salem State University, 127, 131
Witte, Albert, 229
Wooden, John, 58, 180
Woods, Tiger, 288, 299
Woodson, Carter G., 7
Wootten, Morgan, 84–90, 152, 277
Worthy, James, 131, 156–60
Wright, Jay, 311
WTEM talk show, 296–99
Wyatt, Julius, 31, 51, 53, 98, 142, 325
Wyoming, University of, 155

Xavier University, 246

Yeoman, Felix, 117, 138
YMCA, 33
Young, Michael, 178
Yugoslavia, 124–25, 207

ABOUT THE AUTHORS

JOHN THOMPSON was the head basketball coach at Georgetown University from 1972 to 1999, and he won the NCAA championship in 1984. He was inducted into the Basketball Hall of Fame in 1999. He graduated from Providence College and held a master's degree in guidance and counseling from the University of the District of Columbia.

JESSE WASHINGTON is a writer for ESPN's *The Undefeated.*